**The Write Wild Method**
By Sarah Clayton
Published by Write Wild Books Press
First published in the United Kingdom in 2025

ISBNs:
Paperback: 978-1-7394150-2-0
eBook: 978-1-7394150-3-7

Copyright © 2025 Sarah Clayton

All rights reserved. No part of this book may be reproduced, stored in a retrieval system, or transmitted in any form or by any means, electronic, mechanical, photocopying, recording, or otherwise, without the prior written permission of the publisher, except in the case of brief quotations embodied in critical articles or reviews.

The moral right of the author has been asserted.

This book is a work of non-fiction. While every effort has been made to ensure accuracy, the publisher and author accept no responsibility for errors or omissions, or for any loss or damage caused by reliance on the information contained within.

Any references to brands, organisations, or individuals are made in good faith and do not imply endorsement or affiliation. All trademarks and registered trademarks remain the property of their respective owners.

# THE WRITE WILD METHOD

Sarah Clayton

# Contents

About the author ................................................................... 9

What to expect ..................................................................... 11

How to use this book ........................................................... 22

Introduction ......................................................................... 25

How is the Write Wild Method going to help you? ........... 31

The Write Wild Method ...................................................... 34

**THE BEGINNING** ................................................................. 35

    The 10 Principles of the Write Wild Method ............... 36
    Principle One: Reimagining-Reawakening ................... 38
        Your Aim ...................................................................... 38
        Your Objective ........................................................... 45
        Your Goal .................................................................... 53

    Principle Two: Your Elliptic Presence ........................... 56
        Your Aim ...................................................................... 56
        Your Objective ........................................................... 60
        Your Goal .................................................................... 66

    Principle Three: Ebb and Flow ....................................... 68
        Your Aim ...................................................................... 68
        Your Objective ........................................................... 71
        Your Goal .................................................................... 78

Principle Four: Your Illusive Self ............................... 84
    Your Aim ................................................................ 84
    Your Objective ..................................................... 90
    Your Goal .............................................................. 92

Principle Five: The Walking Writer ............................ 97
    Your Aim ................................................................ 97
    Your Objective ................................................... 102
    Your Goal ............................................................ 103

Principle Six: Get Motivated .................................... 106
    Your Aim .............................................................. 110
    Your Objective ................................................... 126
    Your Goal ............................................................ 150

Principle Seven: Your Courage Continuum ............... 129
    Your Aim .............................................................. 129
    Your Objective ................................................... 134
    Your Goal ............................................................ 138

Principle Eight: Ergriffenheit and Humility ............... 148
    Your Aim .............................................................. 148
    Your Objective ................................................... 152
    Your Goal ............................................................ 154

Principle Nine: Your Fairy-tale Self .......................... 156
    Your Aim .............................................................. 156
    Your Objective ................................................... 162
    Your Goal ............................................................ 164

Principle Ten: Impossible Worlds ............................. 168
    Your Aim .............................................................. 168
    Your Objective ................................................... 171
    Your Goal ............................................................ 185

Summary of the 10 Principles with Exercises ............ 188

- **THE MIDDLE** ............................................................... 195
  - The Write Wild Method: Daily Practice ..................... 196
    - Writing is a process. ................................................. 196
    - Your writing goals ................................................... 199
    - Step One ................................................................... 200
    - Step Two ................................................................... 202
    - Step Three ................................................................ 203
    - Step Four .................................................................. 206
    - Step Five ................................................................... 206
  - Working the Method ................................................... 217
    - Animals Don't Follow Laws,
      They Follow Instincts ............................................... 217
    - The Write Wild Experience (WWE) ...................... 219
    - Principle Application (PA) ..................................... 220
    - The Idea: Where Stories Begin .............................. 220
    - Storyline Experience (plot seed) ........................... 225

- **THE END** ..................................................................... 231
  - The Write Wild Method: The Progress Tracker ......... 233
    - Your Writer's Ecosystem ......................................... 233
    - Your Unique Words ................................................. 235
    - Your physical self: ................................................... 240
    - Your Dissociated Self .............................................. 242
    - Your Eco-Subconcious ............................................ 243
    - Your Discovery ........................................................ 244
    - Your Creative Self ................................................... 247
    - Your Reader ............................................................. 252
    - Your Outcome ......................................................... 252
    - Your Result .............................................................. 253
  - Your Growth Ring ....................................................... 255
  - Anxiety and Transformation ...................................... 262
    - Problem Solving ...................................................... 264
    - Nature before writing ............................................. 264

Nature and first ideas..................................267
Nature and first rewrites..............................274
Nature and rewriting....................................282
Nature and plot............................................283
Nature and endings..................................... 288
Nature as Person: The Power of Our Stories........293
Releasing the Orangutan:
What Can Nature Tell You? ........................295

Nature's Impact on Creativity:
Voices from the Wild ................................... 300
    Elizabeth Morris ....................................301
    Craig Russell........................................ 304
    Julie Robertson.................................... 306
    Sophie Hannah ................................... 308
    Norman Bissell.................................... 309
    Terence Blackwell................................ 313
    Ian Banyard ......................................... 315
    Mary Lunan ........................................316
    Liz Webb ............................................. 317
Embracing the Write Wild Coaching Programme......320

Acknowledgements ......................................334

Glossary .......................................................337

Bibliography ................................................ 348

*For Antony, Kirsty and Akira*
*We walk the yellow brick road hand in hand, together forever*

*and for Mike*
*Life is our fairy tale in the making*

# About the author

Sarah Clayton is an experienced writer and dedicated advocate for the transformative power of nature in the creative process. Drawing from a rich background in psychology, philosophy and ecology, Sarah has meticulously crafted *The Write Wild Method* – a groundbreaking approach to writing that combines practical techniques with profound insights.

Sarah's writing path was reshaped when she turned to the natural world—not as an escape, but as a force that sharpened her instincts, restored her confidence, and rewired her creative process. Through seasons of struggle and transformation, she discovered that nature doesn't just inspire—it reveals, challenges, and unlocks what we've buried too deep to write. Her journey has taken her through single parenthood and a whirlwind of jobs—burger flipper, sandwich artist, room attendant, florist delivery driver, and a calamitous taxi driver—before leading her to university, social science research, and running a guest house. Through it all, she wrote, until a chronic illness nearly silenced her creativity. Forced to pause, she began to see the world differently. Eventually, she stumbled upon an experience that rooted her back in nature and creativity, reigniting her writing purpose. From that moment, she reimagined her process, nurturing a new way of writing—one that wasn't about discipline or struggle, but about deep connection, trust, and creative freedom. Now, she helps other writers break through creative paralysis, reclaim their voices, and believe—without hesitation—that they and their words truly matter.

With a passion for guiding writers through their creative journey, Sarah is committed to helping others unlock their full potential and find their unique voice on the page. Through personalised coaching, tailored exercises and immersive experiences, Sarah invites readers to embark on a journey of self-discovery, empowerment and creative fulfilment.

# What to expect

This book is not your typical creative writing guide – think of it more as a supportive companion for you when you're feeling stuck, grappling with creative blocks or are unsure of how to make progress with your writing. I want you to feel that it's a helpful resource rather than a rigid set of rules. It doesn't overpromise, instead it offers straightforward and actionable guidance to cushion you along your writing journey.

But it's more than that. What if I told you this isn't just about writing but about discovering untapped layers of your creativity? That it's about how your connection with nature can transform your writing process and your writing life. The Write Wild Method goes beyond writing techniques. It's about navigating the experiential side of creativity; it's about really connecting with your natural creative flow, uncovering fresh perspectives, and finding your unique voice.

As we take this creative journey together, remember that what you're about to experience is unique to you, as unique as your fingerprint. Creative flow varies externally from one person to the next and it can also vary internally from one moment to the next. Think about that for a moment. Imagine it as if you were rambling through the countryside, your experience will differ from the next person and perhaps from one visit to the next.

While it's true that we all experience our creativity uniquely, there are some common practical challenges that I believe many writers share at some point or another. Here are a few:

- **Writer's block**: getting stuck, difficulty getting started with a writing project or generating good ideas at any point along the journey.

- **Procrastination**: putting off writing tasks or struggling with time management.

- **Lack of motivation**: feeling uninspired or unmotivated to write.

- **Fear of failure or rejection**: anxiety over criticism or rejection from agents, publishers or readers.

- **Lack of consistency**: struggling to maintain a regular writing routine or staying committed to long-term projects.

- **Self-doubt**: feeling insecure about writing ability or the quality of work.

- **Distractions**: difficulty focusing due to external or internal distractions.

- **Real-life harmony**: balancing writing with other responsibilities and commitments.

- **Perfectionism**: striving for unrealistic goals leading to paralysis or dissatisfaction.

- **Harnessing creative flow**: struggling to maintain or reignite creative momentum.

Challenges such as these are multifaceted and deeply personal and fluctuate in impact and resonance from one writer to another. They serve as catalysts for a variety of emotions that can shape the creative journey in profound and complex ways. For example, it's not uncommon to experience some or a range of feelings such as:

- Frustration
- Anxiety
- Self-criticism
- Discouragement
- Guilt
- Overwhelm
- Resignation
- Hopelessness

When faced with creative challenges, feelings can vary depending on the individual writer, the specific challenges they encounter and their coping mechanisms and support systems.

In the midst of these complex emotional challenges, the Write Wild Method can act as your supporter. Unlike conventional writing approaches, it doesn't simply address the technicalities; it's your guide through the emotional highs and lows of the creative journey. By urging you to explore your connection with nature, new perspectives and embrace your unique voice, it equips you with the tools to tackle frustration, self-doubt and overwhelm head on.

The Write Wild Method offers you a roadmap through any uncertainties you may face along your writing journey. It empowers you to confront obstacles with resilience and curiosity, transforming challenges into opportunities for growth. So, in those moments of doubt and uncertainty, remember that the Write Wild Method is here to cushion your path and propel you forward on your writing journey.

In acknowledging the unique landscape of each writer's journey, it's essential to recognise that while the Write Wild Method can be a powerful tool for many, it may not resonate with everyone in the same way. Each writer brings their own set of experiences, challenges and aspirations which shape how they engage with the method. The Write Wild Method's effectiveness hinges on its ability to foster introspection and exploration encouraging you to uncover your distinct voice and perspective. However, what works for one writer may not necessarily work for another. Factors such as individual preferences, learning styles and personal circumstances all influence how writers respond to and implement the method.

Moreover, the Write Wild Method's emphasis on embracing the natural world as the foundation for creativity requires a willingness to step outside your comfort zone and confront vulnerability. While some writers may find this approach liberating and empowering, others may feel intimidated or resistant to change. Therefore, while the Write Wild Method offers a promising framework for many, its application and impact will inevitably vary from writer to writer. It's essential for each writer to approach it with an open mind and a willingness to adapt the method to their own unique journey and creative needs.

Different people think and feel different things so while the method is clear, the results of the method can vary wildly from person to person. Some may breeze through, finding it as easy as walking a familiar path, while others might feel like they're exploring new terrain. I invite you to approach the principles laid out in this book as gentle signposts rather than rigid directions – offering support rather than setting rules.

Whether you embrace the method or find it a challenge, understand that you have choices. This is your writing journey and however you walk it is up to you. The Write Wild Method is just one way of helping you along the route. Take Janice and Brian (names have been changed for confidentiality) for example, two clients I've worked with to help them complete their writing projects:

*Embracing the Method*: Janice wanted to write her first novel but was unable to get started. She was stuck and feeling trapped by self-doubt and making any progress with her manuscript was a huge challenge for her. I introduced the Write Wild Method to Janice as she was intrigued by its emphasis on exploration and creativity. She decided to give it a try, diving into the exercise with an open mind. Fully embracing the method she began to uncover new insights into her writing process. The exercises helped her break free from her creative rut and she felt a renewed sense of inspiration and purpose. With the Write Wild Method as her guide, Janice gained the confidence to tackle her writing challenges head-on, ultimately completing her novel with a newfound sense of joy and fulfilment.

*Finding it Challenging*: Brian, an accountant and writer, was sceptical of the Write Wild Method when he first encountered it. He preferred a more structured approach to writing and was wary of anything that seemed too abstract or unconventional. Despite his reservations, Brian decided to give the method a chance, hoping it might help him overcome his recent struggles with burnout. However, as he attempted the exercises, he found himself feeling frustrated and disconnected. He struggled to connect with the exploratory nature of the method and felt out of his comfort zone. Despite his best efforts, Brian found it challenging to integrate the Write Wild Method fully into his writing process. Eventually, he decided to revert to his familiar strategies, finding solace in the comfort of routine and structure. We continued to work together and it was wonderful to see Brian adopt parts of the method quite naturally into his writing process and make the transformation from nervous to confident writer.

These clients illustrate how the Write Wild Method can elicit a varied response from different writers, depending on their individual preferences, experiences and mindset. While some may embrace its principles wholeheartedly and get huge benefit from them, others may find it challenging to adapt to its unconventional approach. And that's perfectly normal.

So you see that some writers may seamlessly integrate these ideas into their creative toolbox, while for others, it might take a bit of time or it may not be for them. Creativity is a journey that varies from person to person. But if you find yourself embracing the process, there are some potential outcomes you can expect from engaging with the Write Wild Method:

- **Increased Creativity**: you may find that the method sparks your imagination and leads to the generation of fresh ideas and perspectives.

- **Getting Unstuck**: the method encourages you to explore and experiment, helping you break through creative blocks and overcome periods of stuckness.

- **Discovery**: you may uncover and develop your distinctive writing style and voice through the method's emphasis on self-expression and authenticity.

- **Improved Confidence**: you may engage with the method and gain insights into your creative process, experiencing a boost in your ability and confidence.

- **Enhanced Problem-Solving Skills**: the method's focus on exploring different angles and perspectives can sharpen your problem-solving skills, both in the writing and in other areas of life.

- **Greater Resilience**: the method encourages you to embrace uncertainty and navigate challenges with resilience, fostering a mindset of perseverance and adaptability.

- **Deeper Self-Understanding**: you may gain a deeper understanding of you and your creative motivations through the reflective exercises and introspection promoted by the method.

- **Connection with Readers**: by fostering authenticity and emotional resonance in your writing, you may forge deeper connections with your readers and create more impactful work.

- **Joy and Fulfilment**: ultimately, you may experience a sense of joy and fulfilment as you engage in the creative process with curiosity, passion and purpose.

It depends, as I've said, on your individual experiences and engagement with the method. However, these outcomes can highlight the potential transformative effects that the Write Wild Method can have on your unique creative journey.

I want to touch on something significant. When people

engage with the Write Wild Method, some share experiences that go beyond putting words on paper. It can feel almost like a personal discovery, a bit profound. It's important to recognise that there is no 'right' or 'wrong' way to feel or to experience. Instead the method encourages you to embrace your emotions with openness and curiosity, understanding that each feeling, whether positive or negative, has its own role to play in your creative journey.

For example, instead of viewing being stuck as a failure or a sign of inadequacy, the method encourages you to approach writing challenges with curiosity and acceptance. You are invited to explore the underlying causes of your block and to trust that it's a natural part of the creative process and to write regardless. Or you may be paralysed by self-doubt and rather than dismissing this paralysis as undeserved or unproductive, the method asks you to acknowledge these feelings as common challenges that writers face. You're encouraged then to confront your doubts with compassion and self-kindness, recognising that you are on a journey of transformation.

With the Write Wild Method, every experience is valid and there's no concept of 'failure'. Your creative journey may lead you through various emotional landscapes, and that's completely normal. There's no expectation to feel a certain way, think specific thoughts or have particular experiences. Additionally, flow states differ for each individual, and there's no one-size-fits-all approach to achieving them.

It's also important to recognise that nature connection experiences can vary greatly from person to person. While the examples provided in this book offer simple ways to engage with nature, it's essential to understand that your own experiences may differ. You might resonate deeply with some of the suggested activities, finding them profoundly meaningful and enriching. On the other hand, you may not connect with them in the same way, or you might discover entirely different experiences that resonate with you more strongly.

**The strength of the approach laid out in this book lies in its flexibility and openness to individual interpretation, allowing you to explore and discover your own unique connections with your natural creativity at your own pace and in your own way.**

I want to emphasise that while this method empowers you to explore and uncover your personal connections with nature and your natural creativity, there is no right or wrong way to do so. As you engage in the activities suggested in this book, such as natural mindfulness or 'what if ...' problem solving, you may find yourself deeply attuned to the natural world, feeling a profound sense of connection. Alternatively, you might not immediately resonate with the activities and instead discover your own unique way of connecting with your natural creativity, perhaps through music or art. In either case, there's no way to 'fail' in your exploration; every experience, whether traditional or unconventional, is valid and contributes to your personal journey of developing your natural creative connection.

Even if some of the activities don't immediately resonate with you, simply reading the book and considering the suggestions can still be beneficial. It offers insights into what works and what doesn't work for you personally, helping you refine your approach and discover the methods that truly enhance your creative journey. For example, you may not wish to or be able to commit to a daily practice and it may be your preference to write when you're feeling the desire to write and that's okay. What you're presented with in this book is the ability to choose; to choose what works for you and to know the reason why.

Some writers may feel frustrated if they don't see quick results from the Write Wild Method or if the unconventional approach feels uncomfortable. Others may struggle with feeling disconnected from nature or overwhelmed by the breadth of practices. Additionally, impatience with the pace of progress can lead to doubts about the method's effectiveness and this itself will hinder full engagement in the process. The solution lies in acknowledging and addressing these challenges. *Patience and perseverance are key, allowing time for the method to take root.* Exploring alternative approaches within the method or seeking guidance from experienced practitioners can also provide valuable insights and support. Additionally, cultivating a mindset of openness and adaptability can help writers navigate obstacles and continue moving forward in their creative journey with the Write Wild Method.

This process isn't just about creative writing; it's about your personal growth. View it as unlocking doors to parts of yourself you may not have explored lately. It's not about forcing anything; it's about making the unseen aspects of your creativity a bit more visible. Think of it like a ripple effect – your perspectives expanding, your experiences deepening and your senses becoming more attuned. This isn't just about turning you into a better writer; it's about making you a more empowered, creative individual.

For some of you, the Write Wild Method will become a way of life. It's about embracing curiosity, creativity and connection with the natural world in everything you do. Whether you're writing a novel, taking a walk in the forest or simply pausing to listen to birdsong, the principles of the Write Wild Method can guide you along your writing journey to living a more inspired and fulfilling life.

For those who don't necessarily see the Write Wild Method as a comprehensive way of life, it offers valuable tools and perspectives that can enhance specific aspects of the creative journey. While they may not fully adopt all aspects of the method into their daily lives, they can still benefit from its principles in their writing practice. The method provides practical strategies for overcoming creative blocks, accessing inspiration and deepening emotional resonance in writing, regardless of whether it's fully integrated into a way of life. Ultimately, even for those who don't view it as a lifestyle, the Write Wild Method can serve as a valuable resource for nurturing creativity and connection with nature in their writing ambitions.

Now it's time to see where this gentle exploration leads us.

# How to use this book

This book has been written to accompany you throughout your writing journey. It is a book that brings together the writing process and the natural world because once you open yourself up to a deeper, more meaningful relationship with nature, you'll discover something amazing and that is your natural self. With your natural self you'll have the power to release your creativity and completely transform your writing and your writing process in a way that works in your best interests and keeps you writing.

There are different ways you can use this book depending on what you need at any particular moment of your writing process. If you're coming to the book for the first time, you may prefer to read it from start to finish and get a feel for how the elements of the Write Wild Method will work for you in general. Then you may like to go back and begin working through the method. Once you have the method under your belt, you may then decide to keep the book by your side as you write so that should you get stuck you can refer to a particular section of the book to help you work through whatever the problem is, take action and keep on writing.

Alternatively, you may choose to focus on each section of the Write Wild Method separately, starting with THE BEGINNING and learning the 10 Write Wild Principles, practising the exercises until you feel you are developing a strong connection with nature. And then move on to THE MIDDLE and devote your time to developing a daily writing practice, or deciding on a practice that works best for you. Once you have mastered a writing practice, you can then move on to THE END and learn how to keep track of your progress with the Write Wild Landscape. Here you will also put into practice everything you've learned with a particular focus on problem solving at certain points in your writing project.

However you decide to use this book, it's important to remember that:

- you, the writer, have everything you need and are your own influencer during any and all of your writing journey

- however anxious you feel about the writing, you can harness your anxiety as a positive and transformative force when you have a strong connection with the natural world

- you choose to write in spite of ...

Once you begin to practise the 10 WRITE WILD PRINCIPLES, the rest of the WRITE WILD METHOD will fall into place and you may find that your writing process and writing life will look and feel more manageable, more how you'd hoped it would be and you'll reach your writing goals faster and easier, with greater calm and confidence.

Writing is so much more than simply learning the craft. Once you understand the craft of writing, what's next? How do you manage a writing life? How do you harness your creativity to keep on writing? How do you solve all the challenges and make all the decisions that are inherent in creative writing? How do you write well and engage your reader and do that over and over again? How do you maintain a writing practice that doesn't have you feeling guilty, overanxious and afraid? What do you do if you get that uncomfortable feeling that paralyses you and you can't write – what is often referred to as writer's block? What do you do if your books aren't selling, you're out of ideas, you're frustrated and ready to give up, and you're stuck? What do you do if you simply don't know where to start, where to turn, where to go to get support?

All of these challenges are the same and all require the same approach to confronting them and getting on with the writing. The answer is simple, you turn firstly to yourself. That is to your natural self, your courage and your resilience. You understand that you already know the answer and that only you can solve the problem. You know what to do.

**You have invested in your craft. Now it's time to invest in yourself and use the WRITE WILD METHOD to engage in a deeper, more meaningful relationship with the natural world to discover your natural self and harness your unique writing power.**

# Introduction

I used to know an orangutan who liked to blow me kisses. I was about four years old and my gran told me that the orangutan only blew kisses to me and not to any of the other kids in the zoo. I believed her. I told myself this was true. It was around this time that I became aware of this voice inside my head. I'd told myself, the orangutan blows kisses only to me. I could talk to myself and nobody could hear what I was saying inside my head. I remember feeling both exhilarated and terrified by the idea of this voice speaking only to me. I told myself that the orangutan loved me otherwise why would he blow me kisses?

While I was certain back then that the orangutan loved me, as I've grown up, I've become a lot less certain about how this voice in my head feels about me and that is terrifying. For most of my life I've battled with that fear and have found that the more I've wanted to create, to become a writer, the greater that fear manifests as self-doubt, anxiety and pain.

Since developing the Write Wild Method, I've transformed all that doubt and fear and replaced it with confidence, self-worth and courage. I've found my unique connection to nature and the natural world and I now realise that nature is an integral part of my ability to create.

Writing a book doesn't happen solely inside your head, it

is actually a whole body experience. Nature gives us the courage to write because it helps us find the wild places that exist within us. The orangutan was urging me to look inside of myself and share that part of me with him.

I often think about that orangutan and his trick of blowing kisses. As a child, my imagination was free and limitless, it helped me understand the world around me. But as I shifted from puberty into adulthood, my longing to create, my desire to write was something I had to push aside. I had to live in a world of expectations, routines and demands that crushed my natural instinct toward imagination. The orangutan was compartmentalised into my childhood years.

Nature was something that existed outside of me, something to make the concrete world pretty, something that no longer was part of who I was becoming. As a child, the orangutan was my friend. As an adult, it was an animal in a zoo, something of a lesser creature than myself. As if it belonged to a lower class of being. Like I knew Santa Claus doesn't exist, I knew those kisses weren't just for me, that it was best to be better than, bigger than, cleverer than an animal in a zoo who couldn't be my friend because he didn't match up to my peers.

Nowadays, I feel I've come full circle. I have reignited my childhood connection with nature and if that orangutan was alive today I would like to welcome him as part of my tribe, as a being equal to myself, and hope that he too would invite me to become part of his tribe. Because I've finally understood that what matters for me is that I write, and having spent those last few years discovering my connection with nature and my natural self, I now have the courage to create, to achieve my writing purpose. This is why I've developed the Write Wild Method, to give you the courage to achieve your writing purpose too.

**There has been very little said about how a writer can harness the power of nature to fuel their creativity and live a more fulfilling writing life.**

Reigniting your connection with nature allows you access to and awakens that illusive part of yourself where your creativity resides, your natural self. We all have the ability to connect with our natural self. Without it, we may be risking something 'less', something meaning-'less', and worse, we may be inviting our readers to experience something 'less'.

The 10 Write Wild Principles in this book show you why and how nature can help you write your book and live your writing purpose, and each gives a couple of examples of how to supercharge your writing and your writing life.

Those moments when writing is hard, or even seemingly impossible, could be because you're not in touch with your natural self, you've lost connection with your ability to create stories and you're struggling or afraid to write anything or are stuck in the middle of something.

**When you're not connected to your natural self, it's much easier to attend to the fear that crops up around your writing, and with fear comes anxiety. Fear does a lot of harm. It creates needless anxiety. Anxiety is the opposite of connection because it creates unseen barriers that lead to self-doubt and loathing. It is impossible to doubt yourself and write and live well at the same time.**

Do you write with the expectation that words will magically appear and amazing ideas will pop up in your head? Of course, we all do, it's what we call creative writing. We write with our bodiless head, believing that all we have to do is sit down and put our minds to work and if we do that consistently, with all our determination, the story will form itself into bestselling, plot-explosive paragraphs, characters will leap breathlessly from the page, buzzing with tantalising dialogue, conflict and intrigue. If only it were true, I might say to you but I wouldn't mean it. I wouldn't mean it because this thing you and I are doing isn't meant to be easy. It's meant to test us. It has to be painful. We write because we are making meaning. This is big. This is truly huge. We write to make meaning for ourselves because that is our purpose and we want that meaning to matter to someone else too, our readers. That's a big deal.

How does it work, where do all these potentially bestselling words come from? Not from anxiety and self-doubt. Anxiety consists of all the things that might go wrong. Anxiety tells you that maybe you cannot write or find a new idea or present something worthy to your reader. Anxiety has you curled in the corner with the mantra, 'I can't do this!'

If you can gather yourself together, you might ask yourself – what can I do?

You might then be open to discovering your natural self. To strengthening your relationship with the natural world. To transforming anxiety and doubt and throwing open the door to let creativity slip through.

The greater the connection, the more creativity. The more anxiety – the less creativity.

But where do ideas exist? If connection opens the door to let the ideas in, then the ideas must be outside somewhere. Where?

Ideas come from within, from your natural self. This is the illusive part. We don't really understand the magnitude of this yet – our current scientific reach doesn't quite stretch far enough, nor should it, if you ask me – but what is becoming clearer is that this illusive part of you and I is where our imagination and creativity reside.

We at least can understand that our connection to the natural world is beneficial for our creativity as this has been scientifically proven and that is what this book is all about. Ideas exist in the wild places you connect with. What I call, the experience of *you*; your natural self. The *you* that is set free to write compelling prose.

It's thought that the orangutan can teach us about purposeful living and I now understand that these animals symbolise strength and persistence and I like to think that is what he was sharing with me when he blew me kisses that day. What writer doesn't need a bit of purposeful living and persistence and the strength to keep on writing?

What's more important to you? Thinking about your idea, your book, or writing it? It's an interesting question and if you're anything like me, you don't think enough about thinking. Thinking takes time. You want to get on with the process. You want your book out in the universe and in the hands of your reader.

But you have to take a deep breath and pull in the reins. Compelling prose is prose that has had the freedom to breathe and reveal itself. Your writing is your experience and you have to have the experience first. The experience of your natural self. By the end of this book, you will know how to reach the experience of *you*. This is what you will give to your reader. You will also have – really have – the courage to write compelling prose. And knowing this means you're already on your way to achieving it.

Before we forge ahead, I just want to pause for a second and clarify what I mean by thinking. Because it is very easy to get tangled up and stuck in our thoughts. When I talk about thinking in this instance I'm referring to the thought that goes into being present, resting, reflecting, playing, experiencing, learning, crystallising ideas, experimenting with language, testing conflict and drama, rehearsing characters, strategizing your writing process and so on. Thinking, if you like, that helps propel your writing project forward, for with each thought that goes into, for example, realising an idea or deepening a character, stepping away from your work, you are inching forward even if you haven't written a word yet.

There really is no room in the writing process for any other kind of thinking – the kind that has you thinking about doing the writing for example. If you spend a lot of time thinking about whether to write or not, you're at risk of becoming a writer who doesn't write. A non-productive writer or we can simplify it and say, a no-writer. If the thought inside your head is to wait for inspiration you may well be a no-writer and at risk of never getting the writing done.

There exists a seemingly never-ending list of thoughts that we potentially share as writers that impinge on our ability and energy to write. It's useful then to quickly ask yourself the question, is this thought a *write* or *no-write* thought?

# How is the Write Wild Method going to help you?

The aim of this book is to help you reconnect, boost your creativity and supercharge your writing. When I speak of reconnecting I'm referring to your connection with nature, your natural self, your meaning and writing life purpose.

Let's say, for example, that you've jumped right in and started your book with huge enthusiasm but you've hit a bump in the road and you just can't seem to find a way through, over or under.

Or. Your writing isn't happening in the way you want it to, your writing life is miserable, uncomfortable and you can't find a writing process that works for you or even any time to do any writing.

Or. You're working hard but seem to be standing still. The problem is you're not seeing the end of the tunnel, nothing you anticipated is working, and you're frustrated, discouraged and about to give up.

Or. You can't seem to begin, you have too many ideas or not any ideas at all; you have all the time you need to write, or no time. Either way, you can't seem to figure out what to write. You're confused, anxious and even feeling depressed.

Does any of this sound familiar?

You're not alone. Most writers wrestle with these issues and a lot more besides. There's always an issue, it seems and no matter how hard you try, all you feel you're doing is going round in circles.

So, if this sounds like you, what's the problem? The problem may be that you are disconnected. Your creativity is dormant, your ideas elusive and your energy depleted.

It's time to reconnect to your natural, creative self. That's why the Write Wild Method exists for you.

- It's going to help you get to where you want to be with your writing. Whether that's finishing a book, researching a book, beginning a book, deciding a writing practice that works for you, deciding how to find the time to write.
- It's going to help you develop a writing life that works for you and not just a writing life you wish you had. It's also going to help you move toward a writing life that best serves you and not one that beats you with a stick.
- It's going to contribute to you living a healthy balanced life as an author of books you are proud to publish.
- It's going to help you reconnect, boost your creativity and supercharge your writing.
- It's going to get you reconnecting to the natural world so that you can reconnect to your true nature, your creativity and your purpose.
- It's going to show you how to find your path to

discovering your natural self so that you can swiftly overcome hurdles along the way.

- It's going to get you rebooting and reimagining your writing journey and give you the skills that will get you to the finishing line feeling healthy, satisfied and successful.

- It's going to show you how you can transform your fear and anxiety into courage and resilience and the ability to write magical prose and live a more fulfilling, calm and confident life.

The following few chapters are going to describe the 10 Write Wild Principles in detail, but let's pause for a moment because I want you to be sure you're not wasting your time reading this book. There is so much amazing advice and support around nowadays that sometimes it can get a bit overwhelming. I didn't want this method to contribute to that feeling of overwhelm, I wanted to develop it in a way that is easily accessible, available for specific writing problems and as a method that you can adapt so that you instinctively know how to solve a writing problem with confidence and without the fear of being stuck, lost or alone. I want this method to be your companion along your writing journey. Just like writing, learning this method and adopting it is both process and experience. The best thing about this is that as you're learning the method, you're learning how to be a better writer and how to live a better writing life. This is a new approach to writing that requires an open mind and a willingness to put in the effort. In writing, there really are no quick fixes. So, if you're ready, let's begin.

# The Write Wild Method

Just as if we are writing a novel together, the Write Wild Method has a Beginning, Middle and End. The beginning invites you to commit to the 10 Write Wild Principles. Each principle will help you with a particular aspect of your writing and yourself as a writer and together the 10 Write Wild Principles will show you how to engage in a deeper and more meaningful relationship with the natural world and your natural self to improve your writing and writing process.

The Middle section of this book invites you to develop a writing practice that works best for you. For some of you it may be a daily practice and if you would like a writing career I recommend this. But some of you may write for pleasure or may be overcommitted in other parts of your life and you may decide your practice consists of writing at the weekends or every third day. The point is to develop and commit to a writing practice that is going to work for you, be fulfilling and keep you writing.

The End section of this book gives you a means to keep track of your progress. This is the part of the book that invites you to interact with the Write Wild Method and use all that you've learnt to transform your writing journey into an experience that benefits your writing and your life. It gives you the tools to find harmony, balance and calm as you write.

# THE BEGINNING

*- Commit -*

# The 10 Principles of the Write Wild Method

What are the 10 Write Wild Principles and why are they important for writers?

Each principle contributes to the entire writing process and it's as well to think of the order listed here as arbitrary. It's not an order you need be bound by. Ideally, you'll master these principles and whatever you're stuck with in your writing process or writing life, a principle will pop up in your head and you'll be on your way again.

Here is a brief rundown of the 10 Write Wild Principles so that at any point you can return to this page if you need to refresh your memory.

**Principle One:** *Reimagining-Reawakening*: guides you to explore how to make meaning and tell a story.

**Principle Two:** *Your Elliptic Presence*: invites you to embrace the chaos of the creative process.

**Principle Three:** *Ebb and Flow*: encourages focus and helps you become absorbed in your project.

**Principle Four:** *Your Illusive Self*: helps you re-discover your imagination, your natural self, your courage, resilience and creativity.

**Principle Five:** *The Walking Writer*: keeps your writing muscle healthy and willing to show up for you daily.

**Principle Six:** *Get Motivated*: a framework that will guide you along your writing journey and keep you on track with your sanity intact.

**Principle Seven:** *Your Courage Continuum*: reminds you to trust your creative journey and to get your natural self asking questions that will help you achieve your writing goals.

**Principle Eight:** *Ergriffenheit and Humility*: encourages you to develop your natural curiosity and reconnect to your inner wonder.

**Principle Nine:** *Your Fairy-tale Self*: invites you to develop the part of you that will deliver the elements of your story without you having to force the writing.

**Principle Ten:** *Impossible Worlds*: a reminder that you begin a book by writing it for yourself, but your final draft must always be for your reader.

# Principle One: Reimagining-Reawakening

**Principle Aim:** Explore Your Natural Self
**Principle Objective:** Release Your Inner Meaning
**Principle Goal:** Discover Your Hidden Creativity

## YOUR AIM

When you sit down to write, you are *creating meaning* for yourself and your reader. In a fictional story, your protagonist guides the reader and each event is a consequence of the last event. For example, Stephen is in his favourite comic store and he desperately wants a limited edition comic but he can't afford it. He slips the comic into his jacket and makes to leave the store. If you were to write this story you would be aiming to impart meaning for your reader and that requires you to explore. Sit with this for a moment and see what comes up for you. You may have questions about who Stephen is and what his situation is and what has brought him to this point. You may want to delve a little deeper, put your first half dozen ideas aside and continue to explore until something pops up to surprise you.

You can explore meaning anywhere, you are not required to sit at your desk until a bestselling idea pops into your head – which it won't because you're sitting at your desk and for all you know, your creativity is having a nice long sleep.

Meaning is something we as creatives are required to

explore whether we're writing fiction or non-fiction, a poem, lyrics or a screenplay. Otherwise all we're writing is a series of events. You may have a beautifully crafted plot but does it take your protagonist on a journey of transformation that means something to your protagonist, to you, to your reader?

**The quality of your story is a factor of the depths to which you are willing to explore meaning.**

As a social science researcher it was my job to write reports that relayed statistics to government bodies. Statistics are only useful if they mean something and therefore I had to explore and interpret my findings and present them in a meaningful way. For example, I might find that one thousand men requested a bed in a particular homeless hostel on a particular night when normally there would be ten requests. I would have to explore the factors which led to this unusual statistic, of which there may be many; which factors are important? To make that decision I would have to explore a little deeper and I may conclude that none of those factors mattered because I'd found a more meaningful result that provided a means by which government funding could be more accurately informed.

Writing a story demands the same methodical approach: what appears to be an interesting meaning on the surface may prove to be a thousand times more meaningful the deeper we explore our findings, that is, the depths of our inner reserves of creativity.

### *To create is to continuously explore*

Can I invite you to think of yourself as an explorer? If you're writing a romance novel, it appears to me that you're exploring human relationships. If you write a crime novel, are you exploring why people do what they do? I would say so. If you're writing a fantasy novel peopled with turtles and fairies, could you be exploring the fantasy world in order to understand the human world? Perhaps. This makes us, as writers, explorers and the subject of our exploration is what it means to be human. What this tells us is that *writers set out to search for meaning with the aim of communicating what they've understood from the experience through their own words.*

Are you aware that this is what you're doing when you sit down to write? Does it matter? I would argue that it does. **Reimagining-Reawakening** is about really understanding what we're doing when we write so that we can better understand the process, are less likely to become stuck and when we do become stuck, are better equipped to get unstuck.

Why is exploring important? *Unless you're exploring, you're not creating.* Creating is really a problem-solving exercise and when you commit to a creative project, such as writing a novel, you should know and be prepared to spend most of your creative activities exploring and solving problems. There are many bumps in the road to creating a novel, or any other creative project, and these bumps come in even more guises. They do not visit you for you to pull your hair out or threaten to give up or even feel very stuck. These bumps in the road visit you enthusiastically, presenting you with the gift of exploring. Reimagine the problem, reawaken the solution and you'll find you've gotten yourself unstuck and back on the road to the finishing line.

How do you do this reimagining and reawakening? It doesn't sound very intuitive, right? Perhaps not right now but you'll soon be doing it without thinking about it, it will become part of who you are as a writer and a part of how you write. You may well already be reimagining and reawakening.

I'm not going to pretend to you that feeling stuck and actually being stuck is a comfortable position to be in. Reimagining and reawakening is by now intuitive for me but it doesn't mean I don't get stuck. If I didn't get stuck, if this book appeared to be writing itself with little or no effort from me, it wouldn't be any use to you; it would be vacant of any meaning or support and therefore a worthless investment. The point is, you can't reimagine or reawaken anything without putting the effort in, and staring at the page in front of you isn't going to get you to where you need to be anytime soon. A faster and easier way is to walk away and give yourself the joy of quiet time, go outside and practise being in the moment, anything from a fifteen-minute walk to a full immersion in nature. I'm off to do that very thing. You might like to put this book down and try it for yourself. See you when we gather together again and this time I will have an example for you.

There is no better example than one you experience for yourself. This is the idea I'm coming at you with on my return from what turned out to be a twenty-minute mindful walk through my local park. Remember, we're figuring out how to do this reimagine and reawaken stuff.

### *Reimagine the problem, reawaken the solution*

This book exists because of an experience I had around nine years ago. I woke up one morning in excruciating pain all over my body and was unable to move. The doctor visited and administered pain medication and for the next two years I found myself forced into medical retirement, in limbo with no diagnosis and I had stopped writing because I barely had the energy to think. Then I was diagnosed with functional neurological disorder, fibromyalgia and peripheral neuropathy. I was instantly presented with three parts of me: my brain, my body and me. The only part I had any control over was the 'me' part. I couldn't understand any of this and spent a couple of years researching only to find out there was nothing I could do but accept the situation. It's never easy to accept a way of life that we don't want, in my opinion. Neither is it easy to live your life in conflict with the other parts of yourself. I was driving myself crazy trying to solve a problem I couldn't understand.

Then one day I hobbled over some rocks on the Isle of Skye and sat myself shoulder deep in the sea surrounded by huge snakelike fronds of seaweed. This bed of seaweed was so widely spread it was all I could see in front of me, that and the sky. I sat there for three hours and thought of nothing but the seaweed and the sky. At some point, I felt wholly supported by the seaweed, it seemed as if it were wrapping itself around me, healing me and welcoming me until I found myself feeling an incredibly important part of something. I wasn't sure what that something was, but the more I explored the feeling, the better I became at reimagining my then situation and it was at that point that I felt myself reawakening.

The point of me telling you this story is that after three hours I returned to the little cottage we'd rented and for the rest of that day I worked on a story outline for a novel. This was my first attempt at writing since I got ill. Six months later I'd written the first draft of *Light Dawns in Splinters*. I like to think that the natural world reminded me of who the 'me' part of me is: a writer. I was given that reminder as a gift, I feel, because writing is an incredibly therapeutic activity but also because my return to writing reawakened my sense of self and my purpose.

In this instance, emptying my brain of clutter and welcoming in nature's ideas and meanings for me changed my life. Exploring my place amongst all that sea, sky and seaweed demanded me to be open to new ideas and new perspectives, to meanings I didn't know to search for. I learnt that mental exploring is often an activity that requires trust and the belief that I already have the answers, and if I can't dig deep enough myself, nature will do it for me. I also learnt that I still mattered, and there is no better motivator than that.

**A Writer's Exercise**

I'd like to share a brief exercise with you. In a moment, I invite you to put this book down and close your eyes. Practise breathing deeply and slowly, without thinking and without visualising. If you haven't practised breathing exercises before, know that this takes time and lots of non-judgemental practice; the more you practise the better you will get at this. The aim is to let your thoughts fade off into the distance and allow yourself to stare, non-thinking, at the blank space behind your eyelids. If it helps, you may count on the inhale and exhale. For example:

Inhale – count to five
Pause
Exhale – count to six

Breathe deeply and slowly all the way to your stomach. Listen to your breathing as you breathe in and out. This is you beginning to feel your natural self. Acknowledging that you exist within and with-out yourself.

Once you are able to exist freely within this blank space, allow yourself, without judgement, to feel the weight of your body. To listen to the sounds that surround you and smell the environment you exist in. Be curious. Examine the feelings that rise up within you. You are wholly present. You are calm. You may find clarity. You are experiencing in the moment. You are on your way to becoming connected.

While doing this exercise, you may be in your office, in your bed, standing at a bus stop, it doesn't matter where you are because, as you'll begin to realise, the wild is within you. It is you. You the writer. You.

When we practise connecting to our natural self, we are opening ourselves up to the wild places where ideas exist. To where ideas may lead us closer to our potential. We needn't search for our drive to get us there, we already own it. All we have to do is release it. And all we have to do to release it, is to engage in a deeper and more meaningful relationship with our natural self and our place in the natural world. Show up in the moment, immerse yourself in nature, and meet yourself, and your unique connection to your world, inner and outer. We needn't search for ideas or meaning or creativity, it all exists in that place you open up to when you are reimagining, connecting and reawakening.

**Quick Recap**

**Reimagining and Reawakening** guides you to an exploration of meaning. This is the easiest way to remind you that your job is to explore meaning in a way that supports you to tell your story and to do that you must trust and believe that you have all the answers within you and to reawaken them you connect with your natural self.

## YOUR OBJECTIVE

**Preparation**

- Embrace being stuck: look forward to those sticky moments.
- Understand that often being stuck is your opportunity to explore.
- Exploring equates to creating, know that it is part of the process.
- Never stop exploring.
- Keep track of your thoughts; each thought is a footstep along the path to creating meaning. Keep a journal, write your thoughts in pictures, in poetry, on sticky notes, record your thoughts on your phone, keep track in whatever way works for you. If nothing works, keep exploring ways of tracking your thoughts in a simple way. Later in this book you'll have a definitive method of keeping track, but for now, you're aiming for simple notes.
- Trust the journey in front of you.
- Trust the answers and explore the meaning that presents itself to you.

**Purpose**

There are three factors to Reimagining-Reawakening:

1. Exploration
2. Meaning-making
3. Storytelling

EXPLORATION: Imagine you are about to plan your novel. You're on the lookout for ideas so you can build an outline for your story (as brief an outline as you like). Let's keep it really simple. Something happens between two shoppers close by while you're in the supermarket and you think ha! That would make a great book!

*There was only one loaf of bread left and a man took it off the shelf and put it in his basket. The woman standing beside him lifted it from his basket and put it in her own. The man demanded the loaf be returned to him. The woman refused and made to walk away. The man took out the pint of milk that was in his basket, opened it and tipped it over her head. The woman screamed and cried and stamped her foot. Then she shouted at him, 'How am I supposed to feed your son?'*

Can you start to visualise an outline for this idea? Could you get an elevator pitch from it? Can you bring meaning to it? Does it feel to you like an idea that could sustain an entire novel? These are some of the thoughts you may have if observing this incident, especially if these characters resonate with you. You are at the exploration stage.

Imagine that two days later this incident is still playing out in your head. As a writer you're feeling this experience in your gut. Something of what you observed has meaning for you, even if you're not sure what that meaning is. You are beginning to feel, to experience what you observed as if the incident had happened to you. To imagine how you would've reacted in that situation. You are reimagining the incident as your existential subjective experience.

Why? Because this is how you begin to make meaning. This is why, if you and I wrote a novel using this very same idea, our novels would tell a different story, in a different way and perhaps even with a different meaning. In fact, the idea itself may be unrecognisable in comparison. On the surface, if you and I were watching this incident together and we discussed what happened afterwards, we could easily both reach the same conclusion. But that doesn't mean our experience of the situation will be the same. And when we each go on to write the novel, we have reimagined the scenario several more times and it starts to become part of who we are, physically, psychologically and emotionally and it begins taking a shape that is meaningful only to each of us individually and, more importantly, to the connections we've made.

I'll give you an example of how this works. After the supermarket incident, I am so incensed by what happened, I decide that I can write a damned brilliant novel. I begin to write that novel straight away and I write solidly for four weeks without moving from my desk and amazingly I have a first draft. It's magic what I can make happen with a good idea! Boom!

Brilliant, you say. She's got a first draft and in four weeks and all I've been doing is twiddling my thumbs. Is it a good first draft? Who cares, it's a first draft. But ... is it really? In my first draft I've written a story about an abusive husband and a victim wife. In my edit I make ninety-thousand words telling, let's say, a romance story, about a wife beaten and abused by her husband who bumps into her future hero who saves her and they get married. Or a crime novel where the wife hires a hitman to kill the husband and gets away with it because the cop on duty falls in love with her. Is it a good story now? Who cares, I check it for typos and self-publish it. Will anyone read it? Who cares, or maybe I do. Maybe I'll decide to write the next novel and hope that will be my blockbuster. Maybe I will get lucky?

Not all ideas are good ones. Not all ideas show up fully formed. Most ideas are not what they seem on the surface. It is possible that my book will become the next best crime novel ever or the most romantic of romantic novels. There is no way to predict the outcome of our books once we hand them over to the publishing world. But what happens when you retell a story? What's happening underneath the surface of a story?

While you've been twiddling your thumbs, if you are a writer truly passionate about storytelling, you will have both consciously and subconsciously been existing underneath the surface of a story. Buried underneath lies the true meaning of the story *you* want to tell. This is where you may discover that there's a secret between the man and his wife that shines a new and complex meaning on the incident and the people you observed interacting in the supermarket. This new perspective on meaning is deeply rooted to you and your past experience and how you interpret that experience. You were presented with a scenario in the supermarket but to write the story that sparked from it you open the channel between your conscious awareness and your natural self. This will give you access to your Illusive Self, where your creativity exists, and allow communication to flow through the channel. Why? Well for one thing, you'll write a more authentic and compelling story, but to be quite honest, it's a lot easier to write the thing in the first place! Because you'll be writing from your natural self.

If you're wondering what I'm going on about and are thinking you'd much rather be able to just sit down for four weeks and get the first draft written, then read on and you'll see why that's not an easy road to success and fulfilment.

MEANING-MAKING: Opening up a channel to allow your conscious awareness to communicate with your inner self sounds a bit whacky but it's not. Creativity and meaning-making exist within your Illusive Self (the part of you that you have no conscious awareness of – call it your subconscious if you like). Think about it this way. You have conversations with yourself inside your head, right? Remember the orangutan I met as a child and how I told myself it loved me and I discovered the voice inside my head?

When you have a conversation with yourself inside your head, that is you connecting with your consciousness, or more specifically your conscious awareness. Conversation is easy, or at least let's put it that conversation is accessible. Furthermore, you're able to converse with your emotions and this you do through language and thought. Thought creates your emotions so if you think, for example, I am a failed writer, your emotions will throw failure right back at you and you will feel it on a psychological and physical level as well as on an emotional one. So that is conversation of a kind.

> *Your Illusive Self and the natural world have a deep innate connection, via your natural self, and are able to communicate in a way that we don't yet truly understand. But do know that this channel of communication exists for you*

What we aren't able to converse with is our Illusive Self. There is no channel of communication, on any level, that allows us to communicate as we understand the meaning of communication; that is through language, or the spoken/signed word. That would suggest that our Illusive Self (our subconscious) is unavailable to us. So how can we create if our creativity is locked in this illusive chasm within us? Well it's simply not true to believe that we haven't access to our Illusive Self, our creativity, our ideas and our deeper level meaning-making. We do and we access all that amazing joyful stuff via our connection with the other half of ourselves, our connection to the natural world, in other words, our natural self.

When you begin to write any idea for a novel, you are starting to explore a story. It's easy to believe that we pluck a story from what we observe in real life and then write the novel. We don't pluck anything from anywhere. The story we write, the one we choose to tell, comes from within. Ultimately the foundation of all the stories we tell comes from our past experience and our interactions with the world, in other words, our subjective self. This is writing meaning.

We can pluck ideas from thin air and put them all into a book but what will that book say to its readers? What experience will it give them if it's just a bunch of ideas you've strung together without any meaning-making from you?

I am in a stranger's bed. It's 4am.

I am in Pennan on the east coast of Scotland, close to Aberdeen. I've taken myself off to a rented cottage to write this book, or at least to begin to think about it. Earlier in the day, I'd sat outside and watched the sun rise over the ocean. Sitting at the edge of a sea that stretches for hundreds of miles. Swiping at the midges and searching for what it is, exactly, that drives us to create. To write.

Now I can still hear the sea roll lazily over the rocks outside my bedroom window. Through the curtains stream the orange hues of the rising sun. I realise that I have discovered something of an answer to what drives us to create. I can tell it to you in a single word:

Connection.

It means we are choosing to matter.

Could it be that you and I are hardwired to reach our full potential and live a life of fulfilment? Might we, right now, ask ourselves how fulfilling life can be for us if we decide to connect to our potential and reach for our dreams in the short time that we exist in this world? This means that you and I are experiential. We are open, authentic and receptive; we embrace our natural connection and are willing to make the best use of whatever it is that drives us. To reimagine and reawaken.

**Writer's Exercise:** What does all this mean for you as a writer? Ask yourself what does it mean for you to connect? To simply be and to create?

STORYTELLING: Writing is hard. There is no doubt that the four-week draft I talked about earlier would have been a struggle and worse than that, rewriting and editing would have been a nightmare. That heaving feeling of dissatisfaction and resistance, self-doubt and uncertainty – this feeling that I have right now at times writing this book. Like writing a book, like creating anything, this is all a process.

A continuous process. Your natural self is limitless, there will always be something new to learn, something new to discover, a new way to grow, a new path; all of this is available to you while you're exploring. Isn't that very liberating?

> *The Write Wild Method is also a process,*
> *it's about planting your feet and standing*
> *firm and opening yourself up to what nature*
> *has prepared for you and be willing to*
> *interpret it and return with it to your work.*

For a dedicated writer, storytelling is your life purpose. Let's say one of your aims is to live a more fulfilling life – as a writer. Are you on the constant lookout for that moment of euphoria, when the words are flowing and they are full of clarity and meaning? It's easy to forget that the creative process isn't linear. We achieve moments of euphoria only to be hit again with self-doubt and resistance that can often lead to temporary paralysis. This is known as felt experience (Roszak, T., 1992) and is a normal part of the creative process. It's about having the courage to push through resistance and the willingness to tolerate the unknown and find healthy strategies to deal with any fear or anxiety that arises and the motivation to put those strategies in place so that you can live a healthy and fulfilled creative life. It is the method, the Write Wild Method.

Our human-nature connection, that is our deep and meaningful relationship with the natural world, gives us the courage and strength to keep on creating despite self-doubt and the hundred other reasons that threaten to prevent us from showing up. It helps us embrace uncertainty and anxiety. It reminds us that we have a natural ability to become absorbed in our writing, and it allows our minds to remain open to spontaneous creativity.

The reason you want to reach this point is so that you're always on the path towards reaching your writing life purpose. What is your life purpose? Ask yourself, what are you passionate about? Make a list, e.g. you are passionate about painting, crafting, knitting, writing novels, designing hats. If this is your list, then ask, if you couldn't paint, how would you feel? If you couldn't knit, would you die inside? If you couldn't write ...? If you find that you can't score writing off the list as it would be too painful never to write again, then writing is one of your life purposes. Life purposes are different from the things we are simply passionate about; they mean something at a deeper level to us and we would be utterly miserable if we were forced to give them up (Maisel, E., 2005).

Storytelling is about awakening your writer self, opening the channel to your Illusive Self and allowing your inner creativity to burst into your conscious awareness and help you thrive as a writer. This is the way of the Write Wild Method.

## YOUR GOAL

**Writing Exercise 1**

Be willing to explore both with your body and your mind, be open to what you may discover and ready to tackle what the story you're writing demands. Every story you write is your story, and, with your natural self, your own story will continue to grow while you're on your journey to fulfilment.

*Exploring: read a fairy tale aloud*

Either write a short fairy tale or choose one of your favourites and take it outside and read it aloud, feel your growing excitement, your passion for the story, let loose your playful self.

*Meaning-Making: your life purpose*

Work on writing a statement that beautifully describes

your writing life purpose and make this your meaning statement. Refer to it often, polish it, tweak it, make sure it always reflects the work you're doing.

*Storytelling: connecting with your inner storyteller*

Always write stories you love to write. Practise a three-line story – beginning, middle and end – often and keep your creativity working hard for you.

**Writing Exercise 2**

Choose two fictional characters. You can either imagine them right now or choose two from your current work-in-progress.

Make sure to choose two opposing personalities and desires. For example, the selfish sister versus the selfless sister. The greedy boss versus the loyal employee. The villainous dragon versus the timid fairy.

Give each character the same goal. It can be to get a job, kill an enemy, write a bestseller, sail around the world, catch a killer or run a care home and so on.

**First**: One of your characters is someone who exists but never considers his own existence and expects to make no choices or decisions for themselves. The other characters is someone who wants to matter in this life, with purpose and courage and resilience.

**Next**: Rewrite the scene from the perspective of the character who simply exists. Then rewrite the scene once more from the perspective of the person choosing to matter.

**Then**: Wait a week or so. Then find a different place to

write, somewhere you haven't written before. Practise the breathing exercise at the beginning of this section. When you feel ready, think about the scenes you've written. Write down all the thoughts, words, phrases and ideas that come to mind.

What did you come up with? Anything interesting? Are you closer to understanding what drives you?

This is an exercise that will help you practise *Principle One of the Write Wild Method* and help you uncover what exactly drives your characters and why. It will also help you begin to realise that you own your own choices to reach for the writing life you want and to make meaning with your words.

# Principle Two:
# Your Elliptic Presence

**Principle Aim:** Unleash Your Creative Process
**Principle Objective:** Tolerating the Process
**Principle Goal:** Write in Spite of Yourself

## YOUR AIM

Chaos and mess are an inevitable part of the writing process and as it turns out you *will* reach moments of euphoria as you break through one creative decision after another. You've taken the journey and at times you emerge elated – you've discovered something, you've understood something, you've created the thing, etc. – and the joy of that can't be underestimated. So if the mess and chaos is overwhelming and driving you to distraction, try to remember that.

To help you remember you have your Elliptical Presence. What does this mean? We can break it down like so:

The formal definition of the adjective 'elliptical' refers to language that is obscure or ambiguous so that it's sometimes difficult to understand. This is how I like to think of the writing process at the point where you might start to wonder why you're writing, why what you're writing doesn't seem to be working, why what you write isn't what you intended to write, why you feel overwhelmed, perhaps even crushed to the point where you start to believe you can't write (okay that might just be me) and a whole lot of other chaotic 'whys?' That's if you do get these feelings sometimes. I do. If you don't, that's something to celebrate!

In this chapter, I'm going to convince you that tolerating the chaos is something you need to get good at, if you're not already. Embrace the chaos, the messy brain, the uncertainty and the doubt that often goes along with it, and keep going, keep exploring and experiencing. Remain open to experience, new perspectives and new ideas and trust me, those moments of euphoria will be yours to enjoy. You'll find your way; your writing will work and you'll surprise yourself at what you can achieve.

Understanding your Elliptic Presence will make your life easier, your writing more convincing, and disappointments and rejections will be less likely to knock you off track. In fact the better you get at embracing your Elliptic Presence, the easier you'll find yourself looking forward to the chaos, delighting in the mess, with the knowledge that this is how it's supposed to be, that you're moving forward and getting closer to and achieving your writing ambitions.

Understanding your Elliptic Presence is easier when you begin to grasp what all this creative chaos is.

Recent advancements in neurology help. If you thought that creativity belongs only in the right side of the brain (apparently also where our emotions spark from), think again. Neurologists have discovered that both sides of the brain collaborate in the process of creativity. Imagine, if you will, numerous signals and connections in your brain working on your behalf to put your ideas in order ready for them to spring into conscious awareness.

But even if you're not yet at the stage of intentionally accessing your creativity (writing wild), there are ways and means to make your creativity happen. For example, there is a test called the Alternative Uses Test that requires you to think up as many different uses as possible for an everyday object, like a paper clip. The idea is that if you can come up with more than nine different uses of the paper clip, your creativity rises into your awareness and you begin to discover more innovative creative ideas. I've used this test on retreats with writers by getting them to collect three different objects as we walk through the landscape. Then we sit down, choose the object we're most drawn to and write down as many different uses for this object – perhaps a stone, a leaf, twig or seaweed – as possible. Every writer can come up with more than nine different uses. One writer surprised us all and came up with twenty-four! Can you come up with twenty-four different uses for a paper clip? Better still, get outside, find a natural element like a stone or a leaf and try my version of this test. I wonder what you'll discover?

With writers on retreat, I discover new and surprising things all the time. On that retreat with the writer who found twenty-four different uses, we discovered that each of the writers came up with different uses that related to the genre that they wrote in. The writer with the twenty-four uses writes psychological thrillers and she used the pebble she picked up to write twenty-four different uses to kill someone. Another writer of fantasy came up with different uses relating to magic, and a writer/illustrator came up with illustrations of how to use their chosen object. I was excited, as were the writers as this was achieved outside the realms of conscious awareness. In other words, they didn't know they were discovering genre-related ideas and I hadn't expected this amazing feat of genius.

**This is about process. About fully embracing a mindset that is conscious of the present moment and is open and curious about the unknown.**

Getting outside, experiencing new and natural places, observing, being curious about your surroundings, experiencing the now of the landscape – all of these things can and I feel should be part of the writing process. Simply think of it as your journey to a mindset growth, a wild mindfulness, where you're opening yourself up to receiving inspiration from unexpected places. This is combinatory play: the capacity to invite your innate genius to step forward and fill the gaps. This is your Elliptic Presence.

**A Writer's Exercise**

How do you embrace chaos in your writing process? Some of you will find it easier than others. The fastest route to tolerating the mess is to actively notice and confront the way it makes you feel as soon as the writing process starts to feel uncomfortable. That uncomfortable feeling is crucial to creative discovery; you want to get to a place where you get excited about feeling uncomfortable, allowing your courage to step in and shield you.

Keep a notebook and pen by your side as you write. Any time you begin to feel uncomfortable, overwhelmed or at moments when you doubt yourself, ask yourself:

1. How does this feel?
2. What am I thinking?
3. Why am I thinking and feeling this?
4. How might I get excited about these thoughts and feelings?

In our daily lives we always have the opportunity to

practise answering these questions when moments arrive that make us feel uncomfortable and these answers are just as useful as those you note down while writing. For example, I might decide not to make my bed every morning for seven days and each day I'll ask myself the four questions above. This helps me practise how I might embrace those moments of chaos and mess during the writing process.

**Quick Recap**

The writing process is a creative process and it's supposed to feel chaotic and messy at times as this is how we process our creativity and discover new ideas. Neurologists have discovered that both sides of the brain collaborate in the process of creativity and your Elliptic Presence plays a pivotal role in bringing you to the present moment. The aim is to get to a point where you can tolerate the chaos and mess, perhaps even look to embrace this part of the process and get excited about it. This process relates to your willingness to develop a mindset conscious of the present moment and open and curious about the unknown. Combining writing with getting outside and letting nature nurture your courage and creativity is the fastest and easiest route to a writing journey that is exhilarating rather than overwhelming.

## YOUR OBJECTIVE

**Preparation**

- Get outside: combine writing with nature and develop a writing process that is 80% exploring and 20% writing.
- Confront your moments of doubt, imposter syndrome and overwhelm by reframing how you talk

to yourself and how this makes you think and feel, with a view to finding strategies that allow you to fully embrace the chaos.
- Indulge in combinatory play – begin to believe that play is all part of the process and that often, stepping away from your writing to practise another art form or something else pleasurable will help you discover the answers to your current challenges.
- Fully embrace a mindset that is conscious of the present moment and is open and curious about the unknown.
- Be open to experience and new perspectives.
- Acknowledge that it's better to invest more time up front so as to be able to process a problem more efficiently later on.
- Decide to overcome obstacles.
- Acknowledge that creativity is a choice.

**Purpose**

We use our Elliptic Presence in the following way:

- *Preparation* – we begin and continue to gather information.

- *Incubation* – we allow the information to percolate while your Illusive Self (for now, let's coin it your unconscious or subconscious mind) takes over **and engages in combinatory play.**

- *Illumination* – that moment of euphoria, or at least a moment of insight awakens in your conscious awareness. Your creativity has been given the freedom to rise to your awareness.

- *Authentication* – this is the writing part, where you communicate creatively using words to describe the meaning of your insights and illuminations.

Engaging in combinatory play isn't merely exploring another avenue of creativity. Without granting freedom to our creative impulses, how can we effectively and meaningfully convey our thoughts? By likening 'writing wild' to combinatory play, you intuitively integrate it into your writing routine, establishing an ongoing conduit to your creativity that seamlessly enriches your writing.

**Your Elliptic Presence: It's not all about being present!**

I want to introduce you now to your **imagination network**. This might excite you, if you're not already aware of it, because this is when your brain is working creatively on your behalf – the moment you allow your Elliptic Presence freedom and enter the wild places.

The imagination network refers back to my comment earlier that creativity is neither a left nor right function of the brain. Current thinking dictates that different brain regions are recruited during the creative process and, depending on what you're attempting to create, several brain regions combine to form networks that help you achieve your creative task. In the interests of brevity and my determination not to bore you to death, I want to focus in on one particular widely accepted network of creativity and that's your imagination network.

Your imagination network makes up the parts of the brain working creatively on your behalf while you're out in the wild, or walking mindfully or engaging in quiet time in your local park. We can break this down into three separate but combined brain activities that are happening behind the scenes:

1. Personal meaning-making – as you connect with nature, your Illusive Self is busy making sense of your creative ideas and it does this easily via the

imagination network as it activates your unique and innate connection to the landscape. The more you practise meaning-making in the natural world, the stronger your relationship will be with your Illusive Self.

2. Mental stimulation – science shows us that a hybrid writing process – combining writing with time out to explore nature – may actually provide the most optimal environment for unleashing creativity.

3. Perspective taking – imagining other perspectives and scenarios, comprehending stories and reflecting on mental and emotional states, both your own and others. All of the Write Wild principles and techniques contribute to your ability to discover new perspectives, greater understanding and a more meaningful relationship with your natural self, your self as a writer and your optimal writing process.

**But let's not forget why we're here**

Creativity doesn't just happen without your awareness. It doesn't all go on behind the scenes, you have to work just as hard at your writing as your brain is working for you creatively. How best can you do that? By understanding your Elliptic Presence as something akin to your unique creative blueprint.

Sternberg's (1999) Investment Theory helps us do that. As you continue to read, you may want to have a sheet of paper at your side and sketch each of the six factors that combine to make up the Investment Theory of Creativity. The best way to sketch this is to do it in a mind-map style.

*Intellectual abilities*:

Your intellectual abilities allow you to think far and beyond conventional ideas and see resistance and other problems in a new light, and you gain new perspectives. You already have the ability to make decisions about your ideas and the skill set to sell the worth of that idea both to yourself and to others.

The confluence (where two paths merge) is, according to Sternberg, the crucial element. For example, you may come up with what you believe to be a brilliant title for your novel, you take it to your publisher and are told your title doesn't work. What might have happened is that you feel overwhelmingly creative but haven't engaged any critical thinking, i.e. analysed whether your title reflects your plot, and therefore your publisher believes your title idea to be poor.

*Knowledge*

Sternberg cautions us that knowledge can either facilitate or impede creativity. He emphasises that without understanding the current state of a path, for example the reason why you thought your title was brilliant, progress is hindered. However, excessive reliance on existing knowledge can lead to rigidity in problem-solving approaches. Let's say your title exists and for no good reason you can think of, you are dogmatically determined to keep it. At such times, it's crucial to unleash our imagination and remain receptive to new ways of thinking and problem-solving.

**We want to be open to experience and new perspectives and thought processes**

*Styles of thinking*

According to this theory, thinking styles involve choices regarding how we utilise our available skills. To foster creativity, Sternberg suggests adopting a 'legislative style', which entails a preference for and a conscious decision to think in innovative ways. Importantly, we possess the power to make these decisions. Sternberg encourages us to transcend conventional thinking and figure out what truly matters from what doesn't.

*Personality attributes*

Where does our personality come in? It has to count for something. Ask yourself, how far are you willing to:

- overcome obstacles?
- take sensible risks?
- tolerate ambiguity?
- believe that, whatever your personality, you can choose to do or not do any of the above?

*Motivation*

Goals and dreams are our advantage, but we have to take the steps that lead us to our dreams. If all we do is dream, we will never create anything. We decide to be motivated by the creative project we love. Try creating something you have no interest in, or something that goes against your values, or something you're only half loving, you'll feel a lot more pain than you will creating something you love, something you're absolutely captivated by. If you're not captivated by it but you're duty bound to complete it then the best approach is to find a strategy that will get you captivated! And keep going.

*Environment*

The final element to this theory is the environment. To be creative you want to work within an environment that is supportive and rewarding of creative ideas. When environments are non-supportive, it's up to you how you decide to respond. Assessing your Elliptic Presence is a good way of acknowledging the impact your writing environment is having on you at any particular moment. Bring your attention to your body, allow yourself to be completely in the present and acknowledge what you're thinking and how your thoughts are impacting on your feelings, and how your body feels. Your Elliptic Presence is with you at all times and is a reminder to connect to your natural self. Where you write is just as important as your nature experiences. Bring those experiences into your writing space and re-experience, reimagine, bringing all of that energy into your present working environment. Eventually you'll be able to work anywhere as you will instinctively channel your natural self and become almost instantly absorbed in your work.

## YOUR GOAL

**Writing Exercise 1**

Choose to do this exercise adapted from Robert J. Sternberg's *Handbook of Creativity*.

For the next five days, write five stories. When you sit down to write, set a timer for fifteen minutes. Stop writing when the timer runs out. Choose a different title each day from the following:

1. The Penguin and the Gun
2. Five Minutes Before
3. The Sixteenth
4. The Other Half
5. The Glass Stage

I hope by now that if you didn't know already, **creativity is a choice**. The choice you can make is one that embraces the chaos of the creative process. One whereby you endure with joy the messy first draft, the difficult decisions, the complex problems, the resistance, the self-doubt and you discover something about yourself. That you can create. That your Elliptic Presence is your weapon of choice in the process of becoming and being a writer.

**Writing Exercise 2**

The next time you're out exploring and being present in nature spend half an hour sitting in a secluded spot with a notebook and pen. Imagine there are six closed doors in front of you. Take the time you need to form a vivid visual image of the six doors. To open each door you must make a commitment to yourself, your protagonist and your reader.

Write down six commitments relating to your Elliptic Presence and give yourself the joy of opening each of the doors.

# Principle Three: Ebb and Flow

**Principle Aim:** Get the Writing Done
**Principle Objective:** Absorption and Writing Naturally
**Principle Goal:** Bottom Up

## YOUR AIM

In the last section I talked about the writing process and how you as a writer may want to think about ways you might learn to embrace the chaos that the creative process demands. In this section I want to talk about the actual act of sitting down to write creatively. Because when it comes to it, we have to get the stuff written.

Many years ago, as an undergraduate psychology student, I wanted to explore whether creative writers were uniquely inclined to better use their imaginations and what that meant. Back then, in the late 90s I was aspiring to academic genius but I was still writing creatively. And I was still believing I wasn't achieving anywhere near genius in either discipline. What was eluding me, I kept asking myself? I decided to do my dissertation on the subject and compare writers with non-writers on a variety of relevant scales and tests.

My dissertation helped me to discover that the **act of** creative writing itself is what sets writers apart from non-writers. This may sound obvious but stay with me for a moment and I'll tell you something that's much less obvious.

The persistent act of creative writing occupies more areas of the brain than you may think. Of course we employ our cognitive abilities, this is how we get the writing done and how we communicate to our readers on a basic level. But as we write we're also tapping into the emotional centre of the brain, bringing our emotions to the page. For example, we may have a character hanging from a cliff edge and we'd want to do our best to give our readers that experience at an emotional level. Also we bring our unique perceptual abilities to our writing. Your thoughts and feelings about how it feels in your imagination to hang from a cliff edge are different to mine and everyone else's. This is why we read, to learn, to stretch ourselves and widen our perspectives.

**It may surprise you to know that the persistent act of creative writing will more likely than not increase your motivation to write.**

Let's just quickly reflect on all of this for a moment. What does the persistent act of creative writing really mean? That's easy, it means simply showing up and putting the effort in on a regular basis. This act of persistence employs the following abilities:

- Cognition
- Emotions
- Perceptions
- Motivation
- Communication

The basic idea is that the more we *persist*, that is, the regularity with which we show up to our writing, the better we get at each of these abilities and the better we get at writing. We also get better at communicating so I've added that to the list. Don't go mistaking this for the old adage that practice makes perfect because perfection has nothing to do with it. All that's required is that you show up persistently and regularly. Perfection isn't a human brain ability. Perfection is a socially constructed concept, at best a distraction and at worst a barrier to writing ability and productivity.

A host of studies have shown that compared to people who don't write and/or those that write infrequently, persistent creative writers are better able to engage in activities that the creative process demands, such as challenging traditional thought patterns and embracing uncertainties. In other words, if you're persistent, you will be better able to stretch yourself and take risks with your creativity and tolerate the messy creative process regardless of any barriers in your way or any blocks that arise.

What does it mean to stretch and take risks? As creatives, our aim is to wander into the unknown and to do that we have to be willing to take risks, whether that is in our writing life, for example, giving up our day job to become a full-time writer, that's quite a scary risk to take. Or paying to enter a competition may feel risky. But we also take risks with our writing, we may want to experiment, stretch genre convention, stretch our own perception. Make sense?

You may have noticed that I use the word 'persistent' regularly when I'm referring to the abilities of creative writers. To persist is to:

> *Continue obstinately despite opposition*
> *Collins English Dictionary*

Being persistent means being unrelenting.

How might you develop strategies to help you be unrelenting? Stop here for a moment and note down your thoughts. Ask yourself:

- What does unrelenting mean to you?
- How might you bring that to your writing life?
- What strategies can you think of that will help you build your capacity to be unrelenting with your writing life and your writing time?

What happens when you give freedom to your imagination while at the same time you employ effective strategies to get the work done? Does this sound like a growth plan for success to you?

## YOUR OBJECTIVE

At its core, we employ many abilities when we practise the act of writing creatively. The act of writing when we get down to it consists of three components:

- Fantasy
- Absorption
- Dissociation

To sum this up quickly, during the writing process, the greater you indulge in these three components, the easier the writing will feel. We use our imagination to fantasise, to develop our plot, characters and story. During the writing process you are required to write these fantasies and to do that well, you need to be fully absorbed in the act of writing. You need to be absorbed to the extent that you're able to shut out the real world and enter your imaginary one. When you're able to do that successfully, you are dissociating; stepping into your imaginary world and letting your real world fizzle to dust.

Most writers are able to achieve this level of absorption. It's much easier and faster if you have a *persistent* daily or regular practice. It's also more effective if you enter your imaginary world as your true natural self, having thrown aside the identities you adopt as human in the real world and using the power of your creative energy for your creative purpose.

You might associate dissociation with mental health conditions like PTSD or Dissociative Identity Disorder, and indeed, it is linked to them. However, dissociation is also a natural ability inherent in all humans. It's a normal cognitive function, contrasting with association. Dissociation comes into play during hypnotic states and other forms of trance, where we gradually disengage from external stimuli to focus on internal images, memories, and sensations. Even the act of concentrating or focusing attention inherently involves a certain level of dissociation.

This is how you begin to understand your own meaning, your natural self. You are tapping into what makes you unique and as you write, what makes your story unique. You're tapping into your purpose and why your uniqueness is important. Why the world needs to hear your story. The meaning behind who you are and why you write. You are giving your readers your natural self, your unique genius.

You achieve greater Ebb and Flow **if you adopt a natural writing practice**. It's as simple as that. It's difficult to really engage and become absorbed with your writing project if you pick it up every now and then thinking you may write a line or two. Compare this to creating a neural network in your brain that springs into action and shows up on your behalf so that each writing day you pick up your project you take less and less time to become fully absorbed in it to the extent that the real world fades away for most or all of your writing time. Without a natural practice, your brain and energy are having to compete with your indecisive thoughts, your lack of motivation, your procrastinating, your guilt and your temptations.

*A NATURAL daily writing practice takes a different approach to the writing process as it combines tools and techniques from nature that give you immeasurable positive benefits to both your writing life, your writing process and your personal health and well-being.*

The key to developing a natural writing practice is to keep it simple. Keeping it simple helps you to be clear on what you have to do so that once you've mastered it you get on and do it without thinking.

**A Writer's Exercise**

Take yourself out into nature as often as you can over the next week or so. Practise a little natural mindfulness. Then pay attention to the ebb and flow of the land, the sky, growth, movement, sounds and touch. Try to grasp what Ebb and Flow means for you, how it feels, what you're experiencing as you grow your own understanding of exactly how you become absorbed.

Physically embody the movement of the trees, or the ocean or the sky or birds as they fly past.

Pick up some sand, or pebbles or earth and slowly let it fall from your hand and imagine that movement flowing through your body.

Lie on the earth, or get in the water or feel the wind against you and let your body move with nature's movement, focusing only on how it feels physically.

For every feeling or experiencing word that comes to mind try to photograph what it is that brought the word into your conscious awareness so that when you get home you can refer to the photograph and this will instantly take you back to that absorbing feeling with no effort from you at all. You can then use this as a tool each time you sit down to write and the more you develop your persistence, the more your ability to become instantly absorbed in your writing will strengthen.

**Quick Recap**

The writing process *and* the writing become less onerous if you develop your natural self and commit to being persistent with your writing process. If you put the effort in to show up to your writing with commitment and persistence, and you continue to develop your natural self, this combination of activity will greatly strengthen your Ebb and Flow, that is, your ability to instantly become absorbed in your writing without any fuss, stress or confusion.

## YOUR OBJECTIVE

Ebb and Flow is really a measure of how you practise the act of writing creatively. It's about how you bring your natural self and your purpose to your writing. When you're able to articulate to yourself your unique physical experience of Ebb and Flow you will bring that to your writing, making the act of writing a natural inevitability. You will ease into your writing session effortlessly, be more productive and have greater connection to your words.

Deciding whether to commit to a daily or regular writing routine is entirely within your control, regardless of obstacles, setbacks or self-imposed limitations. These choices become available when you embrace a mindset of unwavering determination, when you are naturally unrelenting. When you consistently show up for yourself, despite fluctuations in motivation, you pave the way for a smoother writing process. Your goal is to cultivate a natural habit of showing up and accomplishing your writing goals effortlessly.

**Preparation**

- Discover how you can improve your capacity to be persistent and unrelenting.
- Develop a writing practice that makes turning up to your writing effortless.
- Bring to your writing your natural self.
- Grow your mindset to reach your meaning and purpose.
- Physically experience your own unique Ebb and Flow.
- Let your imagination free.
- Keep the act of writing simple and natural.

**Purpose**

It's reasonable to assume that when you are entirely absorbed in your writing and allowing yourself freedom to explore your imagination you are choosing to neglect or ignore your real-life setting, in particular, your human self in your external reality. You are disassociating yourself from real-world activity.

Have you ever experienced the sensation of returning from a deep writing session feeling as though you've emerged from a hypnotic trance? While researching for my dissertation, I proposed the idea that creative writers often engage in dissociation, viewing it as a key aspect of a 'creative device' activated by their inclination, or rather, their motivation to fantasise. By simplifying these concepts and focusing on their fundamental definitions, and assuming creative writers both dissociate and possess a desire to fantasise, it becomes apparent that the ability to become fully engrossed serves as a crucial link between the two. It appeared to me that there exists a symbiotic relationship between fantasy, dissociation and absorption in the creative writing process, a connection which my research aimed to substantiate.

Relatively speaking, creative writers spend an inordinate amount of their time absorbed in imaginary worlds full of the fantasy scenarios, events and lives of the characters they write about. It's important to note here that while my own research drew on studies from the clinical field where dissociation is generally thought to be a type of defence or coping mechanism, I also extended my study outside the field of psychology and found research that shows dissociation to be a motivational or adaptive ability. I wanted to see if there was, for creative writers, an indication that the relationship between absorption and dissociation could be understood in terms of being a goal response mechanism, rather than a defensive one. In other words, whether this relationship constituted a responsive goal-orientated and voluntary 'tool' used by creative writers to write. A tool? Yes, a tool.

Why do I consider it a tool? I delved deeper into my research by conducting a cognitive-style experiment in addition to the standardised tests assessing dissociation and absorption. Despite working with a small group, it was crucial for me to derive meaningful results. This experiment not only enabled me to achieve that goal but also revealed that writers tend to exhibit a specific cognitive learning style known as field-independence.

The abilities of field-dependence/field-independence individuals were mostly researched by Herman Witkin back in the 50s. I used his 'Hidden Figures' experiment which, simply put, shows a field-dependent person will have difficulty finding a geometric shape that is embedded or 'hidden' in a background with similar, non-identical lines and shapes. The conflicting patterns cause distraction. A person who is field-independent can more easily identify the geometric shape, regardless of the background setting. What I found was that writers have a tendency towards a field-independent learning style.

**Field-dependent = non-writers**
**Field-*IN*dependent = writers**

Perhaps you'd like to think about this for a moment. People who are field-dependent are often thought of as being sociable and able to convey their own feelings in a social setting and they appear to be hampered by a lack of structure in their environment. On the flip side, field-independent people are able to impose their own sense of order and structure on their environment. Socially, field-independent people are autonomous, often thought of as impersonal and task-orientated. Importantly, field-independent people are able to distinguish and maintain their sense of self from the environment. Sit with this for a moment and consider where you sit along the field-dependent /field-independent spectrum. And whether you're aware that you bring dissociation as a conscious voluntary tool to your writing.

In other sections of this book I talk about there being no inside or outside, that the self and the environment are one and the same. This may sound conflicting if writers have a preference for field-independence but it's not. How can your connection with the natural world be unique, if you have no sense of your own uniqueness within it? It is because you may possess this propensity toward a field-independent cognitive style that allows you to see, feel and experience your natural world, however it exists around you. In other words, because you may require no fixed structure to understand yourself within it, you are open to greater experience, new, meaningful ideas and, above all, a greater connection to your world, your sense of self, your words and your reader. Isn't that amazing? It actually defines the foundation of the Write Wild Method and why I've spent so long pulling it all together. As a writer, you have so much more available to you than you can ever imagine. Once you begin to discover your own path, the Write Wild Method can be a transformative force as it encourages you to engage in a deeper and more meaningful relationship with the natural world which, in turn, helps you engage in a deeper and more meaningful creative journey. What we might decide to call an interdependent relationship.

## YOUR GOAL

I invite you to imagine this interdependent relationship as a kind of push and pull string of activity that tests you and your ability to liberate yourself, to detach yourself from total control over the creative process, to not so much manage but be curious about the way in which your writing and your natural self are interdependent.

Does this sound counterintuitive or odd to you? Why

wouldn't you want to dominate your writing? Don't we need to keep control of our words? We do, but not in the sense of our words – we need to control how we convey our meaning to our reader, but we don't need total control over the creative process.

When we stop thinking in terms of having control we give ourselves the opportunity for discovery. We develop a stronger connection to the natural world that frees us up to discover new ideas and new perspectives via our experience. If our experience with nature is reciprocal, we are liberated from fixed ideas and unhelpful processes.

Frank Lloyd Wright is perhaps most famous for designing the Guggenheim Museum and for the Frank Lloyd Wright Foundation. The reason I'm drawing your attention to architecture is that while learning the craft of writing, the terms architecture and structure, often used interchangeably, relate to the way you shape your story. For example, you'll learn the three-act structure, plotting, characterisation, style, voice, etc. A quick Google search results in something like this:

- A sequence of events that culminate in a compelling story. (Structure)

- A series of interconnected, cause and effect scenes populated with characters, plot, pace, motive, concept, theme, voice and style. (Architecture or skeleton)

These are all top-down methods of creating a story. It is possible to write a novel using a structure template. In fact, humans are conditioned to the three-act structure, it was first described in Aristotle's *Poetics* over two thousand years ago and we appear to have an innate fondness or perhaps even preference for it. The majority of movies follow this structure and if you want to study it, I suggest you binge on Pixar movies. It's a fun way of studying structure and story architecture, identifying the extra elements that Pixar are great at, and that audiences adore.

Some writing advice will discuss architecture in terms of the skeleton. You begin your story with the basic bones and add flesh to these bones building up a living, breathing story. Another way to think about it is that you are adding layers, or subplots, as you'll see in the Pixar multi-layered approach to compelling story making.

There are limitless resources, easily accessed, that will satisfy any longing you have to know about all the different methods of designing structure and building story architecture. Here, we're not going to investigate this approach to writing any further. Instead, we're going to start thinking about Organic Architecture and how it can help us strengthen our natural self and transform our reach to our readers.

Note: If you're particularly interested in Pixar's storytelling method (which is sound and well worth studying), I recommend you read the brief and easily digested book: *Pixar Storytelling* by Dean Movshovitz.

Organic Architecture: What is it and why does it matter to writers? Well, Frank Lloyd Wright's architectural designs were inspired by nature. He is quoted as saying,

'*Study nature, love nature, stay close to nature. It will never let you down.*'

Wright's definition of organic architectural design was that a building should be natural, appropriate to time and, more importantly, place. Here, Wright saw reciprocal relationships:

Organic is natural

Natural is organic

When Wright designed the house he called 'Falling Water', he said that the waterfall came first and the house came second. He wanted to design buildings not as mechanical objects but as part of the landscape. Google this house and you'll get a sense of what he was aiming for.

In this sense, natural can be described as existing in or derived from nature, not made or caused by humankind. For Wright, nature was his inspiration. He asks us to look at it, be inspired by it and reminds us that no one else can make the same connection. Your relationship with nature is yours and yours alone. Like a fingerprint. The connection between nature's inspiration and your creativity is a magical process that is impossible to define because it's different for each individual and each individual in space and time. You are more likely to feel it than to be able to define it. This is what we mean when we understand that nature is about feeling and experience.

Earlier we discussed structure and story architecture in terms of a top-down process. Ideas come from the mechanisms inside your brain. In practice, you sit, ready to write, and either hope for inspiration (that, by design, must come from past experience) or detail outlines, plans, character sketches and so on. Does it matter that your character prefers tomato sauce to brown sauce? It only matters if the sauce is a McGuffin or otherwise plays another crucial role in the story. Perhaps the poison was in the tomato sauce and not the brown sauce ...

I want you to start developing a bottom-up approach to your writing and writing process. Put simply, in the business world, a top-down approach relies on historical data while a bottom-up approach is all about drawing data from observation. The top-down approach is backward thinking and the bottom-up approach is forward-thinking. Taking a bottom-up approach to writing means you can't not respond. In other words, you are constantly observing, with all your senses and sensibilities and making decisions based on what you observe in the present (not what you experienced in the past). This allows you to strengthen your relationship between the inner you and the outer you. You are writing from the ground up, from the earth under your feet. This will give you an inner confidence that will flow through you and reach right into the heart of your reader.

**Writing Exercise 1**

Do the opposite:

This exercise is one that you will have to consciously compel yourself to do. It's best done at times when you believe you should be writing but can't, for whatever reason, get yourself together enough to face it. I want you to do the opposite.

Take a notepad and pen and/or your phone out to a place you haven't discovered before. This may take some planning ahead but if you're doing this on the spur of the moment, it's fine to choose a street close by or drive to a location you've never been to. It doesn't really matter, what counts is that you're outdoors and taking your body and mind out for a creative exercise. Walk for ten to fifteen minutes. Stop at a quiet spot and sit. Either write or record on your phone the following:

- Describe the sounds.
- Close your eyes and describe the air on your skin.
- Describe the feeling of whatever is supporting your

sitting position, a bench, the ground, a rock, etc.
- Note down any thoughts you're having about your investment in your writing project.

Take these writings home and sit with your writing project. Choose a word, sentence or paragraph that you've written and write it at the top of the page. Then continue with your writing project (you can always delete what you've written from your notes later).

**Writing Exercise 2**

If you don't already, think about how you may include a daily writing practice into your everyday life. Write answers to the following:

- Why don't I have a daily writing practice? Are my reasons ones that make sense to me? OR
- Why do I have a daily writing practice? Are my reasons ones that make sense to me?
- What would change for me if I developed a daily writing practice? OR
- What would change for me if I stopped my daily writing practice?
- Am I unrelenting? Am I unrelenting enough when it comes to my writing?

# Principle Four: Your Illusive Self

**Principle Aim:** Nature Nurtures
**Principle Objective:** Your Writer's Ecosystem
**Principle Goal:** Creative Aliveness

*Mining your ideas from elusive to illusive: shedding light on your imagination and creativity*

## YOUR AIM

Think of your Illusive Self as the name for your creativity. It lives within you and it needs oxygen to come out to play and it is limitless when it is fully connected to your natural self. Not only does it need oxygen but your Illusive Self also requires you to believe in your creative self. And the easiest way to go about believing in your creative abilities is to understand your Writer's Ecosystem, how it works and why and how you can use it to be your best creative self.

We live in a world where it can be difficult to truly believe in our own capabilities. There's always someone doing it better, an expectation that you can do it better, a word or comment that you can't do it. Often the words and comments come from our own talking head. It's really quite simple to believe that if we're constantly doubting our own abilities then our own abilities are going to be doubtful. Make sense?

Apart from how we talk to ourselves, what others say and think about us has no bearing on our own creative capabilities. Even if you struggle to believe in your own creativity, it's worth trying to believe that. Someone may criticise your book, an agent or publisher may reject your book, a 'friend' may constantly remind you of why you shouldn't be wasting your time writing, all of these supposed self-belief crushing events are actually food for our creativity, our strength and our resilience.

I remember all the way through school I wanted to go to art college but my art teacher told me I wouldn't make it, I wasn't good enough. My family and friends told me to get a proper job and that studying art was a waste of time. I believed all of that instead of believing in my own creativity and didn't go to art school. And yet, as a psychology undergraduate I had to learn statistics and pass regular statistics exams. I failed every one of them; it wasn't until I was at university that I was diagnosed with dyslexia. Failing all of my statistic exams didn't prevent me from spending eight years in a job that required me to do statistics every day. Imagine if I hadn't believed the naysayers bumping on about why I shouldn't go to art college. I'll tell you what I believe, I believe that there isn't a human being alive that doesn't have a similar story to tell.

We all have an Illusive Self, and for you the writer, it's part of what makes up the triangle of your writer's ecosystem. With your writer's ecosystem, you don't have to strive to believe in yourself, it simply comes naturally.

Consider the following statement: *Self-belief possibly comes naturally once you realise you're not in this creative life alone.* You have your writing ecosystem – your unique triangle – to rely on. This is your triangle:

```
        YOU
     YOUR MIND
    ILLUSIVE YOU
```

### YOUR WRITER'S ECOSYSTEM

So what is this?

In each of us there exists three parts. The part that is you – the physical you (including the brain). The part that is your mind. The part that is illusive you. When each of these parts is connected, self-belief becomes less of an issue as it is a natural part of that connection. When the connection is broken, doubts and fears are able to creep in leaving your self-belief vulnerable. So, rather than attempting to improve on self-belief, it's worth investigating where your connection may be broken and fixing that.

Writing is a whole body experience. I believe that the actual writing part is around 20% and the rest of the time we spend 'writing' is all experience driven. However you write it's important to be aware of how your writer's ecosystem is functioning on a daily basis.

Each day, give some thought to each point of your triangle.

YOU: How is your body functioning, physically and mentally? Does this part of you need some attention? If you're physically exhausted, overwhelmed with fatigue you're going to struggle to want to get any writing done and you're leaving yourself open to long-term problems and vulnerable to a crisis of self-belief.

YOUR MIND: Where are your thoughts taking you? How are your thoughts making you feel? Are you mentally striving towards your goals or are you telling yourself lies? Are you getting in your own way? Or, are you trying to cope with a real-life crisis, do you have strategies in place for the unexpected and are you employing those strategies?

YOUR ILLUSIVE SELF: Nature nurtures your creativity. It also nurtures your health and well-being. The stronger your relationship with nature, the easier it will be for you to be creative, come up with original ideas and effortlessly write as your natural self.

The takeaway from all this is that you can't be creative if you're anxious. If one or both YOU and YOUR MIND parts of your writer's ecosystem is in peril it's time to address what the problem is and employ strategies to lessen the impact. One of those strategies may be to stop what you're doing and devote your writing time to your Illusive Self. Get yourself into nature and allow it to heal, nurture and inform you.

Disclaimer: I am not a doctor. Spending time in nature is a great way to heal and a great way of igniting your creativity. However, it is not always the entire solution to maintaining good strong health and mental well-being and you should always seek the help and support of professionals as and when need arises.

*A curious thing*: On a daily basis I have to manage chronic pain and fatigue and I do this with medication. My time spent in nature is only one of the methods I use to manage my daily functioning. I do have a goal, or perhaps it's a purpose, to get to the point where I spend a greater amount of my day every day in nature and the test will be whether I am able to reduce or even stop my medication. But I'm not there yet. I may never be but the point is we have to be aware of our writer's ecosystem and ensure that we're doing what is necessary to keep it functioning at its best.

Nature invites us in, it feeds us, but it doesn't care whether we live or die.

If it's clear there are no issues with the other two parts (e.g. health, illness, exhaustion, real-life demands, etc.), the focus then falls on Illusive You.

This is the part of us we cannot converse with. We can have silent conversations with ourselves – our mind and our body – but we are not able to converse with the illusive part of us. This is the part where creativity thrives. By attending to this part of us, we are giving ourselves our best chance at creativity. Illusive You requires you to become an experiential writer.

**A Writer's Exercise**

Exploring Illusive You:

The Novel Box

1. Think of the end of your novel (or any story you've written or are thinking of writing). What core emotion do you want the reader to leave with after finishing your book? Write it down.

2. Think backwards about the last three steps in your plot that led up to that emotion. Write them down. 1 for the step closest to the end. 2 for the next step back. 3 for the next step back.

3. Imagine: You are lying on the forest floor. It is a warm comforting sunny day. Feel the breeze. Listen to the sounds of the forest. Feel the ground underneath you. This is your place, no one will disturb you. Look up between the trees to the sky.

4. You have a weightless box lying on your chest. The box contains limitless boxes, each smaller than the last. But for now, you can only feel this one box.

5. Think of step 3 on your list. Think about the impact of this step first on you. Then on your characters. Then on your reader. Open the box. Observe what is released. Anything can be released, objects, items, smells, tastes, sounds, mini-scenes, dialogue, memories, something unfamiliar, etc. Keep observing, attending to anything that interests or excites you. Do this until you come to a natural stop.

6. Write about the experience you've just had and what emerged from the box.

7. Repeat this exercise by returning your physical self (via your imagination) to the forest floor. Open the first box, inside you will find another box. Think about step 2 on your list. Think about the impact of this step first on you. Then on your characters. Then on your reader. Open the box. Observe what is released. Continue as before.

8. Repeat this exercise for the final step (step 1).

9. You now have three sets of observations. Combine everything you've written. What are your words saying to you?

These are your words, your creative ideas that you have allowed to emerge from your Illusive Self. If you think about what you're doing here, you are accessing the part of You the Writer that knows more about your creative project than you do. When we're connected, and/or when we connect to our Illusive Self, we have access to that knowledge.

## A Quick Recap

Fully understanding that your creativity is always available to you via your writer's ecosystem is a strength that will help you to tackle doubts and fears and give you a strong belief in yourself that you can and are able to succeed creatively. Remember, you can always be creative practically while exploring Illusive You. In other words, these types of experiential explorations can work simultaneously to move you forward with your writing project.

It's obvious but we tend to forget that whatever we create comes from who we are and why we're creating. Anything less will be either inauthentic, stale or unoriginal and will most likely fail to excite a reader.

When you're writing, you are effectively searching for a meaning connection, the very thing that will help your words stand out and live memorably inside the mind of your reader.

## YOUR OBJECTIVE

### Preparation

- Befriend your writer's ecosystem.
- Discover ways of listening to your Illusive Self via

nature (natural mindfulness, immersion, etc.).
- Pay attention to your body experience – You, Your Mind, Your Illusive Self.
- Become an experiential writer.
- Notice how you're spending the 80% of your writing experiential time: is this time spent working in your best interests?
- Discover natural strategies to help you believe in your self-worth.
- Use your writer's ecosystem tool on page 86.
- Accept nature's invitation and gain from her enduring support.

**Purpose**

Your Writer's Ecosystem, while being a handy at a glance nod to ensuring your writing progress and improvement, can also be used as a tool that we call The Growth Ring (we'll come to that a bit later on, on page 258) by which you can easily keep track of your progress and measure your results. Working with your own writer's ecosystem especially helps you to liberate yourself from getting in your own way. And, especially, liberate yourself from getting in your own way. What it does for you is give you a tool that will point you in the right direction to finishing your writing project. So that while you're dealing with the messy chaotic creative process, you can reassure yourself that you are making progress, even if it doesn't look like you are.

The Writer's Ecosystem may work for you, especially if you like the idea of accountability. Getting insight into your writer's ecosystem gives you a measure of self-accountability and if you're skilled at beating yourself up on a regular basis, this tool will reduce your willingness to give your time and energy to this useless practice. Also, if you're engaging with your writer's ecosystem, you're encouraging your inner critic to quieten down and stop berating you. It works because it brings you together with your natural creative self. It gives you a route to developing your natural connection. In other words, you'll be writing with your creative aliveness.

## YOUR GOAL

Keep this in mind:

*'We are part of nature; we are in the Earth, not on it. We are like the cells in the body of the vast living organism that is planet Earth. An organism cannot continue to function healthily if one group of cells decides to dominate and cannibalise the other energy systems of the body.' (Roszak, T., et.al., 1995, p66 Ecopsychology)*

Hundreds of years ago, society depended on the natural world for its survival. In fact, cultures celebrated and worshipped nature. With the onset of domestication, we as the human race began to rely less on the natural world as part of our survival and more on what we can take from it to progress.

As humans, we are a species like any other animal. We rely on the natural world to survive. It is as much a part of us as our body is. I always hark back to that saying, I have to look after my body as where else would I live? Equally we have to look after our natural world because where else would we live? But it goes deeper than that.

The way we live today we are a lot more detached from the natural world and therefore our natural selves. For many years we've thought we've controlled and dominated the Earth but we were backward in our thinking and we are suffering now because we've lost that important – and necessary for our survival – relationship with nature and the planet we live on. We view ourselves as separate and superior when instead we are truly equal to, related to and dependent upon the natural world for achieving our creative life purpose (Glendinning, C., and Shephard, P., in, Roszak, T., 1995, p62) – this we can refer to as our writer's ecological consciousness and the tool we use is the Writer's Ecosystem.

The Writer's Ecosystem is a tool for investigating your ecological consciousness. It invites you to discover paths to new ideas to solving your writing challenges, achieving productivity, success and self-healing (working along the relationship continuum between you, your words, your reader).

**Writer's Exercise 1**

In your notebook, answer the following questions:

1. What does creativity mean for you?
2. Where does creativity come from?
3. Can I be creative when I don't feel like being creative?

The above are three questions that get you thinking more about who you are as a writer. If you bring to your writing desk what your writing means to you, you are bringing that part of you to the writing process, helping you remain authentic and open to ideas as you write.

Creativity comes from within. Have a look at your response to question two. Are you ready to believe that creativity comes from within you and it can be accessed anytime? In the Write Wild Method, we learn that creativity exists within us, it lives in the part that we call the Illusive Self. This is a part of who we are as humans and the part of us that we cannot directly communicate with. In a sense, it is our subconscious but we normally believe that we are unable to have conscious awareness of that part of our self, that it affects our emotions and beliefs without our control. But what if we could access our deeper self in a different way? A way that allows us an element of control.

We can, via our unique connection to our Illusive Self. That's what you're going to be doing next.

But first I want to quickly talk about question three. What was your answer to this question? Can you actually be creative if you aren't in the mood, can't be bothered or are overwhelmed by a lack of confidence or have hit a snag in the plot?

The answer to question three is normally always yes. Creativity will always show up for you when you want it, there are rarely good reasons for not being creative when you've committed to writing. We can always find something to procrastinate about but procrastination is not a reason for not feeling or being creative. Real life will always get in the way and that is something, as a writer, you will have to manage in a way that best suits your creative goals. These Write Wild Principles will help you with your writing process while managing real life. Keep in mind that whatever you may believe is hampering your ability to write or your creative process, your creativity will always show up for you when you want it.

**Writer's Exercise 2**

This exercise is created using elements of the Reawakening-Reimagining Principle from the Write Wild Method. It's a visualisation exercise that you can do right now from wherever you are. You also have the option of doing this exercise in the natural world, taking yourself outdoors and bringing your present self alive and responding to your creativity. But for now, let's practise this visualisation exercise.

Find a quiet space where you can be alone and uninterrupted for the next twenty minutes.

Read the following instructions then get ready to practise the visualisation:

The Boat Visualisation

1. Lie or sit back and get yourself into a comfortable position.
2. Spend a few minutes listening to your own breathing, making your breathing your focus and not any other sounds you may hear.
3. Acknowledge any thoughts that come into your head, then return your focus to your breathing. Try not to attend to any thoughts.
4. Now, take one deep breath in and hold it for the count of five, then let the breath go as you once again count to five. Repeat this exercise five times.
5. Now, breathe easy, let your breath find its own pattern.
6. Feel your body, be curious about it, wonder about it.
7. Imagine yourself in a small rowing boat bobbing about on the sea. Try to feel what it's like to be in the boat so that you can physically imagine yourself there. If you prefer to watch yourself, that's fine too but as you practise this visualisation you will at some point want to be either sitting or lying in the

boat as it rocks gently on the sea.

8. Look around you, all you see is sky and sea, nothing else.

9. Once again be curious: what do you smell? What can you taste? What can you hear? What can you feel? How does it feel? Spend a few minutes until you feel orientated in your visualisation.

10. Now it's time to pay attention to any thoughts and feelings that crop up. Pay particular attention to any thoughts or feelings that excite you. Keep your eyes closed and remain within your visualisation for at least five or ten minutes, longer if you wish.

11. Open your eyes and pick up your notebook.

12. Sprinting exercise: write fast without stopping. Write every thought in your head that comes with the desire to write. If you don't feel desire for any particular thoughts or have no thoughts at all, simply write and keep writing. This is a stream of consciousness exercise where you empty your mind into your notebook. Write for ten minutes without stopping. Set a timer if you like.

At the end of this exercise, revise your sprinting notes. Is there anything that jumps out at you, anything that may form into a new idea, a new perspective or a new feeling? Write down your thoughts. You can always come back to these notes and review and rewrite. This exercise is a great way to strengthen your connection to your Illusive Self, where all your creative ideas exist, ready and waiting for you to open yourself up.

# Principle Five:
# The Walking Writer

**Principle Aim:** Your Quiet Mind
**Principle Objective:** Walking Mindfully
**Principle Goal:** Discover Your Natural Self

## YOUR AIM

I believe that walking means something different to each of us. Some of us walk every day, as exercise, to get from A to B or to take a break from the everyday. There are a multitude of ways that we can choose to walk. We can walk alone, or with others. We can walk soundlessly or with earplugs or while we're on the phone. We can walk to figure out a problem, make a decision, pick up the shopping, and we can do all of these things without being present. Our minds are elsewhere, fixated with a problem or decision, excited or afraid of the destination or trying to remember what items we need for a particular recipe or even singing along to music while we walk.

How often do you walk silently and mindfully?

You may already include wild mindfulness into your daily routine without knowing it. If you do, that's great, if not, perhaps it's time you did.

There is a wealth of scientific studies these days that provide us with a good clue that getting outside is a great thing for us as human beings. Health wise, our bodies are made for movement, if we don't move, we lose our ability to move.

Cognitively, walking for fifteen minutes a day is enough to improve your executive functioning, restore your attention and it's also a massive boost to your creativity. But why is any of that important to us as writers who must sit ourselves down and write?

**The Write Wild Method helps you transform your writing practice and your writing life because it encourages you to engage in a deeper and more meaningful relationship with the natural world for the very purpose of sitting down to write.**

Even if you're convinced already that being outside is good for you, how can you get the maximum benefits for your writing? I've already said that fifteen minutes' walking once a day is a great way to enhance your writing life, but it's no good if you're not being intentional about your walking.

Interacting is the crucial element here. It's no good spending four hours sitting on a beach with your attention focused on your phone. The effect is a constant drain on your attentional resources, having to deal with distraction and confusion, all of which amounts to cognitive fatigue. Try writing a novel and all you're doing is draining more of your mental resources by forcing yourself to multitask. The end result is that your creative abilities get lost in the fog and your ability to come up with new ideas is severely hampered.

All of this points directly to the importance of letting our minds be quiet. If you want creative insight, understanding and those exciting moments of euphoria, give your mind some quiet time, some wild mindfulness. This is you building a relationship with your creativity, your Illusive Self, and not only that, the benefits include positive well-being alongside reduced stress and you know by now that creativity and stress can't happen at the same time – you choose which it is and if you're on a writing journey, I know which one I'd coach you to choose.

Practising wild mindfulness, whether it's for a week, a day, a fifteen-minute walk or five minutes of focused attention looking at nature from your window or on your laptop, however you do it, whether you keep a routine or mix it up, it continues to work some time after you've returned to your desk. It all depends on how dedicated you are and how often you practise, but wild mindfulness boosts your creativity both at the time and for some time after.

Imagine sitting at your desk for five hours a day, feeling dedicated, determined, making a huge effort to manipulate the creative process. You will get new ideas, you will finish the chapter even though you've no idea what you're supposed to be writing – you will write one thousand words, whatever it takes. Does this sound familiar? Does it sound painful? I would say so.

What if a simple walk outdoors could get you achieving your one thousand words without the effort and pain of trying to be creative? Experimental psychologists, Opprezze and Schwartz (2014) conducted four different experiments, using a combination of an exercise bike and walking outdoors and found that walking increased people's ability to solve problems creatively compared to people sitting. Anything that reduces the stress of writing works for me.

**Writer's Exercise:**

I invite you to introduce a fifteen minutes' wild mindfulness walk into your daily writing practice. Make this part of the writing process for you and you will benefit from it in ways you might not imagine.

How to do wild mindfulness:

Decide that you are going to be present. To do this, while you're out walking, slow your pace down, pay attention to where you're planting your feet, listen to the sounds you're making, feel the air, open your chest and breathe. Now begin Seasonal Breathing.

*Seasonal Breathing:*

This I learnt from my training as a natural mindfulness guide and it's an excellent tool to quickly bring yourself to the present (Banyard, I., 2018).

**Step one**: Spring-refresh. Slowly take an in-breath. As you breathe in – consider SPRING. Imagine you're breathing in new life, life force, awakening, refresh, re-energising or whatever the season 'spring' brings to mind.

**Step two:** Summer-relax. After the SPRING in-breath – hold and relax your breath and consider SUMMER. Imagine nature relaxing, unwinding, and letting go or whatever summer in nature brings to your mind.

**Step three:** Autumn-release. Slowly breathe out. As you breathe out – consider AUTUMN. Imagine you're breathing out and releasing, shedding, easing or whatever autumn in nature brings to your mind.

**Step four:** Winter-rest. After the AUTUMN out-breath – rest a while before you breathe in again and consider WINTER. Imagine stillness, calm, hibernation, inactivity or whatever winter in nature brings to mind.

**Consider the following interpretations:**

Spring Renew = joy, being open to the unknown, beginnings, reignite.

Summer Relax = physically relax your shoulders. Relax your mind, quiet your thoughts. Sense aliveness in your body. Allow time to feel awe. Give yourself space and calm.

Autumn Release = shed your worries, your negative thoughts, your barriers and your blocks. Prepare for comfort, positive experience and wonder.

Winter Rest = feel the present moment. Be open to fluctuations in time. Observe. Observe. Observe. Rest.

**Quick Recap**

As with everything in life it's important to be sensitive to balancing your wild experiential journey and your actual writing time. I like to think that writing is 80% thought/experience and 20% writing. But these percentages don't mean that you spend 80% of your time in the wild and only 20% writing. There are no hard and fast rules and every writing project will demand a variety of ways of working. The thing with developing a strong nature connection is that it will be that connection that will guide you and you'll be able to feel your way to the writing and do it successfully in a way that works specifically for you.

**Writer's Exercise**

Find a quiet spot in a natural space that you're not all that familiar with. Lie down on your back on the ground (forest floor, beach, hillside ...). Do a little seasonal breathing to help you feel grounded and less self-conscious. Spread your arms and legs, really stretch them out. Feel the aliveness in your muscles.

Now, stare up at the sky. As long as the sun isn't blinding you keep your eyes open.

Experience

Experience

Experience

## YOUR OBJECTIVE

**Preparation**

- Introducing a new routine isn't easy and for some, taking a fifteen-minute walk every day may feel easy but for others it may feel or even be impossible. Learn what you need to do specifically to make this happen for you. Tiny steps are better than no steps.

- If you already walk every day make sure you're not wasting all that walk on your phone or otherwise disengaged from nature. Use your time wisely and set aside that wild mindfulness practice, safeguard it, champion it.

**Purpose**

Practise seasonal breathing, but also wild listening, wild walking. Check in with yourself that your focus is on your experience and employ all of your senses.

- Wild Walking: at some point during your walk, slow everything down. Make a conscious effort to walk as slow as you can, be observant, be curious, wonder at what your senses are alive to. Feel your feet on the ground, how do they feel and sound?

- Wild Aliveness: practise really focusing in on parts of your body. For example, how does the air feel on your neck? On your face, on the back of your head. What's happening with your knee? Your elbow? As you become absorbed with the experiences of parts of your body, notice a feeling of aliveness. Does your body, or parts of your body tingle? It's a different feeling for everyone, how does it feel for you?

- How do you experience YOU on an experiential level?

If you'd like a deeper introduction to Natural Mindfulness you might like to read Ian Banyard's book, *Natural Mindfulness* (2018).

## YOUR GOAL

While you're out walking, and outside of your mindful exercises, where might you find connections between You and the land that supports you? Ask yourself and nature these questions:

- How do you define creativity?
- Fill in the following: I am only creative when_____ but what if?
- Reaffirm your meaning statement, make sure it still works for you.
- Reassess your immediate goals, are they going to help you move forward?
- What does it mean to you to be 'Keeper of the Earth?'

**Writing Exercise 1:**

What actions can you take in the next four weeks that will make sure you are being accountable in working towards your goals?

Imagine yourself six weeks from now. Think about your success, your goals and your achievements.

Devise your own specific-to-you definitions for the following words:

- Breakthrough
- Discovery
- Development
- Success

What is truly possible for you?

**Writing Exercise 2**

Creative Effort

- How does the word 'effort' make you feel?
- How do you experience effort?
- Is it a negative or positive experience?
- Is there a way for you to get excited about effort?
- Does the phrase, 'I will create regardless of ...' hold a lightness or heaviness for you? Why?
- What parts of you are getting in your way?

You Are You

- Devise a motivating way of greeting yourself when you wake up:
- Each new day I intend on greeting myself in the following way ...
- Continue to confront the stories you tell yourself,

ask yourself if these are true or false and what impact they're having on your creativity.

- Are you currently keeping track of your progress? How so? If not, how might you go about keeping track of your progress?
- Have you figured an element of accountability into your writing process? If not, how might you go about it ...?
- Do you practise any type of self-coaching? What does/might this look like for you?
- When you think about your creative practice, make a list of your preferences. Analyse whether these are having a beneficial or detrimental effect on your journey to achieving your goals.
- Note down the specific steps for the next four weeks that are required on the journey toward your goals. What actions are required so you can take these steps?

# Principle Six: Get Motivated

**Principle Aim:** Natural Creativity
**Principle Objective:** 12 Steps to Motivation
**Principle Goal:** Discover Your Own Path

## YOUR AIM

What is motivation?

As a concept, it's generally accepted that motivation is the driver to achieving goals. It's thought of as a process, in the same way that creativity is thought of as a process. But is this correct? For example, many people believe that motivation is the process that gets us from A to B and it's thought that there are three ways it does this: initiating, guiding and maintaining whatever behaviour it takes for us to achieve a goal.

Why we want to get our heads around motivation:

- It's going to help you get to where you want to be with your writing. Whether that's finishing a book, researching a book, beginning a book, deciding a writing practice that works for you, deciding how to find the time to write.

- It's going to help you develop a writing life that works for you and not just a writing life you wish you had. It's also going to help you move toward a writing life that best serves you and not one that beats you with a stick.

- It's going to contribute to you living a healthy balanced life full of happiness and joy.

According to current thinking, there are three types of motivation:

- Extrinsic motivation: Think of external validation, praise, winning writing competitions, a publishing deal. Getting great sales for you self-published book. Doing courses, deadlines, getting a writing certificate, getting positive feedback, etc. can also be very motivating.

- Intrinsic motivation: This kind of motivation comes from within you, it is your internal drive and is whatever gets you finishing a task, or creating in the first place. It can also be self-validation and relate to a strong sense and awareness of your own life purpose.

- Family motivation (and I'm including your writing peers here): You may not be able to motivate yourself intrinsically but you may be motivated to finish your book to show your family, to prove your creative worth, or you may be motivated to keep writing for financial reasons.

It goes without saying that wishing or having the desire to be a writer isn't going to get you far. Any creative project takes courage, you have to be able to break down barriers, face challenges and tackle rejections and still maintain your drive to succeed. You have to create in spite of all the pain, hardship and obstacles along the way.

We know from current thinking that there are likely three components you need to have to get and stay motivated.

- Activation: this is all about taking decisions. You decide to write the book you've been thinking about writing and you set aside time every day to do so.

- Persistence: this is what keeps you going. You turn up at your writing desk every day, even if you don't feel like it or if you're tired, bored or would rather do the ironing.

- Intensity: this is the level of concentration and vigour you put into reaching your goal (to write your book).

It all still comes down to you. For example, you might start off great, have bucketloads of intensity and are super keen to get your book finished but encounter several barriers or blocks in the road and your persistence takes a hit and very quickly you're filling up your writing time with other tasks that demand your attention.

Here are a few barriers that will get in your way:

- Perfectionism

- Wanting/wishing the thing was done – wishing there was a quick fix

- Thinking that this course or that how-to book will solve all your problems or thinking that Jenny got a three-book deal because she took that MA course, then taking the course and all you get is rejections – not good thinking

- Depression/anxiety

- Physical health

This is all really great stuff but motivation is painful, why are we bothering with it? Does motivation even exist?

After all, motivation is simply a concept.

Consider for a moment the idea that motivation has nothing to do with writing.

Instantly, you can see that none of us could then say, 'I don't have the motivation to write' OR 'I wish I had more motivation to write' OR 'If I had the motivation of an Olympic athlete of course I'd be writing my book, loads of books, in fact I'd be a bestselling author by now!'

But we've lived with the concept of motivation for so long it's hard just to simply shake it off just like that.

What if:

- a tree couldn't get motivated enough to grow?
- the sea never feels very motivated on a Monday and so doesn't bother making waves?
- the day was tired and doesn't bother to show up for six months?

What if we stopped relying on motivation to show up and decided to show up to our writing anyway? How would that look? How would it work for you?

**Quick Recap**

We tend to think of requiring motivation to get us from A to B, from writing the beginning to writing the end of our book. We might be motivated extrinsically (praise from others), intrinsically (championing ourselves) or from friends, family and writing partners. To be motivated we need to be active, persistent and write with enough intensity to keep us going to the finishing line.

There are plenty of good reasons to get in the way of us

feeling motivated but what if the very idea of motivation is just us getting in our own way?

## YOUR OBJECTIVE

I'm going to introduce you to the **Write Wild 12 steps to getting and staying motivated.** These are 12 steps you can adapt to fuel your writing, your writing process and your writing life and keep the light glowing until your goal has been reached, and then there's limitless fuel available to you for your next writing goal.

Really, this is about showing up to write despite a lack of motivation. The 12 steps will help you to do that.

The 12 Steps to Getting Motivated and Becoming Naturally Creative and More Productive.

1. Writing is Illegal
2. The Interview
3. For All That
4. The Statement
5. My Practice Pledge
6. Bestowal
7. Your Illusive Self
8. Reframe/Reimagine
9. Aliveness
10. Body Check
11. Charioteer
12. Freedom

**Preparation**

**Step One:** Writing is Illegal

Imagine that as of this moment, the powers that be have declared writing is illegal. That only the top echelons of society are allowed to document history, and no other forms of writing is permitted.

What immediate feelings does this idea bring to mind? What thoughts?

Draw a line in the middle of your notebook so you have two columns. At the top of one column write FEELINGS and at the top of the other write THOUGHTS.

EXAMPLE:

Here's how I felt when I imagined that writing is now illegal:

| FEELINGS | THOUGHTS |
|---|---|
| Fear | Loss of identity |
| Outraged | Loss of purpose |
| Mournful | Injustice |
| Frustrated | Resistance |

**Sprint Writing Statement**

Sprint writing is similar to stream of consciousness writing but it comes with a prompt. Begin writing and keep writing without lifting your pen from the paper until you can't possibly write any more. The key is to write as fast as you can. This isn't about the writing, it's about strengthening your motivation to write by completing the following:

Look at your thoughts and feelings and identify WHY you're experiencing these thoughts and feelings. Begin sprint writing and include as many of the thoughts and feelings in your list as you can and write as many 'whys' as you can.

Putting the energy and concentration into doing this exercise will remind you of why you write, why your purpose is so strong and why you're looking to make meaning in your world.

It's good to introduce Step One as a regular part of your writing process. You may want to return to it once a month and rewrite using the same sprint writing exercise and see if something new crops up for you. If nothing new crops up, you get the reminder of why you want to be a writer and that is a great motivator. If something new does crop up, you can assess it and see whether it helps you move toward your goals. If it doesn't, you get to return to your original statement and reaffirm your purpose.

**Step Two:** The Interview

You're not going to get motivated by sitting at your desk if you're stuck. One way to get unstuck and motivated is to revisit your connection with trees. As a child you had an innate connection with the natural world within which you played, observed and were curious about. Play, observation and curiosity are three of the main ways you connect your natural self with the world around you. One of the easiest ways to revisit your connection with nature is to share your thoughts with the trees.

Get outside, find a quiet spot where there are trees and where you won't be disturbed for half an hour. If you come across a selection of trees in a circle, this is the perfect spot. But any trees will do. You may want to take a look at the roots of the trees and see if any roots are reaching out to other trees. Or look up at the branches and see where branches from one tree link with another tree. We don't really know why trees are often observed connecting with other trees, but it feels very companionable for them to do so. Like us, trees may depend on their neighbours for their strength, growth and healing.

While you spend time with these trees, make a point of being mindful. Practise some seasonal breathing to bring your focus to the present. If you're lucky enough to find a circle of trees, sit in the centre of the circle but whatever gathering of trees you find yourself with, sit close to them and spend a few minutes connecting with them.

When you're ready, release all the questions that are blocking your creativity. Any and all questions, one or several, it doesn't matter, ask the trees for answers. Speak your questions out loud so you are physically releasing them into the natural world.

This might feel and sound a bit unnatural, a bit silly, a bit unrealistic. But trust me, if you keep an open mind, allow yourself to be curious, let your playful self free and observe what happens, your creativity will begin to soar and your natural self will reveal itself to you. The more you practise, the more open you are to experience, the more likely that you, like the trees, will experience strength, growth and healing. And because you'll benefit from a constant surge of creativity you'll be more motivated to achieve your writing goals.

**Step Three:** For All That

In spite of ourselves, we get things done

This is one of my favourite thoughts. It reminds me that quite a lot of times, I get in my own way and create unnecessary problems for myself. It also reminds me that I can and very often do get things done.

So, if we're getting in our own way, how do we get on with

being creative and get the job done? We can be daring and step aside.

The next time you're out on a walk, pick up a leaf, a pebble or a twig or something else that attracts your eye that you can take home with you.

Leaves: Leaves are small but significant in nature because they harness the rays of the sun through a process of photosynthesis. They start as small buds on the stem and as we move from winter into spring and the days get longer we have more sun and the leaf takes the light and warmth of the sun and harnesses all of this energy all on its own. The leaves feed the tree and allow it to grow. By keeping a leaf by you at all times, you're reminding yourself that you are the equivalent of the sun for a leaf. You supply life and energy to your creative project, in spite of yourself, it's in your nature to do so.

Pebbles: Pebbles and stones have a long history in spiritual symbolism and are often used in meditation practice to promote a sense of harmony and balance. Pebbles, rocks and stones connect us to the earth in an obvious way, if you hold one in your hand you are connected wherever you are. You can draw on your natural self rather than attend to the self that's getting in the way. Your natural self wants you to succeed, it wants you to achieve moments of happiness and joy and it wants you to achieve your writing goals.

Twigs: I have a twig. I found it while I was walking on Kinnoull Hill. I was exhausted, it was raining so I was experiencing symptoms of fibromyalgia alongside my usual chronic pain and I sat down to rest at the base of a tree. At my feet lay this twig, it was quite sturdy and about nine inches long. The way I was feeling was causing anxiety and I began to panic that I might not have the energy or ability to get back home. I then began to imagine what it would be like to be stranded in the forest, in the dark and all on my own and my anxiety was taking up all my minus energy. Then I picked up this twig and ran my finger along it. I tapped it on my knee. All of a sudden I felt a strong urge to play. This was my natural self guiding me out of an anxious place and into a playful one. I started to come up with different uses for the twig. It was a pen, and I pretended to write with it. It was a magic wand and I changed the ground under me into a beautiful loch, warm and soothing. In my head I was swimming and as those imaginary moments lightened my soul, my body became more relaxed, more energised. I soon found myself laughing, feeling lighter and a lot less anxious and of course I'd make it back home, no problem! Naturally I did make it home and I now have the twig by my bedside so that when I wake in the morning I have a reminder that I can and I will, despite myself.

**Step Four:** The Statement

When we're submitting to agents and publishers we always talk about things like an 'elevator pitch' a 'synopsis' and a tagline. These things all relate to the book we're choosing to submit. They're statements that allow agents and publishers a quick insight into the story we've written.

But what about a statement that gives you something? A statement that gives you motivation? What if you had a statement that gave you insight into who you are as a writer and why you write? What if you had one or two sentences that reminded you of why you're on this writing journey of yours? One that you can glance at and/or say out loud to yourself, as a declaration of your commitment to yourself.

If you write a statement of your commitment to yourself, and it's powerful enough to mean more to you than all the distractions that are pulling you away from your writing project, this may be a great motivator for you.

Can you say with conviction that whatever is stopping you from writing is more important to you than finishing your writing project?

Let's say, for example, that you can't write in the month of September because September is always when you devote all your time to promoting your other business which is selling your handmade Christmas cards. Even if, in September you feel motivated to write, you don't because you never have.

This is only a problem if it's a problem. If you're happy with your decision to not write in September that's fine. But if you're stressed, anxious and viewing a month off from writing as a problem, then it will be a problem and most likely not only impact on your motivation to write but also on your motivation to promote and sell your Christmas cards.

This is where your natural statement will come in handy. The best way to explain this is by testing a couple of examples:

I learnt the value of having a statement from my writing coach, Eric Maisel. His statement is –

'Do the next best thing.'

My own natural statement is: Take the Next Step.

Now when I'm feeling like not writing, my natural self pops up with 'Take the Next Step', and believe it or not, this works for me. It works because my statement was born through strengthening my connection to the natural world and practising other Write Wild techniques. My statement relates solely to my writing purposes (however it also works in other areas of my life when I don't feel like doing something that I will know will benefit my best self).

What do you do then, if you have to work solidly on your Christmas card business in September and you thought it would be a good idea to put aside your writing project for the month but then September comes and you get anxious and stressed about it all? You could try referring to your natural statement. For example, if this was me, I would tell myself to Take the Next Step and that would motivate me to find a way to both write and promote my business. I could record my writing ideas and chapters. I could handwrite a chapter before I go to sleep. I could choose the hour per week I listen to a podcast and use that hour to write instead. I could decide that writing 200 words a day instead of 2,000 is a great compromise. By the end of September I will feel sure of myself, satisfied and proud.

I invite you to write your natural statement:

During those times when you're out being present in nature, take a journal with you and spend some minutes each time noting down ideas of what your own statement might look like. Write a story about an imaginary you. Draw pictures. Journal your thoughts and your ideas of connection and nature. Use this to begin forming your natural statement. From your journal, you may capture something that is unique to you that will keep you motivated and on track with your writing journey.

**Step Five:** My Practice Pledge

Pledge to commit to a daily/regular practice. There is an

unlimited amount of distractions and demands on our time. Beginning, continuing and finishing a writing project can be a long process and if you don't already have a daily writing practice you'll find yourself getting demotivated frequently and all that does is encourage your critical self to take control of your thoughts and feelings and you'll slide further down the motivation ladder as each non-writing day passes you by.

My own writing daily practice works brilliantly most of the time. I write when I first get up, around 9am and finish around lunchtime. Then I get on with the rest of my working day. I don't work weekends.

This is my daily practice; it's how I get my books written. I don't always stick to my daily practice but knowing I have it makes it so much easier to get the job done. I don't have to think about what I'm doing, I just have to get on and do it. And when something crops up that takes me away from my daily practice, like a holiday, my business or family, I'm OK with it because I know that soon enough I will be back to my practice and life will be simple again.

I liken having a daily practice to making my bed. I have a routine that when I get out of my bed I have to make it straight away, before I do anything else. This is a habit I've formed; I don't have to think about it so it takes no unnecessary energy to make my bed. Imagine if I got up and thought, 'will I or won't I make my bed today?' Some days my bed would get made and some days it wouldn't. Worse, I'd be stressed before I even started writing because I'd had to make a decision about making my bed. Making a decision takes energy, we need to reserve that energy for our writing decisions, not waste it on useless decision making, like will I or won't I make my bed today.

The value of having a writing practice on your levels of motivation is magical. If you decide that your daily practice will be 6–7pm every Monday to Friday then it becomes something simple that you do without thinking about. If you decide your daily practice is 8am–8.15am then that's the time you write.

I invite you to pledge to a daily writing practice. You will get writing done, your project will get completed. Whether you choose to write outside of your daily practice is up to you, but as long as you commit to whatever time per day you decide, when it comes to your daily practice, motivation is irrelevant.

**Step Six:** Bestowal

It's all too easy to be critical of yourself, to beat yourself up and to imagine you're worthless. Often we do this without even thinking about it but we experience the same physical reaction whether we're conscious of it or not. The basic physical experience is lack of motivation, demoralisation and sadness and the more we are critical with ourselves, the greater the chance of the physical effect leading to anxiety and depression.

Even if you're aware you're being critical of yourself it's not always that simple to switch to being kinder, more compassionate with yourself. More than likely, you'll have to do this purposefully and set aside time regularly to check in with yourself and be more self-compassionate.

This is a simple exercise that you can do at home or out in the natural world or mix it and do both.

At home, bring two chairs close together. Sit in one and imagine that you're also sitting across from yourself in the other chair. (If you're doing this outdoors simply imagine the chairs or find a bench.) Tell the other you sitting opposite the following:

1. I love you and I care about you.
2. I am right here with you, and I am here for you.
3. There are no words that can express how proud I am of you.
4. Please know that it's okay to feel whatever you feel.
5. You are important to me, and I care about you.
6. I am supporting you.
7. Please let me know if there is anything you need and anything I can do to help.
8. I am taking care of your health, harmony and balance.
9. I am your best supporter.

To stay motivated, it's really important that you're taking care of your emotional health. Compassion is infectious, when you're purposefully compassionate with yourself, the positive emotions that you experience will flow into your daily writing practice and concerns over motivation will stop eating away at your energy levels. Don't forget to check in with yourself and celebrate the small wins and most important of all, gift yourself the gift of compassion.

**Step Seven:** Your Illusive Self

Get into a regular practice of getting outside and finding quiet places where you can practise natural listening. All this involves is that you listen and describe to yourself the sounds that you hear while you're out walking in the park or sitting relaxing in your garden or wherever you are. Really listen to the sounds that you hear. The birds, a ball being kicked about, a train passing, etc.

Get used to being in the moment while you're outside and

listening to the different sounds of the natural world. Don't put any judgement on these sounds. In natural mindfulness we call the outside the 'soundscape' and the soundscape includes all the sounds you hear regardless of the origin of the sound. For example, don't get frustrated when you're enjoying listening to the birds and a train 'disturbs' the birdsong. Just acknowledge that the train is a part of the soundscape.

Natural listening helps you get in touch with your natural self. When you're connected to your natural self, you're connected to the natural world and this helps make you feel like you're standing on solid ground. To acknowledge that you are on a creative journey and whatever that creative journey demands of you, you can do it and you have your solid connection to keep you grounded and on track. When you have this, you'll rarely decide that you're not feeling motivated enough to write.

To read more about natural mindfulness and become part of the growing natural mindfulness community, visit Nature Connection World: community.natureconnection.world

**Step Eight:** Reframe/Reimagine

Just as your natural self likes to get out and play, you like to create and whether your way of creating is to write, to make art or to sing an opera, it feels right to you in some way.

It's mystifying therefore that, as much as you want to create, you often don't want to do it. You want to write but can't bring yourself to write. Bizarre, isn't it?

As bizarre as it sounds, it's perfectly natural and simply a part of the process. If we're having to motivate ourselves we must be doing it wrong, right? If we can't bear the idea of sitting at our desk to write, we must be a rubbish writer, right? If we can't figure out the next step in the plot, we must be crap at plotting, right?

Wrong.

Instead of forcing yourself to get motivated, or deciding that you need a better writing space or that you need an expert plotter to help you out, what you can do first is to acknowledge that this art of creating is one of your life purposes.

Often we talk about our writing as our passion. But for many of us, it's more than that, it's our life purpose. There's a difference.

Our passions can change, we can be excited about knitting in our twenties, making jewellery in our thirties and interior design in our forties. By the time we're fifty we've forgotten how to knit, why we ever wanted to make jewellery and that interior design was fun for a year or two but turned out to not be our thing. But since we were a teenager, we loved art and we continue to love art, in fact, we can't imagine ever not loving art. In this scenario, it sounds like art is our life purpose. Does that make sense?

How often do we acknowledge that something, anything is our life purpose? You can and most likely do have more than one life purpose, for example, family might be another, or running or taking care of the family farm.

When you think of your creativity as one of your life purposes you mean that you are allowing yourself to take yourself seriously. When you take yourself seriously your perspective on your creativity shifts massively, and when a lack of motivation looms in front of you you'll happily swipe it away and get on with what your creative project requires from you.

Other shifts will happen too, for example, you may put less emphasis on what other people think about you because you'll know that what you're creating is about you and not anybody else. You may quite happily do things that you don't like doing, like working in a non-writing job to pay the rent, because you'll understand that this job is taking care of your basic needs while you're creating. You may decide that the pain you're feeling writing this book is valuable and necessary because it's part of the process of you living your life purpose.

You will definitely decide that whether you feel motivated or not, you're going to push ahead and make this creative project happen regardless.

Best of all, your actions in pursuing your creative life purpose will be fun, even when it feels like a slog in the moment.

You can read more about the power of life purposes in Eric Maisel's groundbreaking book: Choose Your Life Purposes (Maisel, 2024. Yellow Pear Press). https://mango.bz/books/choose-your-life-purposes-by-eric-maisel-3220-b

**Step Nine:** Aliveness

This is both a physical and writing exercise to get that alive feeling that you'll need while going through the process of creating.

The physical part of this exercise is simply to go outside and practise connecting to your natural self. This time you want to connect to your inner aliveness. You can do this by stopping and taking a few seasonal breaths. Then hide your hand behind your back and pay attention to how that hand feels. Is it feeling the breeze? Is it cold or warm? Allow yourself time to really let your hand come to life and take up all your focus. Then move your attention to your foot and repeat the same exercise. Move around your body repeating this exercise with different parts of your body until you begin to have the sensation of being alive. How does your inner aliveness feel to you? How is it making you feel? Stay with your aliveness for as long as you feel comfortable doing so.

When you're back at your writing desk, recreate that same aliveness and it will flow into your work.

Aliveness is also a useful tool to bring to consciousness while you're feeling demotivated. Close your eyes, practise a few seasonal breaths then try to capture that alive feeling you felt when you were outdoors.

This takes practice. As you practise you'll learn more about yourself and your natural self that will help guide you throughout the creative process. This is why, once you've formed a strong connection with the natural world, you don't have to be outside to reap the benefits, you get to bring your natural-self experiences to your work at all times.

**Step Ten:** Body Check

Stay in touch with your body and ensure that you're looking after it and giving it health and joy.

Whatever our creative life purpose, we need a body to make it happen. This sounds stupidly obvious but most of us take our health for granted and forget to take good care of our body and mind and check in with it from time to time to prevent missing any potential problems. Like our minds, our bodies need play and if we're not feeling the play in our creative projects, and even if we are, we need to get out and let our bodies and minds have the real experience of play.

**Step Eleven:** Charioteer

This is to get you thinking about where you're going and how much you want to get there. In their day, chariots were cumbersome – just as often life is cumbersome – but the gladiator armed himself with the weapons he needed to win the fight, not just physical weapons but strength, fortitude and resolve.

Start a new journal or open your notebook on your phone. For each day you want the following list:

- Strength
- Fortitude
- Resolve

Now each day fill in each of these three categories' times/experiences that reveal your strength, fortitude and resolve. Very soon you'll have evidence that you are resilient and courageous, and you will carry on creating despite your lack of motivation and, not in spite of yourself, but because of yourself. And this will bring joy to your daily creative practice.

**Step Twelve:** Freedom

When you reach a low point in your creative journey give yourself permission to feel your natural freedom.

Take a walk outside and focus your attention on the wind, how it feels against your body, how it feels emotionally and how it sounds. The wind is a symbol of freedom, it blows where it wants and when it wants without restriction. The wind always has energy and momentum, direction and magnitude. The wind is renewable and sustainable.

I invite you to write down:

- the ways in which you are already renewable and sustainable
- what gives you momentum and what steals it away?
- how do you define freedom in this moment?

The answers to these questions will help sustain you through to the end of your creative project and beyond.

**Purpose**

Nobody but you can understand what natural creativity means for you and how it will fuel your writing. You have to discover your own path to natural creativity, via your Illusive Self and your courage and investment in your writing life purpose. Testing the 12 steps to motivation will help you discover what works for you and what doesn't at any particular time along your creative writing journey. Keep in mind that something may not feel like it's working for you right now but at a point in the future that very thing may kick in to keep you writing so try to remain open to new discoveries.

## YOUR GOAL

Your goal is to get to a point where you believe that you are the only influencer in your creative progress. To know that the concept of motivation can itself be a barrier to productivity – feeling motivated is not necessary to write and make creative progress. You may not feel very motivated but you can choose to write or not write regardless.

## Writing Exercise 1

Identify a character in your writing that feels flat and lifeless. Write a letter to this character telling them in great detail about an event that happened to you at any time in your past that was traumatic. You're not going to post this letter and no one else has to see it so try to write freely from the depths of your heart and be specific. Explain to this character that you're telling them this story because if you can invest so much of yourself into your work, you expect your character to do likewise.

Your own courage and strength should be enough to get you motivated to fulfil your writing purpose. By demanding the same commitment from your characters, you are acknowledging to yourself that your purpose is stronger than the motivation to write and you will write from your purpose and not from your motivation. Keep this letter and return to it whenever you or your characters need reminding of your commitment to your own fulfilment.

## Writing Exercise 2

There are times when you simply will not be able to write, no matter how committed you are or how much time you have. The reason is rarely to do with motivation, there will always be an underlying reason that you may or may not be aware of. You may be exhausted, ill or your brain may need some quiet time to work through a writing problem. You may be overstretched or tested by real-life events. You may be afraid, anxious or there may be an event like a wedding or holiday coming up that is exciting and taking all of your focus. Whatever the reason, these one-off events require your attention and it's okay to step away from your work and attend to them. Give yourself the time and space you need.

If you're not sure of the reason why you can't write at any particular time, take yourself out into nature and spend time being present and giving your natural self the freedom to explore what's going on. Let your natural self do this on your behalf and remain present, enjoying your time in nature, being curious and open to new discoveries. At some point, either while you're out or when you return home, note down words that describe how you're feeling. You don't have to organise these words, just note them, be conscious of them, let the words organise themselves. Hopefully you'll discover something about yourself and what your next step might be. Keep trying and if at any point you feel you want to challenge the words you've noted down, give yourself the freedom to do so. This is you taking action and regaining control. You can do this whether you feel motivated or not. The freedom to play and explore is as much about the writing process as the writing itself.

# Principle Seven: Your Courage Continuum

**Principle Aim:** Trusting Your Journey
**Principle Objective:** Challenge Your Perception
**Principle Goal:** Cherish Your Creativity

## YOUR AIM

It may feel courageous to decide you want a writing career, and that's because it is courageous. Writing one story or one book from start to finish takes bravery. To want to earn a living from writing multiple stories takes courage. The difference is that bravery is a great kick starter, you dive into your writing project without much thought past getting your book finished. But bravery can easily get chipped away as you reach each hurdle, each bump in the road, each time you have to engage in the complex decision-making process, each time you are overcome, overwhelmed, anxious. It is courage that will see you through.

Courage – and we're talking about the courage to be creative here – helps you stand up, get out of your own way, and show up in spite of all the potholes along the way. Courage is what helps you finish one project and go on to the next regardless of how unnegotiable the road ahead feels.

You already possess the courage it will take for you to achieve your writing goals, the tricky part is accessing that courage. You are required to invest in and trust the journey. This is the Courage Continuum.

There are three parts to the Courage Continuum.

1. Understanding that your courage comes from within
2. Accessing your courage
3. Trusting your creative journey

Before we go into this in any depth I want to draw your attention to a Grimm's fairy tale: The Golden Bird. Briefly, this is the story of three prince brothers and a fox. The king sends each of his sons in turn on a quest but it's the youngest son who saves the day. For our current purpose, we're specifically looking at courage, and it's the youngest son who shows true courage. Courage comes in the living form of the fox who travels with the youngest son and attempts to guide him along his true path. After many failed attempts, the youngest son eventually sees what is required of him and there is a happy ending. **You can read the full story on page 324.**

We can learn a lot from a close reading of any of the Grimm's fairy tales, and this tale in particular can be approached and interpreted in various ways for various reasons. For example, we may want to get a better route into the characters we're developing and turn to one of these tales for insight and inspiration. Other useful uses of a close reading of fairy tales is to examine basic human drives, structure, cause and effect and plot arcs.

In this story we can trace the Courage Continuum: the fox acts as the son's courage, even when the son ignores the fox's warnings the fox never deserts him. Eventually the youngest son realises that courage comes from within and to access it he must venture into the unknown despite his fears and uncertainty – and despite his resistance. It's when he learns to trust the journey that he reaches a happy conclusion.

Is the definition of courage universal? I'm not so sure. What do you think of when you think of courage? What other words do you immediately associate with courage? Stop and think about it for a moment, be curious about what comes to mind.

Did you instantly associate courage with fear? Did the word hope spring to mind? What about the word, hero? Bravery?

I want you to consciously separate your instinctive feeling for courage from any of these and other words, concepts and definitions. It may seem obvious but fear is a reaction, hope is a concept, bravery is an action and hero is a judgement. Courage is none of these things. Courage is intertwined with your physical, emotional and mental make-up, in other words, it could be argued that at its basic level, courage is part of who you are. In the Grimm's tale, the fox represented the courage but the boy had to be open to its message, the fox was the conduit to the boy's courage.

When it comes down to it, we're human beings and we are in many ways governed by a very important hard-wired instinct called the flight or fight response. Courage comes into play when we are forced to choose between either flight (retreat), fight or freeze in the face of fear, an obstacle or a threat.

In the face of it, it may seem as if we have no choice when this instinct kicks in. That may be true when we're under threat to our physical selves, we may instinctively run away, or stay and fight or freeze, these are all human reactions to threat and fear, our adrenaline kicks in and works as a system for keeping us safe and alive (even if we choose not to listen to it). In that split second before we run or stand and fight, are we making a conscious choice? I'll leave you to consider that question for yourself.

In our creative journeys we have to make choices at every turn. In everything we do, we have a choice, it may be a difficult choice and/or not feel like a choice at all but however we decide to act in any situation comes down to us making a choice. Not making a choice is in itself, making a choice. So with that in mind, whether we decide to be courageous or not, is a choice.

You may not be feeling courageous or able to be courageous in a particular circumstance but that doesn't mean that you don't have courage at your disposal.

Writing a book is experiencing a journey. You go on a journey when you begin to write a book and hope to experience a learning curve or mindset growth by the end. But it doesn't in fact end there. The bigger desire is that you're able to take your readers along on that journey, have them experience your journey for themselves, in their own unique ways. What you don't want is for your reader to get bored, tired or offended along this journey of yours; you want them to get to the end of your book and for them to experience their own mindset change or mindset growth.

Most of us have heard the saying that writing a book is a journey but how many of us imagine that journey to be a journey of the mind? We sit down, we write a book. Our reader sits down to read our book. In other words, we seem to be giving our bodies a rest during each of these processes. But these processes are not equal.

Have a think for a moment about how you read and why.

For what it's worth I believe that all writers should be avid readers but some are not. Those of you who don't read may want to go and read a couple of books that appeal to you and try this question out on yourself. It will be worth the effort.

*How* you read is less important than the *why*. You have options, you can read a physical or digital or audiobook these days and this no doubt sheds some interesting light on our changing reading habits. But as I said, it's the why that we ought to be attending to. Why do you read?

Apart from the obvious, we read to get better at our craft, what other reasons are there for reading a book? Write your reasons down. This is important at a basic level because it will help you get a greater insight into why your readers read books. However many reasons you end up writing down, they will all lead you back to taking a journey.

I'll say it again just so that you're clear on this: writing a book is experiencing a journey.

No matter how great your imagination is, it will at some point need to be fed along the way. And by that I mean it needs stimulating in some way. Otherwise you'll find yourself repeating the same groundhog journey and so will your reader and who wants that?

**A Writer's Exercise:**

Pick up a book that interests you and as you read it, quickly note down the hero's journey. Simple notes will do, or a word may even be enough. You're not detailing the plot, just the choices and decisions the hero is making in service of whatever it is that drives him.

Once you've finished the book and you have a complete set of notes for the hero of this book, assess your notes and pay attention to what you make of them. Record your reactions on your phone or write them in your journal or just let ideas come to mind as they have a will to do.

How did the author do at communicating the hero's journey to you, as the reader? What would you do differently?

**Quick Recap**

Understand that courage comes from within and that it needs nurturing, cherishing and igniting and the easiest way to allow that to happen is to trust the journey and create in spite of your fears, in spite of the pain and in spite of yourself.

- Spend as much time as you can venturing into the unknown.
- Spend time seeing things not as what they are but as what they may be.
- Create despite not knowing what the outcome will be.
- See your life not as it is, but as it might be. See your book not as it is but as it might be.

## YOUR OBJECTIVE

I want to remind you at this point of the idea that writing is 80% experience and 20% writing. If you don't quite believe this yet, pay close attention to this next section.

Gregory Berns is a pioneer of neuroscience specialising in brain imaging technology and he's revolutionised the way we think about how our brains function. When I was studying psychology at university I was taught that the brain functioned separately from the body. This was called mind-brain dualism. Modern neuroscience and the innovative work of Berns (2010) turns this idea on its head with his research showing how certain people achieve what other people say can't be done. Berns refers to such people as iconoclasts.

*'Creativity and imagination begin with perception. Neuroscientists have come to realise that how you perceive something isn't simply a product of what your eyes and ears transmit to your brain. It's a product of your brain itself. And iconoclasts, a class of people I define as those who do something that others say can't be done – think Walt Disney, Steve Jobs or Florence Nightingale – see things differently. Literally. Some iconoclasts are born that way, but we all can learn how to see things not for what they are, but for what they might be.'*

Gregory Berns (2020)

Now don't get hung up about the word 'iconoclast'. I'm not suggesting that we all become the next Walt Disney. While that may be a possibility, it's definitely not a requirement of being a successful writer. Furthermore, the idea that certain people may have a predisposition to become iconoclasts isn't relevant to us as writers, so don't go getting hung up on that either. If you do find you're telling yourself that 'I can't write because I'll never be the next Stephen King', or 'what's the point of even starting, clearly I'm not predisposed to creative genius', just remember Berns' neat little finishing sentence:

> *'... we all can learn how to see things not for what they are, but for what they might be.'*

## Preparation

When we talk about creativity, we're talking about venturing into the unknown. When we create something, we have no idea how it will turn out. A painter who sets out to paint something doesn't know whether the time spent will be meaningful or not. When you set out to write a book, you can't be sure that the book will work, that anyone will want to read it. **It takes courage to create despite not knowing what the outcome will be.** So while you're not required to attain the status of an iconoclast, what is a requirement is courage and as I've said, you already own that. It's how you *perceive* it that counts and as we've learnt from Berns, we have to experiment with ways of perceiving things, not as they are but as what they might be.

Berns (2010) has written a book called *Iconclasts* if you're interested in reading more, but the point here is to draw your attention to what experience actually is for you and your writing.

How do we perceive things not as they are but as they might be? I give you the answer to this question with one word: **experience**.

According to Berns, imagination and perception share the same neural circuits in the brain. When we talk of perception here we're talking about the process: how the brain makes sense of what you see and how it does this is by presenting it to you according to some past experience. This is why you can walk through a forest and see nothing because your brain is already processing what your last walk through a forest was like and relaying that to you.

It is widely accepted that humans use only 5% of the

functions in the brain. This leaves 95% of the brain left to its own devices. In terms of efficiency and energy conservation this sounds like it's a useful way for us to navigate the world. But it's not such great news for those of us who purposefully want to be creative. It allows us to be lazy and rely on what we know to get us along the journey from initial idea to finished book.

But what if you want more, if you dream bigger for yourself? What if you want to grow as a writer? Or, what if your current writing life or writing process isn't working for you and you're desperate, miserable, demotivated, ready to give up? Or you may not be getting enough readers to sustain a writing life, or the writing life you dream of having? All of these reasons are good reasons to change your habits and find a better mindset, one that works in your best interests and gets you to where you want to be in your writing life.

**See your life not as it is, but as it might be. See your book not as it is, but as it might be.**

**Purpose**

It takes courage to create, and nobody says this more eloquently than Rollo May (1975) in his book titled the same, *Courage to Create*. But it also takes courage to change your mindset, change your behaviour. Bern tells us that if we want to think creatively we must '... develop new neural pathways and break out of the cycle of experience-dependent categorisation' (May, 1975, p40). In other words, we must garner our courage and stride forth into the unknown.

If you attempt to do this purposefully it will be difficult because our brains are stubborn, they don't like change and they resist fiercely. How often do you sit at your desk and try to think up some magical creative solution for a plot hole, or a character trait or poorly executed scene? The harder you try, the less creative you'll be. It's true that creativity resides within, but it has to be cherished, fed and loved, it doesn't respond well to being beaten with a stick.

## YOUR GOAL

**Writing Exercise 1**

Cherish Your Creativity

This exercise allows you to practise developing new neural pathways and feed both your courage and your imagination. There are two parts to it whereby you will be bringing together your mind with your body and thus experiencing.

**Part One:**

Write a story in 300 words (approx.).

Reminder: a basic story must include the following:

- A beginning, middle and end
- Conflict and resolution
- Cause and effect = action/reaction/reflection/action/consequence (for each event)

Cautionary note: This exercise is not about the writing itself. So you don't have to worry about whether your writing here is any good or not, you're going to be writing your 300 words quickly. Neither is this exercise about whether you're writing a good story or not, you're simply required to write a story, it doesn't have to have an original exciting plot. So please don't waste time on polishing your words or coming up with a unique idea. Or even ensuring you have all the elements of a story. Of course, if you want to come back to your 300 words at a later date and work on them for another purpose you then can take the time to satisfy the requirements of the story.

Now it's time to get to work. This is an exercise you can do as often as you like. It's a good idea to set a timer; you don't have to, just be aware that you want to spend no more than ten minutes on it.

I'm going to work through an example for you here so let's get started.

- Think quickly of an idea: example, father and boy separate for reasons of survival.

It's always good to start with a title. Take a minute or two to think one up (no longer). I've come up with:

- The Summer Dream beneath the Tamarind Tree

Now write your 300-word story (no longer than ten minutes):

Let's quickly think up a story.

The Summer Dream beneath the Tamarind Tree

'The gods tell us that those who exalt themselves will be humbled,' the father tells the son.

'What use am I to a dying tribe, Father? Why not let me free to roam?'

The father sighs, discomfited by his son's conceit.

In a barren land brought on by drought three years long, father and son sit under the shade of the tamarind tree.

The father waits, undaunted, for the first rumble that will signal the rains.

'Freedom is indolence,' the father barks. He fears for his son, a boy stricken with disloyal dreams. 'All life is declining,' the father reminds the boy. 'We must prove our usefulness, and the gods will take great pity on our people and save us from drought.'

The father senses that his son is not satisfied with this judgement and turns his back on the son. 'Instead my son wants to roam idle,' he whines. The father strokes the bark of the tree. 'What good can come of it?' he asks the tree.

'Not idle Father. But this tree is dying. How can I love you and deem you to be wise?'

'The answer is you cannot. Love instead the weeping branches of this tree. Those who hunger and thirst for righteousness will reap its fruit. Son, there is only this way. It is not for dreamers but believers to seek a perfectly justified satisfaction in the sentence of the gods.'

'Alter things with those peering eyes of yours, Father. Who among us is satisfied?'

The father has no answer. 'You seek shelter in some happier star? Preposterous.'

'I will seek new ways to bring life back to this wasteland,' the son replies, and rises to begin his journey.

The son walks many paces before turning back for one final glance at his father. The light is fading. In the shadow he sees a vulture swooping low, circling the tamarind tree.

You'll see that I haven't taken time up figuring out all the story elements and neither should you.

Now that you have your 300-word story, rewrite it and begin with the ending. In other words, write the same story backwards by picking out the events and rewriting them beginning with the end and finishing at the beginning. Here's how the above example looks:

The son walks many paces before turning back for one final glance at his father. The light is fading. In the shadow he sees a vulture swooping low, circling the tamarind tree.

His last words to his father were, 'I will seek new ways to bring life back to this wasteland.'

His father had turned away, believing him to yearn for something better. It's not true. He yearns for something better for his father, not himself. Now, as he walks, he's ashamed of the harsh words he spoke.

'Alter things with those peering eyes of yours, Father. Who among us is satisfied?'

How can a man so wise be so ignorant? His father talks of 'believers'. But he means, slaves to fear.

'The answer is you cannot be idle. Love instead the weeping branches of this tree. Those who hunger and thirst for righteousness will reap its fruit. Son, there is only this way. It is not for dreamers but believers to seek a perfectly justified satisfaction in the sentence of our gods,' his father had argued.

Sinfully, he'd argued back, 'Not idle Father. But this tree is dying. How can I love you and deem you to be wise?'

He, as son, must be a dreamer in action.

Father had stroked the bark of the tree, begging it for answers. 'What good can come of it?' he asks the tree.

'Freedom is indolence,' Father said. He fears for his son, believes him to behold disloyal dreams. 'All life is declining,' Father remonstrates. 'We must prove our usefulness, and the gods will take great pity on our people and save us from drought.'

The gods will not save us. It is our duty to save ourselves.

In a barren land brought on by drought three years long, father and son will no longer sit under the shade of the tamarind tree. Father waits, undaunted, for the first rumble that will signal the rains. He, the son, seeker of salvation.

Father, discomfited by his son's conceit, will rejoice on his son's return.

With the freedom to roam, to explore what is yet unknown, he will become the celebrated saviour of a dying tribe.

Read both versions of your story, note down anything that springs to mind. Then write the answers to the following:

- How do you feel?
- What have you discovered (if anything)?

Before we move on to Part Two of this exercise, I want to talk briefly about your answers to that first question: How do you feel?

Negative feelings are a major barrier to creativity and ultimately to you being able to write confidently and with purpose and joy.

I accepted a long time ago that negative feelings are a part of being human. We can't stop negative feelings, they are useful for us in many ways. For example, feeling afraid stops us and makes us think about our current situation, are we in danger?

But ultimately, negative feelings aren't often going to get us writing and writing well and consistently. Negative feelings about ourselves as a writer and about our writing in general can put the brakes on you finishing your book or even starting it. And if you have a habit of feeling negatively about many or all aspects of writing, you'll find it difficult to get as far as publishing your book.

Where do these naturally occurring negative feelings come from? They come from our thoughts and the language we use to express them. In answer to the question, 'How do you feel' you may have written something like either of the following:

- Brilliant. I've just written 600 words in twenty minutes.

Or

- I've just spent twenty minutes writing a whole lot of rubbish.

The first answer will make you feel good. The second answer will make you feel rubbish. Which would you rather feel? What are you telling your brain?

It's good writing practice to get into the habit of confronting your negative thoughts and reframing them. Like this:

- I've just spent twenty minutes writing a whole lot of rubbish. (Barrier thought)
- Great. I've finished this exercise, learnt something

> about myself and now I can't wait to move on to Part Two. (Best Interest thought)

We're about to move on to Part Two. This is the experience part of this exercise. This chapter is all about the courage of creating. Learning and understanding the concepts and principles in this book is a creative endeavour in itself and therefore requires courage and courage requires persistence and determination. Within that is being able to accept that when we don't get it the first time, we return to get it the next time, or the next time. Like taking your driving test, you want to be able to drive, if you don't pass the test first time round, you'll take a few more lessons then try the test again. Hopefully you'll pass next time but if you don't, you'll go around again and keep trying until you do. This is the process. This is what it takes. It doesn't mean you're a bad person or are rubbish at driving, it just means that you still have things to master before you meet the requirements of the test. There is no test after you finish this book. That doesn't mean that if you haven't yet mastered the idea that writing is about experiencing, you give up on the whole idea. Instead, you go back and read this chapter again with the understanding that once the idea reveals itself to you in all its glory you will be super excited to get on with Part Two of this exercise.

> *'The real voyage of discovery lies not in seeking new landscapes but in seeing with new eyes.'*
>
> Marcel Proust

**Writing Exercise 2**

Cherish Your Creativity

**Part Two:**

This exercise will invigorate you, refresh you and reboot your creativity.

Schedule a time for yourself when you can go outside for a minimum of twenty minutes. Preferably to somewhere quiet, with few or no people around. A forest, a hill, park or beach will be ideal.

If all you can manage is your garden, that will work. If all you can manage is to open your window and lean outside, that will work. But I encourage you to take this practice outside as and when you can.

Take with you a paper copy of your rewritten 300-word story. Take your phone, without headphones. When we can be out in nature, headphones are a barrier to achieving your wild nature, communicating with your Illusive Self and healing your mind and body.

Wherever you are, your aim is to find a peaceful spot with sparse potential for uninvited human guests. Taking your dog along may or may not work, depending on how willing your dog is to sit quietly while you fulfil this part of the exercise.

This is what you're about to do:

- Hold the piece of paper with your story out in front of you, in a position where you can easily read from it.
- Prepare your phone to record.

Now, practise some Seasonal Breathing

Here's a quick reminder of Seasonal Breathing (Remember the four Rs):

Spring: Breathe In: Rejuvenate

Summer: Let the breath flow through your body: (Relax)

Autumn: Breathe Out: Release

Winter: Breathing normally, return your attention to nature (Rest)

Back to the exercise. Press record on your phone and read your story aloud. You can either record yourself reading or turn the phone to your natural surroundings, it's up to you.

If, before you begin to record, you're feeling self-conscious (we all do the first few times), this is a great opportunity to reframe your thoughts. For example:

- I can't do this! (Barrier thought)
- This is so easy, of course I can do this and I am going to do this. (Best Interest thought)

Or

- This is too silly. (Barrier thought)
- This is so exciting. What discovery might I make doing this exercise? (Best Interest thought).

The aim of this exercise is to cherish your creativity, feed it and allow it to bloom. But can you see that by taking your writing practice into the wild, by experiencing your writing life as something that is intuitively linked with the natural world, and by including experiential practices into your writing process and trusting that your discoveries will make a difference, you are simultaneously strengthening your courage. That means, you are breaking the cycle, forming new neural pathways that allow you to see not what is but what might be.

If you're wondering what the point was of writing your story backwards, it's worth taking a few minutes to return to both versions and re-examine them. Alternatively, try the same exercise with a scene in your novel. In my example, the point of view changed and I hardly noticed myself doing this, it happened quite naturally. That told me something about the story, that it required me to take the reader closer. It also told me something about myself, and that was that I'm always moving forwards, even if sometimes it feels as if I'm moving backwards.

# Principle Eight: Ergriffenheit and Humility

**Principle Aim:** Writing Effortlessly
**Principle Objective:** Ignite Your Sense of Awe
**Principle Goal:** Your Natural Space

## YOUR AIM

Ergriffenheit is a German word and the simple English translation is emotion.

For writers, it means much more than that.

For writers, Ergriffenheit describes the moment we want to reach, that moment of our creative freedom. Carl Jung used the word Ergriffenheit to describe the experience that occurs when two different selves come into conflict and the resolution of that conflict leads to an increase in our capacity to create. The conflict reaches the deepest part of ourselves and from this clash we experience Ergriffenheit. Jung developed this idea and the definition of the word Ergriffenheit to describe moments of heightened emotion, marvel and wonder.

This is an interesting framework within which we can map our conscious awareness and our Illusive Self. It describes the moment when you are deeply involved in wild mindfulness and letting your natural self out to play, and when you let go of your preconceptions, release your creativity and become open to marvel and wonder.

The word 'wonder' comes from the Old English for 'wundor'. It refers to words such as 'astonishment', 'marvellous' and 'rapt'. Without wonder, we have no curiosity and our writing has the potential to be stale and unimaginative and boring to a reader. Wonder is a necessity for writing magical prose that will connect on an emotional level with your readers.

Read the following story. If you can, take this story outdoors and read it aloud:

Once upon a time there was a man, his son and a camel. They were on a journey. As they walked along, they heard a bystander say: *'How foolish, they've got a camel and they walk.'* Heeding these words the man climbed onto the camel's back, whilst the son lightly led on foot.

Soon the man heard a passer-by comment: *'That man has no pity. Look at that poor tired boy.'* The man immediately descended from the camel and allowed the son to ride the animal instead.

Then they encountered a group of women and one woman scolded the son: *'Have you no shame, letting the old man walk.'* So the son reached down to help his father onto the camel's back.

They had not gone very far when a passer-by urged them to take better care of the poor camel, who carried such a heavy load. *'Have you no heart? Are you not ashamed of yourself for overloading that poor camel of yours – you and your hulking son?'* a man yelled.

They saw only one solution. They carried the camel.

I invite you to answer the following question:

Q: What is the reality of lived experience?

When you're thinking about this you may like to consider the following:

- Start by defining the question. It's about how you see and understand the world around you.
- Think about your own perspective. What shapes your view? Is it different from others?
- Use your imagination and reflect on your experiences and how they influence your understanding of reality. Are there any moments that stand out to you?
- Think about viewpoints and imagine how someone else might see the same situation. How might their perspective differ from yours?
- Write your thoughts and feelings and pay attention to the language you use to express these. What makes your view unique?
- Embrace your creativity and don't be afraid to think beyond your current beliefs and understanding. Creativity is limitless, be more creative than you ever have before.

Unless we are open to trust, continuity and transformation, we will be less likely to experience anything close to Ergriffenheit, wonder or joy in our writing. Trust relates to challenging our assumptions and being open to experience. Continuity means consistency, resilience and self-belief, all things a writer wants to aim for. With trust and continuity, we reach transformation, a state of Ergriffenheit.

Re-connecting to your inner wonder takes practise and persistence. You can think of it as your imagination, your creativity, your determination to create. Reaching for it is the first step.

Exploring and interacting with the world outside is the optimal route to you discovering wonder. That is, to becoming a writer who is an explorer and curious, interactive and experimental, one able to transport a reader and deliver an emotional experience.

Try this next exercise as you begin to practise getting outside and developing your sense of wonder and joy.

**Writer's Exercise**

Character Goals

Imagine there are three people who live in a house. Right now, each of them is staring out of a window in a different room. Choose one occupant and write from their point of view (you have ten minutes). Include the following:

- The Motivator
- The Obstacle
- The Solution
- The Desired Outcome (goal)
- The Actual Outcome
- The Resolution

Repeat for the other two occupants.

Now write a scene bringing all three occupants into the same room where each of them shares their experience.

What can we learn from imaginary and actual goals when we share our thoughts on them?

**Quick Recap**

Walking in nature, exploring and strengthening your connectedness will help you hone your observational skills, help you recognise Ergriffenheit and align your external world with your Illusive Self to reach a greater level of authenticity in your writing. You will form a unique and powerful emotional connection with your reader.

- Reconnect and Reimagine.
- Keep track of your small goals ensuring they're supporting your larger goals.
- Listen to your natural self.
- Breathe.
- Savour your precious moments.
- A sense of awe is worth sharing, otherwise decide whether your sharing time could be better spent exploring so that you have something worthwhile to share.
- Write a list of things you do that surprise and delight you and refer back to this list when you need a boost.

# YOUR OBJECTIVE

Ignite Your Sense of Awe

Exploring the outdoors and reconnecting with your natural self will lead to a sense of awe, which is essential for keeping us well-balanced emotionally, physically and creatively.

Scientists refer to that tranquil feeling you get while on a hiking trail or gazing across the sea – where your mind is completely at peace, taking in the scenery and maybe letting thoughts drift – as 'soft fascination'. In comparison, when we're intensely focusing on something loud like an ambulance siren, our brains go into 'hard fascination' mode. We are exposed to experiences of hard fascination continuously in this modern world which is why we want to discover and explore wild places, let our minds and bodies experience awe and give our creative selves a chance to reimagine and reawaken.

**Preparation**

Wilderness therapy aims to foster self-development through a deep connection with nature. Individuals or groups are placed in natural settings as a transformative force shaping their perception of and responsibility for their own experience and forward journey. The experience is a source of empowerment, fostering personal growth and resilience.

You can practise your own form of wilderness therapy in a variety of ways:

- Plan a solo camping trip or nature retreat to disconnect from technology and immerse yourself in the wilderness.

- Join a wilderness therapy programme or writing retreat that combines outdoor activities with creative writing workshops.

- Incorporate nature walks or outdoor writing sessions into your daily routine to reap the benefits of spending time in nature regularly.

- Use nature as a source of inspiration by observing wildlife, studying plant life, or simply soaking in the beauty of natural landscapes.

Overall, practising wilderness therapy can help you rejuvenate your creativity, gain perspective and find deeper meaning in your writing.

**Purpose**

Your purpose is to foster a profound appreciation for life and a sense of interconnectedness with all living beings and bring to yourself a sense of awe from the experience.

The aim of seeking awe in the wilderness is to ignite a feeling of astonishment and deep respect for the magnificence of nature, spanning from the vastness of the sky to the intricate beauty of a solitary flower. These experiences will help you cultivate a deeper connection to nature and recognise that you are not separate from the Earth but rather an integral part of its ecosystem. Discovering awe in the wilderness can serve as a catalyst for personal growth and healing. You may often experience a shift in perspective, transcend your everyday concerns and tap into a deeper wellspring of inspiration and creativity. This heightened state of awareness can bring clarity and facilitate inner peace and self-acceptance.

# YOUR GOAL

Your goal is to find a sense of awe, to rediscover your meaning and purpose and cultivate a deeper appreciation for the wonder that surrounds you. In doing so, you can embark on a journey of profound transformation, aligning your life with values of gratitude and harmony with the natural world.

**Writing Exercise 1**

This exercise is for those of you who spend time on

social media. For one week, only post videos of yourself exploring nature and practising wild mindfulness. Share the joy and wonder of nature and the uniqueness of your connection.

**Writing Exercise 2**

Write a 300-word story about a character on a hiking trail. Include the following:

Beginning – character has a difficult problem.

Middle – character experiences something out of the ordinary in nature.

End – character solves the problem.

Compulsory: the events in your story must come from your own experiences in nature. That doesn't mean that you can't use your imagination to expand on those experiences ...

# Principle Nine:
# Your Fairy-tale Self

**Principle Aim:** What Makes a Good Story?
**Principle Objective:** Your Unique Words
**Principle Goal:** Delivering to Your Reader

## YOUR AIM

If chaos is all we know when we create, then chaos can be accepted as the way of the creative world. Writers like you and me; we want to write good stories. Stories that readers adore. That is no easy thing so we must take care that the effort we put in is working for us. Within each of us is our Fairy-tale Self. Fairy tales are enduring, adored and often they astound us as readers. On a surface level, studying fairy tales is a good use of a writer's energy. On a deeper level, igniting your Fairy-tale Self will get you closer to writing those good stories and becoming a great writer.

What accounts for the enduring popularity of fairy tales? The explanation is not straightforward; it's a question that revolves around what constitutes a compelling narrative. Writers grapple with this mystery, striving to create stories that resonate with audiences. The subjective nature of storytelling means that what captivates one person may not engage another. However, fairy tales endure because they possess the essential elements of a captivating narrative. Therefore, writers on a quest to unravel the secrets of storytelling excellence would be wise to study fairy tales closely.

Practise close reading fairy tales and you're practising good storytelling that will filter down to your own writing.

What are you looking for on a close reading – the elements of story:

- The planting of seeds
- Rich experiences
- Curiosity and Ergriffenheit
- Fantasy, imagination and metaphor
- Reasoning
- Emotional development
- Anxiety problem-solving
- New perspectives and aspirations
- Real-life resonance and fear resolution
- Fulfilment, satisfaction and hope

When you sit down to write a story, novel or any kind of creative book, it won't do you any good to have this list by your side in an attempt to tick it off by adding each element at a conscious level. Your writing will feel forced, awkward, preachy, inauthentic and it's unlikely to flow well.

Instead, you want to ignite your Fairy-tale Self, the part of you that will deliver these elements of story without you having to force anything. The Fairy-tale Self resides within your Illusive Self (see page 84). You awaken it by investing in the practice of close reading and there is no better text to practise on for this purpose than fairy tales themselves. This is where you get to tick off that list.

Choose a fairy tale. Read it two or three times. Put it aside for a day or two then read it again. Set aside time for the close reading when you won't be interrupted. Then read the story again. Next, take your list and think about each item in turn. Write your thoughts as they crop up. Refer back to the story as often as you wish or not at all. When you've completed one close reading and have noted comments for each item, ask yourself if you've read close enough. Read your comments again. Could you dig deeper? Once you're satisfied that you've uncovered all you're going to uncover for now, write a paragraph about any key revelations that come to you. Revelations may not come to you right away, it may take a day or two, or a week or they may come and go without you having observed them, although this is less likely to happen if you try to remain curious and observant. Life gets in the way, we get in our own way, but there's no need to worry because new revelations, ideas and perspectives will be stored in your Fairy-tale Self, ready and waiting for you to access when the time is right for you.

Repeat the above exercise with other fairy tales and keep going. Anytime you feel like taking your fairy tale out to a wild space and reading it aloud, do it. You'll surprise yourself each time. Especially do this if you're struggling to find any or all story elements in a particular fairy tale.

Eventually this practice will be something you do naturally and without thinking about it. You will have your friendly Fairy-tale Self to guide you in writing a truly authentic and compelling story.

**A Writer's Exercise:**

What can you learn from listening to and reading aloud traditional stories?

Answer the following with your ideas:

How to propel your story from the ordinary to the extraordinary

Ideas:

- 
- 

How to energise your characters and make them memorable

Ideas:

- 
- 

How to present character motivations in a simple but powerful way

Ideas:

- 
- 

How to tackle difficult themes, engage, shock, entertain your reader

Ideas:

- 
- 

How to know what you want to say, and say it engagingly

Ideas:

- 
- 

How to know you can write strong and compelling stories

(hint: by being first compelled yourself)

Ideas:

- 

- 

**What is Fairy-tale Self and how can it help you?**

It's quite simple really; it's a measured way of tracking your progress towards your writing life purpose. The very idea of tracking your progress begs these questions of you:

a. Do you know where you're going with your writing career?

b. Do you know where your writing project is heading and how you're going to get to the finish line?

c. Do you prefer the idea of not knowing any of this?

d. Do you prefer to wait to see what will happen?

e. What does it mean to you to take responsibility and be accountable for your writing progress?

Have a think about these questions and answer them. They are questions you can ask yourself at any point in your writing journey to remind you that you are on a journey and that writing is a process.

Your Fairy-tale Self brings nature and the writing process together to form a connection and at the centre of that connection is YOU. Your natural self. Your natural self comes from being in nature and setting your Illusive Self free to roam and find the creative answers you need to keep going with your writing life.

Recognising that we are not just on the Earth but also

within it rekindles the innate connection ingrained within us. We are as integral to the Earth's nurturing cycle as the cells forming our physical beings.

Consider my personal example: Our bodies consist of countless nerve endings that relay messages to the brain. In a healthy state, this communication ensures appropriate responses, like withdrawing a hand from fire upon sensing pain. Yet, in instances like mine, when this communication breaks down or is severed, the body's functioning is disrupted. Faulty signalling from nerves to the brain leads to misinterpreted sensations, such as feeling pain without a physical cause.

Just as our bodily functions rely on efficient communication, our relationship with the Earth is similarly intertwined. When we detach ourselves and assert dominance over the Earth, we sever this vital connection, causing harm to both the planet and ourselves. Conversely, nurturing our bond with the Earth fosters the well-being of both our planet and humanity.

When we work to keep the natural world healthy, the Earth returns the same a hundred times over and we find limitless benefits to our health, well-being and creative capacities.

- We interact and cooperate with the Earth.
- In return we find ourselves with a system of interconnectivity and cooperation integral to achieving our writing goals.

## Quick Recap

The Fairy-tale Self resides within your Illusive Self. You awaken it by investing in the practice of close reading and there is no better text to practise on for this purpose than fairy tales themselves. On a surface level, studying fairy tales is a good use of a writer's energy. On a deeper level, igniting your Fairy-tale Self will get you closer to writing those good stories and becoming a great writer. Eventually this practice will be something you do naturally and without thinking about it. You will have your friendly Fairy-tale Self to guide you in writing a truly authentic and compelling story.

Recognising that we are not just on the Earth but also within it rekindles the innate connection ingrained within us. We are as integral to the Earth's nurturing cycle as the cells forming our physical beings. Your Fairy-tale Self brings nature and the writing process together to form a connection and at the centre of that connection is YOU. Your natural self. Your natural self comes from being in nature and setting your Illusive Self free to roam and find the creative answers you need to keep going with your writing life.

## YOUR OBJECTIVE

While the soft approach to understanding that only you can write your story is digging into who you are as a writer and the whys and hows of what you write, the ultimate approach to what Your Unique Words mean is accepting that you have to show up to write. Your story will never get written if you don't park yourself and do the writing. Your Unique Words mean something to you, but they will only mean something to a reader if you release them into the world.

## Preparation

Remember, Your Writer's Ecosystem is a tracker system to guide you, encourage you and finally to get you to the finishing line. Knowing you have to show up isn't something you have to track; it's something you must choose to do and make the decision to show up. How and when you show up is worth tracking. But getting to that point may be the thing that's keeping you stuck. Tick off the following:

- You are a writer
- You are able to solve all writing problems
- You can write in your own words
- You are confident
- You are able
- You are committed
- You are creative

## Purpose

### Writer's Exercise

Imagine your current writing project as a person rather than a thing. What kind of person is it? What shape? How does it sound?

Now imagine you are introducing your Fairy-tale Self to this person (your WIP).

Answer the following:

- What's happening?
- Who is saying what?
- What are you laughing at?
- Suggest somewhere playful to go together
- What game will you play?

Decide between you:

- How does the ocean connect to the rocks?
- How are trees communicating with each other
- Like the leaves on the tree, when I fall, what will I re-emerge as?
- When was the last time you felt completely engrossed in each other?
- How did you both feel then?
- How might you recreate that feeling?

# YOUR GOAL

*Your creative self*

Your Illusive Self is where your creativity lives, where your courage, tenacity and uniqueness releases.

Nature and your natural connection open up a channel to your Illusive Self so that all of these things can come into your conscious awareness.

Take a moment to think about what your overall solution would look like on the journey to reaching your writing life purpose. Write it down, refer to it often.

- What does that solution mean to you now, in a year's time, in five years?
- What impact does your solution have?
- What impact does it have on your self-worth right now?
- What are your intentions right now?
- How resilient do you see yourself? How might you best use your resilience or best strengthen it?

Part of the creative process is getting used to the idea that creating anything will, at some point, require you to get comfortable with coping with a messy brain. Describe one experience from the past when your brain has felt incredibly messy and write about how you got through that experience.

From the mess comes wonder.

During the creative process your brain becomes messy because you are putting it into situations it has no experience over. You've just read your first draft and you've found ten plot holes. Your brain freaks out and twists itself around trying to fill you up with solutions to old problems that won't work in this new situation. But by working through this situation you grow, you learn, you discover and you create and you emerge at the other side with both your brain and your sanity in harmony.

*Your Reader*

How do you intend to reach out and grab the heart of your reader?

Write your thoughts on this and keep adding new ideas and new perspectives as you journey through your writing project.

Remember, writing is all about experience.

Track:

- The why of your project
- The why of your experience
- The why of your heart
- Imagine your reader experience
- Imagine your reader expectations
- Think beyond your initial ideas

- Think beyond your goal: open an experiential channel to your reader – what does this look like? What does it feel like?

*Your Outcome*

Your outcome is everything that surrounds your goal achievement.

- Your anticipated outcome
- Where might it fall short?
- Write about your self-belief
- Commit to your writing goals
- Commit to your daily practice
- Your achievements
- Your promise to your self
- Your promise to your reader
- What next?

Pay attention to when you might be getting in your own way. Develop strategies to walk right through yourself while at all times loving who you are.

**Writing Exercise 1**

Read the following fairy tale

### The Maiden with the Wooden Bowl

A long time ago there lived an old couple with their young daughter, a lovely, graceful child. After her husband died, his widow grew concerned about the daughter's future. She spoke to her child, 'My beloved daughter, the world can be a cruel place. You are too fair to live alone so I am placing this bowl on your head. You must wear it always. The bowl will protect you against those who would do you harm.' Soon after, the old woman died. The maiden, with the bowl on her head, went to work in the rice fields to earn her keep. Those who saw her laughed at the strange sight of a maiden with a wooden bowl on her head but the young girl paid little attention. When young men tried to pull the bowl off her head, it would not move. After a while they stopped trying, contenting themselves with calling her names.

1. Imagine you are your eight-year-old self. Write about this story.
2. Imagine you are your reader self. Write about this story.
3. Imagine you are your Fairy-tale Self. Write about this story.
4. Compare your three pieces of writing and note any differences, surprises and/or insights.

**Writing Exercise 2**

Take yourself out into nature and be your eight-year-old self.

# Principle Ten: Impossible Worlds

**Principle Aim:** Reader Engagement
**Principle Objective:** Transitioning Worlds
**Principle Goal:** Recreating Wonder

## YOUR AIM

Connectedness reminds us that we as writers are not setting out to simply put words on paper. We want to aim higher than that. Writing is about experience and about feeling. We are interacting with our words, our environment and our readers. We aim to share our natural self, our connection, with our readers and offer them the gift of meaning and awe.

The focus here is the writer-reader connection. How we connect, relate and interact with ourselves as writers, and how we connect with our readers and our world. All of this is important. Writing isn't simply about sitting at a desk and writing a story. We first talk our stories inside our heads. Writing stories is simply an exercise in communication. But we have to make sure that we're communicating exactly what we mean to communicate to our reader (this is not always what we mean originally), and that we are offering an experience to our reader that we've connected with and thus created experientially. Otherwise the act of writing fails in its duty to elicit wonder for us and our reader, our writing is lacklustre and we become disengaged from our creativity.

Readers rewrite our stories as they're reading them. This idea may not have occurred to you before, or you may have wondered what a reader does or how a reader feels when they're reading your stories and what a reader thinks about your stories. As writers, we know that we are writing for a reader. We want our stories to be read. Unless, of course, we're simply writing for ourselves. Even then, try putting a story away in a drawer for a year then returning to it and you'll read it differently, feel and most likely think differently about it. In all likelihood, your experience will have changed. With any luck you've developed your writing muscle and your confidence as a writer and you'll rewrite the original story as you read it anew. The literary scholar and critic, Marie-Laure Ryan (1992), embraced the notion that during the reading process, readers construct imaginary worlds from the story that mean something particular to them. They do this by filling in the gaps in a story with a fictional world that resembles their own lived experience of reality. Ryan describes the fictional world of the story (from a reader perspective) as a 'possible world'. An alternative from the fictional world in the text and one that means something particular to the reader. This possible world then acts as the actual world, we call it a relatable world, while the reader is immersed in the text.

What all this means is that reading stories is just as important to a writer as writing them. I mentioned earlier that readers fill in the gaps. This is them forming their possible world. It's part of a reader's cognitive make-up and something they do subconsciously. A writer who pays attention to how a reader might fill in the gaps of the story they are writing is one who is serious about their craft.

The difficulty is in trying to discover these gaps in our

stories that give readers the opportunity to develop their own possible worlds. Think about it, a reader who can reimagine a possible world from your story is a reader who will be more likely to invest in your story. It's not that difficult really, all it takes is practice.

Let's have a look at the following

'When the border guards ask, I say I'm a writer,' remarks Bringhurst. 'If they ask still more, I'll say I write both poetry and prose. That's usually enough; they'll shake their heads and wave me on. I wouldn't attempt to tell them the truth, which is that writing is just a disguise. I do my work by talking to the air. Sooner or later the talk is disguised as writing and printing, because those are the simplest, least obtrusive ways of miming something spoken.' Robert Bringhurst, *The Tree of Meaning*, 2006

Your aim is to discover the gaps as a reader so that you can write like a reader and learn how to grab your readers' attention to keep them reading and loving your stories. The best way to achieve this is to practise reading, as hinted previously. But reading alone is not enough. You need to focus on the text and by that I mean experience it, feel it. Feel the story and create your own possible world from it. By comparing the fictional world of the story with your personal possible world (as it relates to your actual lived experience) you'll begin to get a feel for the gaps that hook a reader's subconscious, and for what is likely to keep them reading. The best way to feel a story is to read it aloud. As Bringhurst suggests in the quote above, we write by 'talking to the air'. In this practice, you want to do more than talk to the air. Take your story outside and tell it, out loud, in a setting you're comfortable with and, if you can, record your voice while telling the story. Once you've completed this practice you'll discover a host of reasons why this is the best route to writing like a reader. But for now, trust in the process, be open to the experience and we'll come together at the end to discover the leap you've made toward improving your writing.

## Quick Recap

How we connect, relate and interact with ourselves as writers, and how we connect with our readers and our world are all important. Writing isn't simply about sitting at a desk and writing a story. We first experience then talk our stories inside our heads. Writing is simply an exercise in communication. During the reading process, readers construct imaginary worlds from the story that mean something particular to them. They do this by filling in the gaps in a story with a fictional world that resembles their own lived experience of reality. If you can take a reader from developing their own fictional world to this world becoming something your reader resonates with (an actual world) you will successfully captivate them, ensuring they return for more of your work.

## YOUR OBJECTIVE

Let's get down to practising transitioning from fictional worlds to possible worlds. There are five steps. Take your time, there's no need to rush this. Each step is designed to get the maximum benefit for you and your writing. Complete the steps in order and don't read ahead. Let yourself be open to new experiences. Don't worry about getting it right or even fully understanding what you're doing. Your subconscious will retain it for you when you return to your writing desk.

## Preparation

**Step One:** Read the following Cherokee folktale then rewrite it so you experience it and you have a physical copy:

At the start of the people's time on earth, they decided that life would be greatly improved if there was only day and no night. They petitioned the Ouga, or Creator, and the Creator agreed. They soon realised their mistake, however – the days were long and hot and they had to work harder than ever – and they were not happy with things like this. So they went again to the Creator, asking instead for it to be night all the time. This went no better: crops stopped growing, it was impossible to see in order to hunt, and people were cold. Weak and hungry, a small number of people perished. Realising their mistake, the people petitioned the Creator once more, begging for both day and night to exist as they had before. The Creator agreed, and the people were happy, as things returned to their previous, contented state. The people were happy and grateful, but the Creator was sad that so many had died. In their name, the Creator formed a new tree, and put the spirits of those who had died in the long night into it. It was named a-tsi-na tlu-gv – cedar tree.

Chainey and Winsham (2021)

## Step Two

- 2a: Plan a trip outdoors with a definite destination. It doesn't have to be far, or adventurous or even a wild landscape. Things to think about are what you'll encounter on the route. The best route/location for this is a place of few or no fellow humans, the least amount of distraction and somewhere you can spend ten minutes alone without a care. Take a copy of the story with you and if possible, your phone so that you can record yourself telling the story out loud.

2b: Just before you embark on your trip, note down how you're feeling in the moment. Then note what thoughts are in your head.

2c: As you embark on your trip, try to be in the present. Consciously notice things as you walk by and name them, either aloud or to yourself (no need to write them down and a flower is a flower, no need to know the name of it).

2d: Once you've reached your destination take a seat or at least rest for a moment. Take a few conscious, deep breaths. Check in with yourself. Can you be present in this moment? Try your best. Remember, thoughts of the past/future are not welcome at this time. It's perfectly fine for these thoughts to crop up, don't try to banish them, simply don't attend to them, acknowledge them and then let them pass by you without engagement.

2e: Once you're ready, set your recorder (if you can) then begin reading the story aloud.

**Step Three:** Re-presenting Story:

As writers we navigate, explore, dig up and discover our story world and its content from within.

Remind yourself that the words we write are our unique representation of the story we are telling.

Answer each question as it relates to your reading of The Cedar Tree.

1. Think about how you feel like interpreting The Cedar Tree. What kind of story world comes to mind for you? What resonates with you? What story or stories are circling about in your head?

As you continue with these questions, answer each one as it relates to The Cedar Tree but feel free to note down other stories, ideas, characters etc. that come to mind from your direct reading of The Cedar Tree and apply each question to your own story worlds also. In a sense, this exercise helps you develop your own interpretation of the fictional world of The Cedar Tree and extend that development into a possible new world that resonates uniquely with you.

2. Whose story is it – who is the main character? Who is telling the story? Are these different characters or the same?

3. What problem does the main character have to face?

4. Does the main character have enemies? Allies?

5. What does the main character want to achieve?

6. What obligations does the main character have?

7. What does the main character know about the other characters?

8. How does the main character face the problem and by what means?

9. What is different about the main character by the end? Are there changes to desires, feelings, obligations, etc.?

10. What does the main character gain? Or lose? What are the consequences of the main character's actions in relation to him/herself and others?

Adapted from: Efthymia G et al. *Narratology and Creative Writing in Primary Education* UPERC 2017

Did you discover a possible story world derived from the Cherokee folklore tale, The Cedar Tree? Did you decide who the main character was? Perhaps you approached the story separately from the Cherokee people and the Creator? You can always come back to this practice sheet and experience the story once again and continue to develop other stories that resonate with you.

Let's untangle all of this. How do we transition from fictional to possible world in The Cedar Tree? I can give you a brief summary of my possible world and that's fine. It will be different from yours and that's how it should be. How often do we imagine the obligations of our characters when we're writing our stories? It's an important clue to who we are, what kind of writer we are and what kind of writer we want to be.

For example, if I approach the story from the point of view of the Creator, I imagine he is obligated to the entire Cherokee people, to the natural world, the close environment, the sustenance of the earth. Does he consider he has obligations to himself? Is he a people pleaser? Or is he the type of character that sits back and watches others make mistakes knowing he can and eventually will leap to the rescue?

I view the Creator as someone who takes the Cherokee people to his heart and wants what's best for them and is willing to put them before himself but you may see a rather more cynical side to him. Neither of us are right or wrong, all this does is tell us a little about our possible world (one that resonates with us), which in effect means we've translated the text into something that more resembles our actual world, that is, our lived experience.

The main thing is to practise this exercise as you move

forward in your writing. Let it inform your reading, your writing practice and your inner editor. The more you practise this transitioning, the more you will be writing like a reader. Keep in mind that the closer you pay attention to how a reader could possibly fill in the gaps of your story, the better you will get at your craft.

**Purpose**

Let's say, for argument, that I am a people pleaser. That my understanding of The Cedar Tree is based around the notion that my first reaction is that I always put other people before myself. This is a very simplistic understanding of the story but it's useful to make a point. What good does it do to know this and how can I use it to improve my writing?

It is likely that all people pleasers who read this story will easily relate to it (i.e. form a possible world that becomes an actual world while the reader is immersed in the story). That's good to know. It gives me pause for thought as a reader – what good does people pleasing achieve? – and as a writer it helps me understand how my words and meanings may impact, influence or affect a reader and why a reader may be attracted to my story or otherwise.

Equally, some people may approach the story in an entirely different way and see the Creator as weak and ineffectual. This reader may form a possible world that confirms their own self-belief and may relate that way or they may find the story itself weak and ineffectual. I may point out here that for the purposes of this task we've viewed this tale as a fictional one. We recognise that it is folklore and that there is a difference between folklore and fiction but in this instance the difference is not within the scope of this exercise which is simply an exercise in reading a story, fictional or otherwise.

A good writer must be interested in how their words and meanings impact, influence or affect a reader and why a reader may be attracted or otherwise to their stories. Considering fictional, possible and actual worlds gives you a method of ensuring that you are writing like a reader, which, ultimately, means you are writing for your reader.

I want to conclude this section by briefly discussing the 'read aloud outside' aspect of this practice. Most writers are aware of the benefits of reading their work aloud. However, I have no idea how many writers consider the benefits of doing this outdoors. I practise this with my own writing, but more often than not I am outside reading other people's stories and tales and myths from around the world. Wherever I go – the local park, forest, the beach, somewhere wild, beautiful and remote – what matters is having the confidence to do it and feel the benefits from it.

You will have already felt something by reading The Cedar Tree outdoors. If you were able to record yourself, watch the replay, observe yourself and see your self-confidence, enthusiasm, drive and hope growing as you read. Getting outdoors with a focus on your writing practice, your writing self and your work in progress is a transformative experience and the benefits are limitless. See for yourself, get out and about, read aloud, read a range of stories, read your work in progress. Read aloud with gusto and joy.

Then you can tell me of your transformation and how much your writing has improved. And I'll smile knowingly and congratulate your successes.

**Step Four:** Observing

Read one book and watch one movie. For each, answer the following:

1. Name one specific note/episode/sentence/image or any other aspect of the film/book that made you feel something.

2. In what way did you feel – what emotions were going on for you?

3. Name a point in the story where you felt you belonged in the story. If you didn't feel you belonged, why was that?

4. Was there anything that irritated you while watching/reading?

5. In your opinion, what would have made this film/book stronger?

6. Did anything in the film/book make you change the way you think or perceive of who you are as a writer?

That last question (6) is worth thinking about. When we have a strong connectedness to self, our characters, our story and our reader, when the story flows seamlessly within this sphere, we discover new things about our self and our world and our reader does too, in a meaningful way for them. You don't experience what your reader experiences, or vice versa, but you both experience something that changes you in some way, however subtle. If part of the connectedness is broken, disrupted or missing, that change is unlikely to occur.

As a reader, when a story resonates with you, you feel a sense of the distance between you and the world of the story shortening. This is what's known as Closing Distance. Closing Distance refers to the writer's ability to bring the reader in, closer to the world of the story.

As a writer, it's not about closing the distance between writer and reader or text and reader, the technique is more about bringing the reader closer to your natural self, you as the creator of the story world. There is a difference. Closing distance refers to measuring and reducing the distance between your natural self, your story world and your reader.

Obviously we're not talking about physical distance here or even imaginary distance.

We could write a truly compelling story of two characters, let's say one is in Wisconsin and the other is in Ireland. Each character – and the reader – imagines the distance between them in a different way. Unless the writer can connect these imagined distances and deliver a potential possible world for the reader, the story may not resonate with them.

If you've read, or choose to read, *Letters from Skye* by Jessica Brockmole, you'll get a good sense of what I mean here. Brockmole's book is a series of letters (as you may have guessed) between a romantic couple. For me, this story was all consuming. I was gripped by this one. It's a great example of closing distance. The distance is closed through the emotions of each of the main protagonists, and the way the author has been able to transmit those emotions in a way that mean something specific to me as the reader.

First I want to make the distinction between closing the distance between reader and writer and bringing the reader closer to your natural self.

The distance between your natural creative self and your reader is worth paying attention to. You want to engage your reader as much as possible so it's a good idea to find ways to make that happen.

One of the most commonly used techniques to close the distance between writer and reader is point of view (POV).

First-person POV is the most effective. The reader is directly inside your character's head.

e.g. 'I hate this house.'

not

'She hates the house.'

It's easy to see why this works well. The reader is party to all your character's thoughts, feelings, emotions and if it's done well, it can grab the reader from the beginning.

As writers, we want to close the distance so that we can create an emotional connection between reader the story journey, make the reader think, make our books memorable. But we want to do this from a place of authenticity, from our natural creative ability.

Third-person limited POV can also be effective at closing the distance. The reader is still able to be inside the character's thoughts and feelings but not necessarily all of them. There are varying levels of distance between the story and the reader depending on how the third person is executed. A writer connected to their natural creative self has a better chance of controlling the distance. Because it is the story that dictates which POV you choose. Some stories demand first person and others benefit more from third-person limited, or even third person which creates slightly more of a distance.

e.g. 'She grabs a paintbrush and slaps paint on the walls, making sure that he can see the tightness of her jaw. She isn't clenching her teeth for no reason. He has to pay for what he's forcing her into.' (Third-person limited)

'She starts to paint the wall. The sunlight has dimmed and the room is in shadow. He hasn't said anything for at least ten minutes. She wonders what his plan is.' (Third person)

The omniscient narrator is the furthest from the reader but a good narrator can capture a reader's attention. *Little Women* by Louisa May Alcott for example. There are memorable books written with an omniscient narrator and it can be a useful tool if done well. The comfort and familiarity of your story world that you achieve when you're connected physically, emotionally and creativity can't be underestimated and helps to bring to the page an omniscient narrator that is wholly alive and compelling.

Second-person POV is subjective in my opinion and not a popular choice for most writers.

**Example:**

You left the door open hoping she would follow you in and you waited alone for some time until you decided she'd rejected your offer of friendship.

Think about how this line makes you, as the reader, feel.

When reading a story written in the second person, you may feel, as a reader, that you are the character or you may feel resistance or take a defensive position. It depends on the story and the character and the ability of the writer to do it well. A perfect example of a well-written story in the second person is *The Sound of My Voice* by Ron Butlin.

Give it a go and take note of your reactions so you get a good feeling for how you, as reader, form a possible world.

Publishers and agents are always on the lookout for an original story and it's your unique connection with your reader that will take your writing forward, not what is popular or what is considered 'out of fashion'. Remember, we're writing from the inside out, and closing distance, when we get there, will take you forward. But first, just a brief word on style and setting. Each of these techniques can help to reduce the distance between reader and story.

Style is subjective but when carefully considered is a good means of attracting the reader to your story. Style isn't simply genre, for example, whether your story is a tragedy, comedy, romance or fantasy, etc. Once you're clear on the (approximate) genre of your story paying attention to style becomes important. Style is both genre specific and unique to you. It is the intertwining of both these things because no one can write in the same style as you. You bring your uniqueness to your writing. It has been said that you have to write ten thousand words before you can identify your own style. I say, write from deep within, from your natural creative self and you'll find that your style is already fully formed, ready for you to discover.

Setting can be a good route to your readers' emotional psyche. Again, this is subjective. You could write a beautiful account of your setting, with rich and compelling detail. Not all readers will appreciate your efforts. If a reader picks up your book from the thriller shelf of the bookstore, he won't be best chuffed if he can't see the wood for the trees. In other words, if he has to trawl through pages of setting to get to the action, he's likely to throw your book out the window. On the other hand, there are certain genres where the setting sells the book. The bestselling, *Where the Crawdads Sing* by Delia Owens is a good example. How you create your world and present it to your reader is important.

All of these techniques to shorten the distance between your story and your reader only work well if you, as writer, have a strong and close connectedness to yourself, your story and your reader.

We write to seek change, in the way that nature adapts to changes, and likewise, we adapt to nature. Nature is about feeling and experiencing. If you can believe that human nature and nature co-exist as one interactive entity this helps to connect more easily. We accept that we aren't merely observing but interacting and experiencing. We acknowledge that as we invite nature in, we are at the same time, asking nature for an invitation. (Wulf, 2015).

**Step Five:** Riff Writing

Riff Writing is something you can do with any text: books, scripts, poetry, screenplays, advertisements, newspapers, web content. You can also do it while observing visual media.

Think about what the word 'riff' means to you personally, how does the word sound to you? How does it feel? The term 'riff' is associated with the music industry, i.e. guitar riffing. Other ways to think about riff is to browse, to rifle, to skim, to thumb or to glance. You're looking to approach your subject, whether your own writing, a book, a film, from a feeling perspective, how do the words feel to you? This is about getting you into yourself, allowing your subconscious to soak up your experience so that, later, when you come to write your own work, you can develop a channel to your reader and connect with them on an emotional level.

So what is Riff Writing? Let's look at an example paragraph from one of my stories. This paragraph needs editing and I'm going to approach it with a bit of riff writing. When you're Riff Writing, the way in which the words/sounds make you feel will be the route to gifting your reader an experience.

Here is a paragraph from an old draft of mine:

It's been exactly four weeks of nothing. But this morning, while I was sat up on the roof watching the sunrise, I felt something. It was like something inside of me shifted. The air smelt sweet and the leaves danced in the sky before settling at the root of the tree, waiting to be reborn. I know today is going to change everything.

There's a lot wrong with this paragraph but I want to focus on the last sentence because it's the worst offender. When we're examining a text or observing a movie we're looking for that unique connection, the one that draws us in and makes us feel something. Riffing this line I immediately pick out two words that would fail miserably at connecting with a reader: 'change everything.' Change is a signal word but the signal gets lost because while it alerts us, it leaves us with nowhere to go. Worse still, 'everything' is a dead end. What does 'everything' mean? Do either of these words elicit a feeling? Definitely not. Combined, these words do next to nothing for a reader.

Riff Writing helps us to be more specific in our writing, to pay closer attention in our observations and to focus at a deeper level on what matters most, delivering an experience for our readers.

Think about your readers' expectations. The simple way is, let's say, you're watching a film, a piece of music comes along and you know instantly what to expect, that something is about to happen. Watch an episode of Agatha Christie's *Poirot* and when you reach the denouement, listen to how the music sounds. It builds our expectations. This is a great way of connecting with your readers, understand the music of your words, the rhythm, the emotions. Get outside and feel the rhythm of the wind, listen to the sound of the rain. Try to feel the experience with every inch of your body, all of your senses, observe your thoughts and make contact with everything around you. When you have this level of connection it filters through to your writing, and when you come to edit, your Riff Writing will contain reimaginings that will enhance or even subvert reader expectations and give them a memorable experience on a deeply emotional and potentially physical level.

A few minutes Riff Writing – noting down how I feel, what does or doesn't resonate, ideas for words and phrases, rewriting exactly the experience of the words for myself, my character and my reader. Being curious about what might happen and writing about that curiosity, challenging perspective. Riff writing is simply about putting words down for your brain and your natural self to wonder about.

'I know today is going to change everything' becomes:

'I stand tall on the roof and stretch my arms above me as if, in this minute, I can clasp the clouds, as if I am part of them, all knowing and all seeing.'

Better?

## YOUR GOAL

The next time you take a walk outside, pay close attention

to the way in which you are observing and stop when you can to interact with your immediate environment. Pick up a leaf, a pebble, a stone and try to use each of your senses to absorb the feeling you experience in that moment. You don't need to try to find words to describe the experience, just feel it. Be open and in the moment and interactive. When you're fully present in the moment, words will pop into your head. If the words are about anything other than the moment, acknowledge them and let them go on their way. But if those words are related to your immediate environment, explore them, imagine, wonder about them. This will help you connect with your natural self.

Good writing is unfused with values and experiences, holding both collective and personal significance. It necessitates trust, consistency and an openness to transformation, all of which relies on interactivity.

**Exploring Wonder**

Although we covered Ergriffenheit at Principle Eight, I want to bring your mind back to the human-nature connection and the joy of writing. Both rely on us as humans observing and seeking out moments of wonder. The Write Wild Method encourages symbolic and value laden experience that relies on a degree of trust in the writing journey and continuity of practice and being open to transformation, all of which is supported via the human-nature connection. You can check your progress every now and then by answering the following questions and reflecting on your journey.

**Answer the following:**

1. What does Ergriffenheit mean for you (see Principle Eight, page 148)

2. How do you define trust as it is in reality for you and your writing process?

3. What are your thoughts on the concept of continuity?

4. Do you believe you have or can achieve an openness to transformation? What aspects of yourself would aid you in this practice?

# Summary of the 10 Principles with Exercises

1. **Reimagining-Reawakening:** Guides you to explore to make meaning to tell. This is the easiest way to remind you that your job is to explore meaning in a way that you can tell your unique story and to do that you must believe that you have all the answers within you and to release them you connect with your natural self.

*Example Exercise:*

Outer exploration – when you're practising wild mindfulness outdoors, being present, quieting your mind, be curious and focus on the aliveness within your body. Practise wild listening and wild walking. Use all of your senses and wonder at new ideas and new perspectives that come your way. Pick up one item that you can take home with you to remind you of this experience so that when you're at your desk you can reimagine the experience and with it will come aliveness, curiosity and absorption, all of which will fuel your ideas and your writing.

Inner exploration – write your meaning statement: sprint write for ten minutes each day for a few days focusing on what's important to you, what brings you alive, what your purpose really is. From this writing, devise a meaning statement. My statement is 'Take the next step'.

2. **Your Elliptic Presence**: This is about allowing yourself to embrace the chaos of the creative process. Creativity is a process, therefore writing a book is a process that encourages you to endure the chaos of meaning-making and combine it with strengthening your natural connection to allow freedom to your creativity.

*Example Exercise:*

At any point in your writing journey you start to think you can't do this, step away from your work and get out into nature. Practise wild mindfulness. Then when you return to your desk, reaffirm with yourself that this writing project is a process and that part of that process is **taking the step into the unknown and trusting the journey**. Remind yourself of your meaning statement. Remind yourself that you are an authentic writer with a purpose. Now, try to identify what the problem is and find a solution. One of the best ways of getting out of a block in your writing is to interview your protagonists and ask them what their life purposes are, what is meaningful to them? This is especially great if you're stuck and you don't know where the story is going.

3. **Ebb and Flow**: Ebb and Flow is like a feeling of the tide, nothing will stop the tide from its focus, little

will dissuade it from its regular pattern (as long as we don't allow our glaciers to melt as if that happens, the sea will become solidified). Without oceans, humans couldn't survive. This principle is a reminder that you are as connected to the planet as the sea, and you do have the ability to focus and become as absorbed as the sea in your task. Don't let external pressures get in the way of your purpose.

*Example Exercise:*

If you get stuck, get physical. If you can't concentrate, can't focus, don't feel like writing, get physical. If you have no time to get out and practise wild mindfulness, reacquaint yourself with anything you've collected from outdoors. Move your body in an Ebb and Flow way, reimagining yourself as the sea, then decide to be relentless. If you need more, take the last paragraph of the last thing you wrote and write it backwards. All of this together will inform your brain of your intentions and that you expect it to cooperate. Remember the sea never gets bored.

4. **Your Illusive Self**: We can think of our Illusive Self as the name for our creativity. It lives within us, it needs oxygen and let out to play and it is limitless when it is fully connected to the natural world and your natural self.

*Example Exercise:*

Take yourself out to a quiet place in nature and read a fairy tale aloud, record yourself. Watch the recording back and feel the joy of watching yourself become absorbed in the tale. Then take a few moments to sit and practise some seasonal breathing. Remind yourself that your creativity resides within your Illusive Self and it needs air to breathe and for you to quietly listen.

5. **The Walking Writer**: We all know that old saying, an apple a day keeps the doctor at bay. Well I'm prescribing a fifteen-minute daily walk. A walk a day keeps the writer in play. In other words, taking time for at least a fifteen-minute daily wild mindful walk will keep your writing muscle healthy and willing to show up for you daily.

*Example Exercise:*

Be alert for changes in shade and colour while your senses are alive during your walk. How do you relate to shade and colour? What are the shadows telling you? How do you feel when you hear the birdsong? Walking reminds you that you are alive and that you have a purpose in this world. State your purpose, speak aloud your meaning statement, to things you walk past, like a tree, a bush or a rock. Have a giggle, this stuff is supposed to be fun, writing is fun. Walking is fun. All of this will fuel your writing.

6. **Get Motivated:** Motivation is a decision. You make the decision based on your creative life purpose and your meaning statement. You also must consider your physical self and your health and ensure you have a good balanced and healthy writing life.

*Example Exercise:*

Decide what a daily writing practice might look like for you. What are your thoughts, beliefs and feelings about a daily writing practice? Are those thoughts, feelings and beliefs working in your best interests?

7. **Your Courage Continuum**: This is to remind you to trust your creative journey and to get your natural

self asking questions that will help you achieve your writing goals.

*Example Exercise:*

Get outdoors and practise wild mindfulness. State your purpose to the natural world and ask it to strengthen your courage to continue. Lay yourself on the ground (in a safe place) and spread your arms and legs. Gaze at the sky then close your eyes and be curious about what you're experiencing. Really feel the earth beneath your body then allow yourself to feel the awe of seeing only sky surround you and feeling the earth supporting you. Here is your quiet space, for both your body and your mind. Believe it or not, this turns out to be fun as well as having a great boost to your courage continuum. And that is not only building courage but resilience and determination also. You are reaffirming your life purpose.

8. **Ergriffenheit and Humility**: This is about developing our natural curiosity and reconnecting to our inner wonder. Returning to our childhood imaginations and connecting with a state of awe.

*Example Exercise:*

Release your inner child, reconnect with this past you and let yourself be guided by your childhood imagination. Climb a tree, jump in the ocean, whatever makes you smile. Build a fort or a castle in the woods or in the sand. Fish for tadpoles. Send yourself a card from your inner child.

9. **Your Fairy-tale Self**: This is developing the part of you that will deliver the elements of your story without you having to force anything or write from a place of inauthenticity. Your Fairy-tale Self helps

you find meaning in what you write and what you communicate with your readers.

*Example Exercise:*

Fairy tales transport us and take us out of our own way. Spend time with a fairy tale, especially when the writing isn't working. Study it, interpret it in different ways, make meaning from it. Understand it and what it's trying to teach you. Each fairy tale can offer you a new perspective on your own writing. Take it outdoors and read it aloud and experience it with your body, mind and all of your senses. Feel it and take that feeling back to your writing.

10. **Impossible Worlds**: This is a reminder that you begin a book writing it for yourself, but your final draft must always be for your reader.

*Example Exercise:*

Read a chapter you've already written. Write down what this chapter means to you. Now write down what you want this chapter to mean for your reader. Now write down other perspectives the reader may take from this chapter. Compare the three worlds, are they connected? Is there something that doesn't feel right to you? This will help you go deeper with your writing and bring more clarity and relatedness to your reader.

# THE MIDDLE

*- Writing is Process and Practise -*

# The Write Wild Method: DAILY PRACTICE

**Writing is a process.**

When you begin a writing project, you're taking the first step in the journey to completing your project, whether that's a novel, an anthology, a memoir, a poem, a script or screenplay and so on. If you're aiming to publish your writing, the simplest way of reaching your goals and creating success for yourself is to have a daily writing practice. Whether or not you decide to fully commit to a daily practice is entirely up to you but knowing is all part of learning and knowing that a daily practice is available to you if you want it is a great way of taking charge of your writing journey.

Developing a NATURAL DAILY WRITING PRACTICE, is all part of becoming and being a writer and by taking the natural approach you'll have a daily practice that will stay with you as you adventure along your writing career.

It's worth working through this section of the book even if you have no intentions of developing a daily practice. There are some ideas, concepts and exercises to get you thinking about the writing process and developing ideas to overcome any obstacles that get in your way.

The process towards developing a daily practice demands forward momentum and can be categorised into five main steps. Each of these five steps takes you further towards completing your project and the best way to completion is to follow the steps in order, beginning with step one and ending with step five.

The five steps are:

PREPARE
PROGRESS
DEVELOP
SIMPLIFY
TRANSFORM

Before you begin, it's important to know exactly where you are right now and to have a clear foundation to spring from. The first few exercises are designed to help you do just that; build a foundation from which you can embark confidently and creatively on your writing journey.

By the end you will have a NATURAL daily writing practice that takes a different approach to the writing process as it combines tools and techniques from nature that give you immeasurable positive benefits to both your writing life, your writing process and your personal health and well-being.

Before beginning Step One, it's a great idea to assess where you are now on your writing journey. Fill in your writing goals and map your road to success. These questionnaires and assessments will help ground you and also give you a measure to compare to when you finish Step Five.

Here's a first glance at what to expect:

**Step One**

PREPARE: Getting Fit for Purpose

We often forget that writing is a whole body experience. The best road to success is to be prepared, physically, psychologically and emotionally.

**Step Two**

PROGRESS: Tracking Your Road to Success

Only you can write your story. This means getting the writing done and rewarding yourself at the end of each day.

**Step Three**

DEVELOP: To Bravely Go ...

Develop Courage and Resilience to Push Through.

What life looks like when you embrace the process and are able to tackle any bumps in the road easily and swiftly.

**Step Four**

SIMPLIFY: Simplify the Process

It's easy to spend a lot of time developing a daily practice only to find out that you've made it too difficult to sustain. Make sure that doesn't happen!

**Step Five**

TRANSFORM: Transform your Writing Practice

Are you ready to supercharge your writing? This is a guide to get you writing. Develop yourself a daily practice, brilliant! But above all, write!

## Your writing goals

Know where you are: before you get started, it's a good idea to take note of where you are right now on your writing journey so that you can ...

Know where you're going: deciding on definite goals for your writing will help you commit to a daily practice and make quick and easy progress.

Start to think about what a daily practice means to you right now.

Make a list of all the benefits that having a daily practice will have on your writing success.

Ask yourself the following and begin to assess where you are right now.

Score yourself out of 10 (1 = not a lot / 10 = I've got this)

1. PREPARATION: How prepared are you to easily keep on track with your daily writing practice?

2. PROGRESS: How much progress do you believe you've made towards developing a daily writing practice?

3. DEVELOPMENT: To what extent do you believe you've made new discoveries and developed your writing in a way that's helped you get closer to your writing goals?

4. SIMPLIFY: How much do you believe you've been able to simplify your daily writing practice so it feels easy and achievable?

5. TRANSFORM: How positive are you feeling about maintaining a daily writing practice and reaching your writing goals?

**Assessing the road ahead**

Assess the score you gave to each step. For each step answer the following:

Is this score a true reflection of where you are right now in the process?

If you scored yourself less than 8, what action might you take next to increase your score for this step?

Does this score offer up any new perspectives or new discoveries about your writing practice?

Have a think about where you are at now and answer the following to work out what your next steps might begin to look like:

My next steps:

What works?

What doesn't work?

What can I celebrate?

# Step One

**Prepare**

In this section, you'll find everything you need to get you

started. Step One is designed to guide and prepare you to develop a daily writing practice that works for you; one that helps you take your writing forward.

Value yourself, value your writing. It's crucial that you find a way of valuing yourself, otherwise, all the effort you put in will be valueless. Does that make sense to you?

Developing a writing process, developing yourself. You can't develop a writing process that works for you without also developing yourself. This is worth noting and worth celebrating.

Here's a list of seven statements.

Answer the following statements with whatever comes into your head when you read each one.

1. Why should I bother?
2. My life, my choice
3. What's all this about process?
4. What, who? My natural self
5. It can't be all work
6. I am staying alive
7. I value me

When you get to statement seven, ask yourself if you believe yourself to be of value. If you do, give yourself a cheer and move on.

If you hesitate or do not believe at all that you are of value, stay with this exercise for a time. Re-assess your answers to the statements, re-evaluate your beliefs, and see if you can find a way that will get you ticking off statement seven with gusto!

Now that you've ticked statement seven, what are you waiting for, move on.

As you probably know by now, part of a good daily writing practice includes a daily fifteen-minute walk. Let's get you beginning that practice right away.

A: What does life look like to you right now?

B: What does life look like to you when you finish your writing project?

Now, go for a fifteen-minute walk and think about the individual steps you'll be required to take to get you from A to B.

## Step Two

### Progress

Answer the following questions:

What does your writing progress look like right now?

What does creativity feel like to you?

What does the opposite look like?

How does making no progress feel like to you?

How does feeling uninspired or uncreative feel like to you?

Write the following statement: DEVELOPING ME

Now, read aloud these seven statements to yourself:

1. I know my purpose
2. I am steadfast
3. I stand up for myself
4. I am my own cheerleader
5. I am full of self-compassion
6. I respect my creativity
7. I take action

Note down how you feel. Write these statements down and practise and learn them so you can repeat them to yourself every day and at times when you're feeling less like writing.

## Step Three

**Development**

Turning problems into curiosities is an effective method of investigating how to free up time for your writing in your busy life without causing overwhelm. Ask yourself:

How might you turn the problem of time into a curiosity, then a means by which you can show up for your writing?

How might you turn the problem of a lack of energy into a curiosity, then a means by which you can show up for your writing?

List all the problems that are preventing you from showing up and getting the work done.

Dust comes and goes like the wind. Problems actively behave in much the same way. One problem after another, after another to be curious about. The act of curiosity naturally encourages us to detach ourselves from our problem and look at it from an objective stance.

If we embrace the idea that problems will always be lingering around somewhere like dust, we can exist as our whole natural selves and act accordingly. This is not to ignore or demean your problems nor is it to measure the weight or impact between one problem and another. Take a look at the example below:

*I am too anxious to write today:*

Action: I don't write

I don't write.

Curiosity: What is anxiety? What if anxiety didn't exist? What if I wasn't anxious, would I write? Where is my anxiety, is it close, far away, in the dark or in the light?

Action: I write while I figure out what I can learn about anxiety from my curiosity.

This is not to simplify the often uncomfortable feelings of anxiety and/or reasons for anxiety. The thing is, if you want to write you have to write, in spite of the things that get in your way, and in spite of yourself.

Here's another example:

*I have no time to write today:*

Action: I don't write

I don't write.

Curiosity: How am I approaching the concept of time? Is time a process in the way that writing is a process? Can I manage the idea of time differently?

Action: I write while I learn from my curiosity about time.

I write.

This may all sound too simplistic but what if it turns out that this is exactly what's going to help you achieve your writing goals? When you're curious, you're in control of what actions you choose to take on a daily basis.

Make a list of all the things you can be curious about while going about your daily life.

Making progress can be a slow and painful process. The reason for this is because we don't tend to collect on the small wins. Put another way, we don't notice half the time when we are actually making progress. Time well spent interacting with nature is making progress. It's opening you up to new ideas, new perspectives, more curiosity, more energy and greater creativity. Writing an idea is making progress too! One unsuitable idea leads to the next suitable one, then the next better one, then the next and so on …

Making decisions is also making progress. Creativity is all about making decisions. Having to make those decisions can sometimes feel like a bump in the road and halt your progress but embarking on the decision-making process is indeed, making progress. Writing words is making progress, even if those words don't end up in the final draft, they are taking you on a journey towards that final draft.

Being a writer means you'll have some losses which are also wins because, again, they are all part of the writing process and your writing journey. You'll encounter small wins, medium-sized wins and huge wins, it all counts. These wins and losses truly count as progress and you will benefit from celebrating them. But when it comes down to it, these wins only mean something towards your writing life purpose if you actually show up and write regularly.

Making progress and being accountable for your own success will help keep you on track to meet your writing goals.

## Step Four

### Simplify

For the next five weeks I invite you to write for a minimum of thirty minutes, Monday to Friday. The time of day you choose to write is up to you. You are welcome to write for longer than thirty minutes if you choose. If you write for less time, this still counts, after all you've shown up, just keep an eye on it and try to stick to the thirty-minutes slot as often as you can.

Try to be accountable to yourself. Take note of each thirty-minute slot and each fifteen-minute walk and any changes you feel or experience along the way

Fifteen Minutes Wild:

Examples of interacting with nature can be anything from watching a nature video to spending a day somewhere wild and remote. Mix it up. A walk in your local area, a trip to the beach, a five-minute nature video on your phone. As long as you're using that time to quiet your mind; be observant, be curious and connect with your natural self. Practise wild listening, wild walking, wild breathing.

## Step Five

### Transform

How quickly do you think it will be before you settle into this routine?

Have a guess:

    1 week   2 weeks   3 weeks   4 weeks   5 weeks

What next? This is entirely up to you.

My Questions to Me:

Find a quiet time in a place where you won't be disturbed for the next half hour or so.

Practise some quiet breathing.

Then bring two chairs to face each other (if this isn't physically possible, close your eyes and imagine this space with two chairs facing).

You sit in one chair and the person sitting opposite you is you.

Now, ask the you opposite the following questions:

In what way have I or have I not made progress with my writing, my writing journey?

How do I feel about having a daily practice?

What felt right, what felt wrong, what worked, what didn't?

What next step/s am I going to decide to take?

**Courage and Resilience**

Writing will demand of you strength and devotion. Building your courage and resilience will be necessary if you want to reach your goals and especially if you want to make writing a career. This step gets you thinking about your own reserves of courage and resilience, particularly the reserves you're not currently accessing.

This step invites you to ask yourself questions and discover where you may be getting in your own way.

Check back in on yourself regularly on your answers to all the questions in this step, question whether your answers are working in your best interests and if not, give yourself permission to discover a new perspective, or different approach.

1. What kind of writer am I right now?
2. What kind of writer do I want to be?
3. Think about the kind of writer you want to be and ask yourself, why?

**Answer yes or no to the following:**

QUESTION 1:
Courage will always show up for me when I need it.

QUESTION 2:
I don't wait for courage to show up before I take the plunge.

QUESTION 3:
I believe in my writing capabilities more when I get validation from others.

QUESTION 4:
I quite often feel disappointed in my own writing capabilities.

QUESTION 5:
I am impatient to reach my writing goals.

QUESTION 6:
With my writing, I quite often feel like I don't know what I'm doing.

Regularly reassessing your thoughts on your progress is a good way of reframing any thoughts that may be getting in your way and stopping you from showing up.

**Answer the following:**

My thoughts on my YES answers

My thoughts on my NO answers

**Progress Tracker**

The key to developing a daily writing practice is to keep it simple. Keeping it simple means that you're clear on what you have to do and you get on and do it.

**On the next page is a quick chart to fill** in at the end of your daily practice to make sure that you're keeping your daily writing practice simple and workable. This chart helps you to see which areas are working for you and which areas need a bit more thought or action. Tick whichever box correlates with how you feel; one, two or three.

| | |
|---|---|
| **I show up to my writing most days.** | 1: Yes, this is working... ○<br>2: I'm making progress... ○<br>3: This needs more work... ○ |
| **I have lots of energy for my writing** | 1: Yes, this is working... ○<br>2: I'm making progress... ○<br>3: This needs more work... ○ |
| **I believe I am making good progress** | 1: Yes, this is working... ○<br>2: I'm making progress... ○<br>3: This needs more work... ○ |
| **I love this daily practice** | 1: Yes, this is working... ○<br>2: I'm making progress... ○<br>3: This needs more work... ○ |
| **I am being accountable to myself** | 1: Yes, this is working... ○<br>2: I'm making progress... ○<br>3: This needs more work... ○ |
| **I no longer worry about writing time** | 1: Yes, this is working... ○<br>2: I'm making progress... ○<br>3: This needs more work... ○ |

Congratulations if all your ticked boxes are number one. Ticking a box two gives you a great clue that there may be positive change you can make; be curious and begin looking for what that change may be. Ticking box three requires you to take action and you have a great indicator that tells you what area deserves your attention and transformation.

Ticking box three on your checklist indicates that you need to take some form of action to simplify the process and move you from three to two . Here are a few ideas of the kinds of action you may take for each of the categories on the checklist.

I show up – Only you can write your story. Nobody else is going to show up for you. Pick up your prompt sheet (page 215) and write.

I have lots of energy – Give yourself a regular health check. If your health is your 'normal' get outside and revitalise your aliveness. Engage with your natural self

I'm making good progress: The obvious question is why. Are you showing up? Are you stuck? Creativity is problem solving: work through the problem. You'll stay stuck if you try to go over or under or duck the problem completely.

I love my daily practice: Is a daily practice what you need? Is it what you want? If so, re-evaluate your investment in yourself. Reassess your meaning and purpose

I am self-accountable: Procrastination here may be as a result of previous rejection, perceived failure or a need for external validation. Check in with yourself and make sure you are your own best cheerleader.

I no longer worry about time to write: With a working

daily practice time shouldn't be a concern. If it is, the rest of this step is devoted to time.

Keeping your daily writing practice simple means finding time for your writing and time is often felt as either a burden or a hurdle when all you mean to do is write. Here we look at a couple of big reasons for why that is and what you can do about it.

Are you telling yourself a lie?

You might like to journal your thoughts as you begin to develop your daily practice and keep an eye out for any stories you're telling yourself that may be making time feel heavy and unforgiving and especially unavailable.

Things like: 'I've always been lazy,' or 'If I were as skilled at writing as I am at procrastinating I would be a bestselling author by now'. Or, 'I'm far too busy with everyone else's demands'.

Ask yourself, are these stories really true? Where's the evidence? If these stories are true, they have to be true all of the time, if that's not the case then you're telling yourself a lie.

You're then able to reframe your thoughts and your daily practice will feel less of a challenge. For example, you may choose to say instead, 'I work hard and I am proud of my achievements'. Statements like this will have you making the time for your writing rather than putting the time off and doing something less productive instead.

**In search of meaning ...**

As a creative, you have no need to go in search of meaning. Instead, you make meaning. Meaning mainly occurs for you when you make it. Making meaning requires your time but it also pays dividend to your happiness and fulfilment. No matter how busy you are and how many demands you have on your time, once you begin to invest in your own meaning-making and show up for it, time shows up for you.

Instead of trying to organise time, try instead to organise your meaning-making. That means implementing a daily practice!

Then you'll feel like you're on the right track and making progress toward your goals.

**Transform**

To make any kind of change in your life, you have to believe that what you're doing to make that change, and how you're doing it, will work. If you're having doubts about these steps to a daily practice then there's still more work to be done. If you're not doubting this or yourself, well done, you're on your way to reaching your goals.

It's super easy to cling to the idea that someone knows how to do this stuff better than you. This simply isn't true because anyone can find out anything these days, but not everyone will put the effort in.

You've reached the end of this process and that means you have put the effort in and I congratulate you. Huge congratulations!

I invite you to put some music on and have a little dance. Yes, right now, you deserve to spend a few moments congratulating yourself.

Now I'm going to ask one more thing of you. That is to complete this final step. The aim of this step is to get you to focus on your writing.

You have been writing. Now it's time to let this idea of a daily practice sit with you in the background while you get back to fully focusing on your writing.

You want to get to the stage where you automatically absorb your natural daily practice so that it requires no thought, you simply write every day (five days).

Complete the following checklist to check your progress.

**Answer yes or no**

QUESTION 1:

I am able to write every day (five days) without thinking about it.

QUESTION 2:

I write with more clarity and more conviction.

QUESTION 3:

I feel content that my writing is progressing and I am on track to reaching my goals.

QUESTION 4:

I get strength from my natural daily practice.

QUESTION 5:

I have surprised myself with what I am capable of.

QUESTION 6:

I feel happier and more alive now that I have my natural daily practice.

Regularly reassessing your thoughts on your progress is a good way of reframing any thoughts that may be getting in your way and stopping you from showing up.

Write down your immediate thoughts regarding the questions above:

My thoughts on my YES answers

My thoughts on my NO answers

Reassess your beliefs, if you're not fully committed to this natural daily practice process it's time to decide whether or not it works for you and why.

Return to the questions on page 210. For every YES answer, write a letter to yourself explaining why.

Return to the questions on page 210. For every NO answer, write a letter to yourself explaining why.

Write, write, write: however you do it, do it. If after these five weeks you hate this natural daily practice then ditch it and write anyway. However you do it, get the writing done.

Put this book down and go and work on your writing project. Right now.

Do it now. Don't think about it. Just do it.

If you're feeling panicky, there is a list of prompts on page 216. Use one to kickstart your writing process. Choose only one, complete it then move on to your writing project. If you're halfway through a prompt and get a sudden urge to work on your own writing, ditch the prompt and get writing.

Don't be tempted by the prompts, allow yourself one per writing session. Remember, it's you're writing project that counts.

You may find that a prompt sparks an idea or a paragraph, line or word that will make it into your writing project. That's a win!

## DAILY PROMPTS

Set your timer and don't spend any longer than fifteen minutes on a prompt. You can come back to it later or on another day but after fifteen minutes it's time to get on with your writing project.

- Begin your next sentence with: 'Now I know why you're crying ...'
- Write three sentences detailing your protagonist's deepest innermost thoughts.
- Your protagonist walks along an important street. Write her description of the street while she's wrestling with a problem.
- Write a paragraph about why one of your characters doesn't listen.
- Your protagonist wants to do one thing but someone else expects her to do the opposite. Write this scene.
- During your fifteen-minute walk, find three objects, photograph them and then include them in your next page of your writing project.
- Put your protagonist on a train. Who is there to wave her/him off and why?
- One of your characters visits an antique shop. What does she buy and who does she buy it for and why?
- Choose a novel from your shelf and begin today's writing session with the first sentence of your chosen novel.
- Sit down with your protagonist and describe to her in one paragraph the emotions you felt on today's fifteen-minute walk.

# Working the Method

## Animals Don't Follow Laws, They Follow Instincts

I've borrowed the title of this chapter from a truly immersive and thought-provoking book that's well worth your time. It's called *Animal Vegetable Criminal*, written by Mary Roach (2022) and it considers real-life examples of when nature breaks the laws of humankind. I won't say any more about that but I do want to draw your attention to the reason I've chosen this title for this particular chapter.

This chapter concerns how the Write Wild Method can work for you, whether you're at the initial idea generation or editing the third draft of your book. Laws are a part of the human condition, without the practice of lawful behaviours, life would be utterly chaotic. There is no suggestion here that we shouldn't be bound by our laws of society, equally we don't expect animals to follow our human laws, why would we? Animals no doubt follow their own laws and sets of rules.

At the basic level, writing a book also involves following certain rules and conventions and the more we practise writing, the better we become at understanding and following these rules. I'm talking about basic rules of word length, story structure and plot points and conventions of genre and publishing houses; these rules are in place as part of our apprenticeship to becoming a writer. However, once we've learnt these rules are we bound by them? Why would we be? Why should we be? As creatives we aim to create something unique and wonderful, something with great meaning, and as writers we want to write a story in a way that delights our audience and perhaps reassures them or offers a new perspective. How can we do that if all we do is rely on the rules of writing?

It should come as no surprise that a huge wealth of writing advice we all have access to in books and on the internet is packed with conflicting rules on any and all subjects of the craft.

I chose the title of this chapter deliberately and by now I'm hoping you're getting a sense of the direction I want to take you in. That is, specifically, don't ignore the rules once you've learnt them but equally, as animals do, give yourself permission to follow your instincts and by that I mean, your natural self. That is the essence of the Write Wild Method.

Let's dig a bit deeper into the method so you can be sure you know how it works and, more importantly, how it will work for you in particular.

There are 10 Write Wild Method Principles. There is a chapter in this book that covers each of these principles in greater detail. For each principle, there are two methods of application.

These two methods of application are:

1. The Write Wild Experience (WWE)

2. The Principle Application (PA)

I'm going to define each separately and then show you how, using these methods of application, each of the 10 Principles can be applied to any part of the writing process, from developing the initial idea of a book to getting it ready for publication.

Let's be honest, writing a book is hard enough so if there are only two things you have to remember, that's a lot easier than having to learn rules for every aspect of the writing process. Know your WWE and your PA, and you'll be ready for anything that comes your way during the writing. With practice, the two methods of application will become ingrained in all your creative work, you'll begin to apply what you know naturally and without thinking and then it becomes even easier.

So let's take a closer look at both these methods of application, beginning with the Write Wild Experience.

## The Write Wild Experience (WWE)

I tell the writers I mentor that writing is 80% experiential thought and 20% actually writing. Many writers, especially those new to the writing process, believe that writing is about writing, i.e. sitting down at a desk and slogging it out from the first word until you type The End. This simply isn't true. Writing is so much more than the basic cognitive application, it's about creating. When you write, you're creating something, something more aligned to meaning than the end result suggests, the collection of pages of the written word. Fortunately, once you have the 80% experiential thought under your belt, you'll have the story and all you need to do is write it down, or type it up.

This section is about how this all works so let's get down

to it and see how this eighty-twenty divide actually gets your book written. We're going to be talking mostly about the 80% here as I assume that you can already write and/type onto a page and that what you're most interested in is how to create a novel, or a book in general.

People read books because they're looking for an experience. The concept of experience is a bit vague, all it really means is that we read to learn, understand, to feel, we read for new perspectives, answers, comfort and for entertainment. What this amounts to is that meaning is subjective. This makes it difficult to judge whether the meaning you've created with your book will resonate with a reader. But there's one thing that we all have in common, we are all human and we all share a longing to understand meaning. Your best chance to be a writer of memorable books is to present to your reader a meaning experience that is uniquely yours. And the only way you can do that is to commit to the actual experience of your idea. This doesn't mean you carry out your plot, or your character's motivations – you don't need to be a serial killer to write about one. What it does mean is that the work of your storytelling ought to grow not from words but from the experiential reawakening of your imagination.

## Principle Application (PA)

Let's move on to Principle Application and look at how a book gets written from initial idea to finished product and you'll begin to see how this works in action.

## The Idea: Where Stories Begin

How do you get ideas for a novel? Ideas come from your

inner creative self, you're Illusive Self, you can read all about that in the section on page 84.

To keep things neat and tidy, let's stick with this chapter's title – Animals Don't Follow Laws, They Follow Instincts. True, this sounds like it's more suited to a non-fiction book, but as an idea, it could be workable into a fictional story.

Animals Don't Follow Laws, They Follow Instincts.

How does this statement speak to you? Let it play about in your head for a while, any bits that pop up and excite your imagination, note them down. Don't do anything else yet, let it all float loosely for at least a couple of days while you're attending to the everyday things of life.

**The Idea**

Now it's time to experience this idea. You have several Write Wild options at your disposal. You could put your Fairy-tale Self (page 156) into action and practise ruminating, rearranging and fantasising, sharing your experience with the natural world and open yourself up to potential new ideas and new perspectives. You could combine this part of yourself with ideas from The Walking Writer (page 97) and practise a little wild mindfulness at the same time. The main thing is that you give your creative self wholly to this new idea, giving your Illusive Self time to mix it up and throw ideas at you, and ensuring that you're ready for these new ideas. Reawaken your sense of wonder and be a curious observer of your amazing ability to reimagine. This is you engaging in your unique Write Wild Experience.

I really can't stress enough that if you practise these

experiential principles, you're giving yourself your best chance at grasping the big idea that will help you achieve your writing goals. The big idea that will have you writing a tantalising hook that will attract readers and creating a compelling and memorable and not least authentic story that will delight your readers and have them waiting expectantly for your next book.

Before all that, we want to get to work on this current idea. Here's a refresher of our initial idea:

Animals Don't Follow Laws, They Follow Instincts.

Now we want to begin to think about the premise.

**The Premise**

The idea is the seed you allow to grow into the premise. The premise is what you base your plot on. In the Write Wild Method we think of the premise as The Impossible Void. The Impossible Void is the visual representation of your idea, or at least, this is what you want to be working towards. The Impossible Void contains opposition and opposites.

What is this impossible void? I want you to imagine the sea crashing against a rocky shore. The rocks are stubborn and don't budge. The sea retreats with the tide, only to return relentlessly forward to battle the rocks. What's left when the sea retreats is The Impossible Void. Can you visualise that space? What does it look like? How does it feel?

Visualise that space and ask yourself:

- What frightens you?
- What angers you at the deepest level?
- What frustrates you?
- What makes you cry?

Now, throw all your thoughts into your visualisation of The Impossible Void without judgement and imagine them swirling about in the void. Allow yourself to be curious and simply observe. Does anything seem larger or more forceful? What feels greater? Anger, fear, frustration or sadness?

To write a novel from start to finish requires you to be wholly invested in the process and doing that is much easier if you're working with a premise that stimulates an emotional response from you. If you're visualising your Impossible Void and the greatest share of that space is anger then you want to be creating your premise based on something that truly angers you. What you're looking for is an idea that contains something immovable, something relentless and something impossible.

This is quite complex so I want to give you an example:

Quite often when I visualise that deep empty space between the rock and the retreated sea I observe frustration more than anything else and without me having to give it much thought, I can wonder about the initial idea and will come up with a premise based on what frustrates me.

Something that might look like:

Initial Idea: Animals Don't Follow Laws, They Follow Instincts.

Sample Premise: He's Proposed. He's Everything You Want. Except He Killed Your Son.

This is a beginning of a premise for a crime novel. The immovable aspect would normally be that it's likely to be impossible to believe that anyone would marry the killer of their son, but what if your character does? Would he be relentless in pursuing her or is she the relentless one? How did he kill the son and why? Is there any moral reason why it would be okay for her to marry him?

Are you beginning to see a story or stories developing here? Remember that the ideas have to come within you. It's no good building a story up with other people's ideas, it needs to be your frustration, your impossible, etc. It needs to be your premise.

How many premises can you begin to make using this initial idea?

You can make a premise for any genre in the same way. For example, He's Everything You Want. He Doesn't Want You. Until You Meet His Mum.

A premise isn't fully worked until you have everything else in place. So let's move on and keep building.

**The Setting**

At this early stage, the setting is important in relation to mood, atmosphere and the tone of your story. You may already have a setting that feels important to you. But return to your Impossible Void and experience your idea at a deeper level now that you have something to work with – your premise. When you're visualising, don't try to force ideas to the surface, simply relax and allow whatever happens to happen. Don't rush it, if nothing happens you have options. Try Sprint Writing (page 111) or Reimagining (page 44). If you're still not getting ideas that excite you take a break, practise some wild mindfulness. If you can, go to the sea and the rocks and observe the actual gap between them as the sea recedes.

I'm going to choose an island for the setting for my example story because I already know that I have a deep connection with islands, the sea, rocks and also it's a great setting for a crime story. And because I live in Scotland, I'll choose a Scottish island.

## Storyline Experience (plot seed)

Remember, at this experiential stage, you're not trying to write your book, you're trying to experience your story, feel it, become intimate with it. You're experimenting with the experience. By the end of this practice, writing a detailed plot (if you want to outline) will be so much easier.

The best thing to do here is to go for a walk and pick up three natural items, like a leaf, a twig, a stone, grass, sand, etc. Find a quiet spot and lay these items out side by side. Take your time and pick each item up in turn, feel it, smell it, either taste or imagine its taste, listen to it. Be curious about each item. Then replace them side by side and think about how each item is connected. Then imagine a line that connects the first item to the second and the second item to the third. What does that line look like? What if you reimagine each item as something else, what might that be? Take your time with this, again no rushing. You're giving your creativity time to do the work for you, these workings are illusive but the greater your connection to the natural world the easier ideas will filter into your awareness.

Let's go with: She marries him. Everyone on the island turns against her. She discovers he's taking the blame for someone else.

There is a line that sticks by the premise and offers a satisfactory conclusion.

It doesn't end there though. Between the lines, is it really satisfactory? She married the man who murdered her son before she knew his secret.

## The Characters

Two characters are all you need at this point. Your protagonist and your antagonist. For this example story, I'm going to make my protagonist the female and the antagonist the male. Nothing is fixed at this point, we're simply experiencing. I could have done the opposite, it's an interesting idea but I just need one example here for you so I'll stick with what I've got.

It's time to play about with your creative ideas and lay them out just as you did your natural items when you were on your walk. All stories have a beginning, middle and end. You can experience as many ideas as you like, laying each idea out as either a beginning, middle or end. Here is my idea.

## The Beginning

Female marries her son's killer

## The Middle

She is hated by the island but finds out something that suggests her husband is covering for the real killer. She investigates.

**The End**

She learns that she should've trusted her instincts (whatever those are/were).

You see, you're not detailing the plot here, but your drive to tell the story.

**The Story**

Your story demands two main characters that, when they come together, the impossible happens.

For this to work, you need two opposing characters, imposing in every way. In this example, my female protagonist is intelligent, stubborn and goal driven, she has certain rules for herself and those rules drive the way she lives her life, makes her decisions and choices. My antagonist is indecisive, simple in his needs but highly intelligent. He wants a quiet life. He is loving and kind. He has PTSD from his previous job on the mainland as a police officer when he was sacked when a robbery went wrong and his treatment of the robber was deemed illegal and excessive.

No characters in a story behave without motivation and basic drives; if you have opposing forces it means you're more likely to uncover these authentically. Revisualise your Impossible Void for this initial idea and delve deep to see what you come up with. If I imagine my protagonist behaves like the sea and the antagonist (her husband and her neighbours) behave like the rocks. You can see that there's lots of movement within the void to try ideas out, you're looking for cause-and-effect ideas.

For the example story, I'd have to come up with a reason why she would marry the man who killed her son. And

I'd have to know why her husband is covering for the real murderer. Until I know this and all the consequences that come along with possible answers, I don't have a real story. It's about feeling for the right ideas, allowing yourself to let ideas float away and new ideas to reach the surface. You have to work at this and not just go for the first ideas that spring up in front of you. Search for the impossible. Impossible drives, personalities, obstacles. In fact, it's best if you imagine both your protagonist and antagonist as being on an impossible journey.

You may be wondering about why I've chosen the husband as the antagonist as the plot seems to suggest him to be the hero. But what if she turns out to be the hero? Or a third person, even the island? Don't be prescriptive when you're practising experiencing the story.

If at any point you get stuck, get out and release your Fairy-tale Self (page 156).

Experience is everything. I'm not talking about experiencing the setting or the subject or anything that will end up in your book. Instead, I'm talking about experiencing your idea, your meaning, your intent, because once you do that, you will write authentically and with a better chance of producing writing that is compelling for both you and your reader.

# THE END

*- Transform -*

# The Write Wild Method: THE PROGRESS TRACKER

## Your Writer's Ecosystem

This section – THE END – is all about keeping track of your progress. At every juncture we want to be celebrating our achievements, big and small. If you managed to show up to your writing today, that's worth celebrating as much as getting a three-book deal. More importantly, it's very easy to be blind to our own achievements and successes and especially our progress as we journey along. This section will help you do that, it will help you see that you are making progress even if you're convinced you're not and it will help you stay accountable to yourself.

There is the option to keep a journal and a detailed record of your progress but if you're not keen on keeping a journal it's not obligatory. As well as the option to journal, you have use of the Growth Ring which we'll get to later in this section. It's good to track how you're doing on each of the points of the Growth Ring and if that's all you feel like doing that is a good way to keep track. The journal helps you go a bit deeper and so it's worth giving it a try while you're working on the next few sections of this book. You never know what will work and what won't unless you try.

'We are part of nature; we are in the Earth, not on it. We are like the cells in the body of the vast living organism that is planet Earth. An organism cannot continue to function healthily if one group of cells decides to dominate and cannibalise the other energy systems of the body.'

Metzner (in Roszak et al., 1995, p66)

Read the quote above again and, if you like, write a few thoughts that come to mind.

**Your Writer's Ecosystem**

Your Writer's Ecosystem helps you keep track of your Elliptic Presence. Remember, your Elliptic Presence is concerned with your creativity, your ability to tolerate the process and your willingness to write in spite of everything else.

By attending to your Writer's Ecosystem, you will have a better chance of instilling a harmonious, calm, creative process and writing life.

To delve deeper and keep track of your progress, the Growth Ring (we'll come to that in the next chapter) has been developed as a tool for monitoring and experimenting with your Elliptic Presence. Its aim is to help you discover new ideas to solving your writing problems, achieve productivity, success and self-healing (working along the interrelationship continuum between your natural self, your words, your reader).

The Growth Ring encompasses all the eight unique aspects of your Writer's Ecosystem. When you attend to each of these aspects you're giving yourself and your process the care and attention it deserves. There is no requirement to use a journal, although you may like to keep one by your side and use it if it feels right to do so.

The Growth Ring makes it easy to track how you're doing along your journey and to celebrate your individual growth.

Simply knowing this ecosystem exists for you may help you solve a problem or make a decision or keep on writing.

Let's look at each aspect of your Writer's Ecosystem in a bit more detail.

## Your Unique Words

Only you can write your story. Connecting to nature is the quickest and smoothest route to developing and writing your story. This is really quite simple; all it takes is for you to include experience in nature as part of your writing process. There are various ways to do this but the point is that the stronger your connection to nature is, the easier it will be for you to come up with new and authentic ideas and write your story from a place of confidence and authority.

With a strengthened connection to nature you are addressing three different writing aspects of your practice:

**Your writing problem:**

Writing a book is a huge undertaking but it is a process and as with all processes, it attracts a variety of problems along the journey. Whatever your writing problem is, it won't be solved by either not turning up at all or turning up at your desk and forcing yourself to solve what in the moment appears to you as unsolvable and increasingly begins to feel an overwhelming task.

Think of the problem as a triangle: Your Illusive Self/your creativity/your courage

If you think of this triangle objectively, you can take comfort from the knowledge that each side of the triangle is working in your best interests and will reveal the answer to your problems if you quiet your mind.

When you hit a problem, down tools and go for a walk. Take a day off and go exploring in wild places. If you can't, for good reason, then let nature come to you. Whether you're in nature or sitting at your desk, practise your seasonal breathing a few times to orientate yourself and reduce overwhelm. The greater your connection to nature, the easier it will be for nature to come to you. This sounds a bit like the chicken-and-the-egg problem but trust the process. A day at the beach or a walk in the forest goes a long way in terms of opening you up to new problem-solving ideas and new perspectives.

The effects of nature are lasting, make the best use of this on days when you're forced to remain inside. For example, once you have a strong connection to nature it becomes very natural for you to re-experience your nature connection when you're sitting at your desk. It works exactly the same way with your writing process, if you write regularly your brain gets used to you writing and accepts it as what you do. When you practise your connection with nature, your brain will quite happily conjure up those nature experiences for you if you give it the quiet time and space it needs to do so. All that means is that you sit back, close your eyes and take yourself back to your nature experience and you will benefit mentally and physically in the same way almost, as if you were actually there. You'll also find that you'll have a calling to get yourself out into the natural world if it's been a while and listening to that calling, rather than attempting to forge ahead, is a smart move. It's about reinforcement, reimagining, rediscovering and re-experiencing. Just as you do, your nature connection needs nourishing.

Your own words are what give you and your reader meaning. When you hit a writing problem it's often because you've lost confidence in your own ability to write. Try this exercise:

Write the Lost Boy story: Write a story about a boy lost in a forest. It can be in any genre, any length. There are three things you must do.

1. Write by hand
2. Make sure the boy is found
3. Write the story in ten minutes (no longer)

You've solved the problem of the Lost Boy in only ten minutes. You can now tell yourself:

- You are a writer
- You are able to solve all writing problems
- You can write in your own words
- You are confident
- You are able
- You are committed
- You are creative

Remember, trust the journey. And if you've not experienced your journey for a while, give yourself permission to go for a mindful walk and be present in nature, give your brain some quiet time.

**Your writing psyche:**

All creative individuals have an impressive ability to flood their minds (and bodies!) with negative, destructive and debilitating thoughts. I do mean ALL creatives. Writers are especially good at this ability because they can form their thoughts eloquently and powerfully so that these thoughts both appear and feel true. No thought is a truth unless you agree it is so. And that includes the metaphors we use to describe ourselves and our experiences.

For example, when I first began to experience my chronic illness, I often described the pain I was feeling to myself and my doctors as being hit by an articulated lorry then run over by a herd of bison then buried under a falling building ... you get my drift. This may have given my doctors a sense of how much pain I was in but more likely it raised awareness of my heightened and broken central nervous system. It took a long time before I realised that this way of perceiving my pain was self-destructive. Of course, I knew I wasn't being hit by a lorry etc. But simply telling myself these untruths, I was increasing my level of pain. Because our brains don't distinguish between truths and lies. Our brains believe and act on what we tell them. I was telling myself my pain was as bad as if I'd been hit by a truck and so my brain reacted as if I had and not only increased my pain but increased my shock reaction too and I became even more hypersensitive to pain.

What I'm getting at here is that if you tell yourself you can't solve a problem, you'll find it more difficult to solve the problem. If you tell yourself you're a rubbish writer, you'll struggle to write your own words and write them authentically, and your writing will be mediocre, flat and uninspiring.

There are a few things you can do to ensure your writing psyche is healthy and working for your best interests.

**Your Authentic Thought:**

This is a breathing exercise you can do either inside or outdoors. A great time to practise this is when you wake up, when you're ready to write and before you go to sleep. And, importantly, whenever you have a negative, self-destructive thought.

Before you start, make sure you're in a quiet space and sitting down.

1. Close your eyes.
2. Pay attention to your breathing, notice it.
3. Notice the kind of thoughts at the forefront of your mind.
4. Choose a thought that doesn't feel as if it's working in your best interests.
5. Speak the thought out loud.
6. Reframe it to a thought that is in your best interests.

**Examples:**

Barrier thought: What makes me think I can be a writer?

Best Interest thought: A tree behaves like a tree, a writer behaves like a writer. I am a writer and when I write, I'm behaving like a writer. I will write.

Barrier thought: My first draft is such a mess, there's no way I can make my novel publishable. I may as well give up.

Best Interest thought: I'm excited to have written my first draft, what an amazing achievement! I accept that writing is a process. I'll take the next step in the process and plan my editing. Giving up is not an option. I am as relentless as the sea and when my novel is ready, I will be amazed at my tenacity.

We don't always pay attention to our thoughts, especially our negative thoughts. Often they're chipping away at our Illusive Self and wander about our busy minds like pale shadows that we hardly recognise. We have to intentionally identify the thoughts that are impacting on our ability, confidence and motivation to write. We have to identify them and call them out. Then we're able to reframe them and each time we do this, we're giving ourselves our best chance at being our authentic natural selves, being creative and getting the work done.

## Your Physical Self

Your body is important. By now, I hope your idea of being a writer is something more than logic and language and healthy brain functioning. Keeping yourself physically healthy is all part of your balanced and harmonious writing life. Clearly, getting outside, walking, exploring and discovering in nature is a great way to keep physically healthy. That fifteen-minute walk per day that you integrate into your writing process will benefit your physical self as well as your creative and imaginative writer self.

There are simple ways you can strengthen your nature connection that I call Wild Mindfulness. These ways are adapted from my training as a natural mindfulness guide and tailored specifically to writers.

### Wild Awareness

Take yourself outdoors. Bring yourself into the moment by paying attention and observing what's around you. If you're in the forest, for example, slow your steps down and use all your senses. Touch the trees, pick up a leaf.

Listen to the ground under your feet, the birds singing. Feel the wind through the trees, the air on your face. Taste the air, a blade of grass. Smell the leaves, the earth, the foliage. Open yourself up to the forest's welcome, wonder at feeling a part of it all. Wait and be receptive of new ideas and new perspectives. Feel whatever comes to mind and be interested in any memories that spring to mind unannounced. Be, feel, acknowledge.

**Wild Resolve**

This is a great technique if you're wrestling with a problem or are all out of ideas. Take yourself off to natural surroundings, somewhere quiet where you won't be disturbed by other humans or their dogs. Find a space where you can comfortably lie down and do so. Lie flat on your back with your arms and legs stretched out. Stare up at the sky and begin slowly to feel how your body is connected to the earth. How do your hips feel, your back, your arms, legs? Now feel your body as a presence and imagine how it's a part of the earth and sky.

Allow your mind to wander freely. Only pay attention to thoughts that excite you or cause you to wonder. Engage with discovery. Lie for as long as feels comfortable.

**Wild Connections**

This is something to notice while you're out exploring and discovering nature. You may have to go further than simply noticing, you may want to seek out these connections. What you're looking for are instances where you find nature connecting with itself. For example, in the forest you may come across a tree and by tracking the roots or branches of this tree you notice that they're connected to another tree nearby. And that tree may be connected to yet another tree. Nature understands the benefits of reaching out and connecting. Trees need trees. Writers need writers.

The other day I was out exploring and came across a trunk of a tree that was dead. Growing on this tree was green moss, glistening and thriving on the dead trunk. I sat on the trunk and pressed my hand on the moss and the feeling I got was filled with energy and belief. It's not always easy to define what we're feeling when we're connecting with nature. I didn't need a definition, I allowed the feeling to nestle within me and trusted that this was what nature knew I needed in that moment. Just because we have words and language, it doesn't mean we have to use those tools to try to label something we don't quite understand yet. Trust and openness to experience, being willing to enter into the unknown is all part of the process of connecting. Does that sound familiar? Creativity is about having the courage to journey into the unknown. It's all part of your Elliptical Presence.

You want to keep track of:

- the bumps and the blocks
- the problem
- your writing self
- your physical self

## Your Dissociated Self

The what to do and how to do it.

Theodore Roszak (1992), in his book *The Voice of the Earth, An Exploration of Ecopsychology* gives us a strong non-clinical definition of dissociation as a part of being human. We dissociate when we drive, when we walk, when we do many other things so that we can get on with thinking. For writers, natural dissociation is crucial, it allows us to become absorbed in our imaginations and the imaginary worlds of our stories. Without the capacity to dissociate, writing would be mechanical and we'd produce something akin to AI.

Getting out, practising Wild Mindfulness and strengthening your connection to nature will help you quiet your mind, develop new ideas, revaluate your story elements, etc. and prepare you when it comes to writing.

One way to really practise your natural dissociation is to connect with the soundscape of your environment and bring that to your writing. When you're out exploring and practising your seasonal breathing and the other wild mindfulness techniques, deepen your mindful listening to a point where everything you hear is connected to the soundscape. I learnt this technique in my natural mindfulness guide training. It's about committing to being non-judgemental about sounds you hear in nature. For example, you're finding joy taking a walk through the woods and then a plane flies overhead and instead of feeling annoyed or irritated you accept the noise as simply part of the natural landscape in that moment. As you get used to this you'll strengthen your absorption skills and be more focused with your writing.

**Exercise:**

Try writing in front of the telly. Either on your laptop or on paper, it doesn't matter. If this isn't something you've ever tried you may need to practise it. The aim is to reach a point where you've written a body of text without realising your attention hasn't been on the TV. With this exercise, you're teaching your brain what matters and reminding it of your writing life purpose. You're also strengthening your neural network responsible for dissociation, absorption and focus.

**You want to keep track of:**

- the ways in which you reinstate balance (or not)
- how you quiet your mind
- the influence of your meaning connection

## Your Eco-Subconscious

This is all about monitoring your natural connection as you progress through your writing journey. Ultimately you want to achieve balance and harmony and to feel connected to your natural self, your Illusive Self and your physical and mental self. This is what will help you face any challenges along your creative journey.

If you're feeling out of balance, or you're feeling as if you're trudging along your writing journey alone or if you're experiencing overwhelm, try to think how you might reinstate balance and harmony. What might you do right now to make a shift, make progress or simply give yourself a nudge in the right direction?

- You may want to remind yourself of your meaning statement.
- Find a wild place and quiet your mind, feel the ground underneath your feet.
- Begin or resume a daily practice of walking and seasonal breathing.
- Be curious.

Being curious is a great thing. Doing nothing isn't going to help you progress. Find something to be curious about.

Play around, let your Fairy-tale Self free.

Go out and discover something new in a place you're familiar with. Imagine your surroundings are a fort or a princess's castle. Or are you in a jungle full of friendly giants? Whatever it is, let your imagination soar. Touch the ground and ask questions. Become a part of the natural landscape. Bring it all back to your writing. Rediscover the wonder of your words.

**You want to keep track of:**

- what your connection means to you in this moment
- areas of self-development
- areas of self-liberation
- change and transformation

## Your Discovery

It's important to be open to and curious of any and all discoveries however small. Why has that tree reached out to its neighbour? What makes that moss grow on the dead trunk of that tree? What if my protagonist was here, what would she do?

When you return to your writing take a quick note in your journal of the discoveries you've made, your thoughts and feelings about them. This will help those discoveries to grow into new ideas and new perspectives. Try to remember what you were doing when you made the discovery and write that down too.

You don't have to wait for a discovery to come to you. You can make discoveries happen naturally as you explore. Touch the bark of a tree and share your aliveness and ask yourself what positive influence you can control over your writing and your writing life. The answers are there, directly or indirectly, if you're quiet and are listening and prepared to note even the tiniest discovery, however irrelevant it may seem. Walking the creative journey is an unknown experience and something you discover right now may be just what you need a bit later on.

See what you may discover from this exercise:

*'Close your eyes, prick your ears, and from the softest sound to the wildest noise, from the simplest tone to the highest harmony, from the most violent, passionate scream to the gentlest words of sweet reason, it is by Nature who speaks, revealing her being, her power, her life, and her relatedness so that a blind person, to whom the infinitely visible world is denied, can grasp an infinite vitality in what can be heard.'*

Johann Wolfgang von Goethe

Read the passage another couple of times.

**Part 1:** Answer briefly the following questions. Don't think about it, just write down what comes into your head:

Question 1: How did this paragraph make you feel?

Question 2: Imagine the narrator of this paragraph is a protagonist of a story. Describe the narrator, what he/she portrays on the outside and what his/her beliefs and emotions are on the inside. Who is this person?

Question 3: What does this protagonist want most in the world?

Question 4: What or who is stopping him/her from getting what she wants?

**Part 2:** Write a piece of non-fiction narrative, around 500–1,000 words, about your writing.

Return to the paragraph as if you're reading it for the first time. Read the paragraph again, this time, read it out loud or have it read aloud to you.

Question 5: To what extent does the Goethe paragraph contribute to your personal understanding of nature?

**You want to keep track of:**

- what you've discovered
- new perspectives
- new ideas
- new approaches
- new practices

## Your Creative Self

This is about releasing your Illusive Self, connecting with your natural self and bringing all of that to your creative project. You should know by now that creativity resides within you and it's up to you to release it so that your creative ideas shift into your conscious awareness. Your creative self is hugely important to your writing progress, your writing practice and your writing life. If you're not giving space to this part of yourself, it will be difficult for you to feel motivated to write.

The simplest means of releasing your Illusive Self is to engage with the natural world. Get yourself outside, explore and be curious. Especially if you're feeling anxious, demotivated, fearful, overwhelmed, getting outside will help you keep on writing in spite of how you're feeling. Schedule your walks, schedule time with nature, schedule variety if you can and visit new places.

While you're out, engage all your senses. Touch the earth,

smell the air, listen to the birds, slow yourself down, focus on the thoughts that keep you present. Give yourself permission to become fully immersed in nature and let nature give you what you need.

**You want to keep track of:**

- your solution
- your engagement with nature
- your impact
- your worth
- your intention
- your resilience
- your messy brain

## Your Reader

Your reason, purpose, connection, end goal.

As you write, it's as well to regularly remind yourself why you are writing, why this means something to you and you also want to keep in mind what you want your reader to experience when he/she comes to read your story. It's likely that as you redraft, reimagine and rewrite your story, the end goal for your reader will change along the way and be something completely different by the final draft. The key is to remain aware of these changes as this speaks a lot to the overall goal for your particular story. If you're regularly checking in with your goals for your reader, you are gaining clarity, being in charge and listening to what your story is telling you.

When you begin writing you may not know your end goal for your reader. That's okay. It's important to keep track of where your creativity is taking you, recognising what that end goal may be and begin to understand how, why and what you're working towards on behalf of your reader. What is true for your story has to feel true for you before it can feel true for your reader. Even in fiction, there is truth.

The main mission of Write Wild is to help you create a meaningful channel between your natural self, your words and your reader. In other words, we want to write to reach out and grab the heart of our readers and give them the unique experience we've created for them.

To fully understand what this means for us as writers we need to look at what this 'reach' means.

David Mamet is a playwright, screenwriter, poet and essayist. In his book, *Three Uses of the Knife*, he boldly states that he doesn't believe reaching people (audiences, readers) is the purpose of art. He claims that:

'In a drama, as in any dream, the fact that something is 'true' is irrelevant – we care only if that something is germane to the hero-quest as it has been stated to us.'
(Mamet, 2002, p26)

What he's telling us is that truths and realities are not what audiences/readers are searching for in drama (or fiction), rather what your reader wants from you is a clear statement of intent. One that makes sense to your story. One that stays true to your story. So if your story is about a detective solving a crime, it must show us the crime solved by the detective. Not only that, your audience/reader wants to know how the detective solved the crime and the 'how' must be true to your detective's actions, purpose and personality.

Language is amazing in its subtlety.

'Mamet goes on to claim that, *'The power of the dramatist ... therefore, resides in the ability to state the problem'* (Mamet, 2002, p26).

Here, he's referring to the premise of your story. The premise of your story is taken from your story's concept: What was it like to be on the *Titanic* the night it sank? That's the story concept for *Titanic*. To figure out the premise we take the main character's goals, fears and motives and obstacles. It may be, will this unyielding love survive the sinking of the *Titanic*?

In the same book, Mamet also talks of our innate adaptive mechanisms and feeling vicarious fear. As an audience, or reader, we are tuned to the ability to project our own 'truth', our desires, wants, needs, onto the protagonist reaching for his/her goal.

It turns out that we don't have to put much thought into the protagonist's goal once it has been laid out for us, clearly and precisely. We can easily sympathise with Jack when he's framed by Rose's fiancé for stealing the blue diamond and we can cry with Rose when she holds the blue diamond in remembrance of Jack and then drops it into the sea as a tribute to Jack and a metaphor for their reunion in the afterlife.

Do we need to care whether Jack and Rose and the blue diamond actually existed in the history of the *Titanic*? No. What we care about is the truth for Jack, for Rose and for us as audience/reader in relation to their premise. How did this story make us feel? And how did the production of the film/book achieve that feeling in us?

1. What is your story concept?

- 

- 

2. What is your story premise?

- 

- 

Remember the ingredients for a story premise:
- Goal(s)
- Drives
- Fears
- Motive(s)
- Obstacles

Also, in most stories there are at least two protagonists, the hero and the villain. Each of these protagonists should have different (actually opposing) motives even if they share the same goal. Different fears, obstacles. In most detective stories, the hero is usually the detective and the villain the murderer. But the villain could easily be a non-human object, like the sea or a nuclear plant. There should be some tension between the two characters, e.g. the detective wants to find the murderer, the murderer wants to not be found. Rose wanted to be with Jack, Jack was a 'second-class' passenger.

Now, write the premise of your story.

Tip: If part/s of a likely premise is/are missing, fill in the missing parts to your story concept, then check back to see if you can unearth a strong premise.

Tip: If you get stuck, remember what it felt like to read out in the wild. Take the core outline/idea of your story outside and read it aloud. Try to reimagine yourself feeling those same feelings. Close your eyes, take deep breaths, transport yourself to the time and place of your story. Look around and consciously see what is all around you. Look for what you can't see. Nature is within us, all we have to do is experience it.

**You want to keep track of:**

- the why
- reader experience
- reader expectation
- beyond your goal

## Your Outcome

Making progress

It's important to track your progress but in my experience it's even more important to keep how you do that simple. Making progress isn't just about how many words you wrote today or how many books you've written in a year. It is about that but it's also about how you as a writer are making progress. It's easy to count words but it's also all too easy to forget about how you're growing, how far you've come and how you're transforming into a better writer who is living a better writing life.

Your outcome and your results work together to help you get to where you want to be.

You want to keep track of:

- your anticipated outcome
- your self-belief
- your writing schedule
- your daily practice
- your transformation

## Your Result

Personal outcomes, future goals

Keeping on Keeping on Writing

This is a brief look at some of the problems that writers must sometimes work through before continuing their writing journey.

1. Describe your experience of procrastination and how you manage it.

   •

2. Describe your experience of being present, in the moment.

   •

3. Decide whether procrastination, writer's block and writer's fatigue are present actions or past.

   •

4. How can being in the moment help you solve barriers to your story?

   •

5. Where to begin. What actions can you take to overcome barriers to writing?

- 

6. How will you work for the long term and measure progress in the short term?

- 

7. What if the faster you complete a short-term task, the more your day feels productive and you feel effective, satisfied and accomplished.

- 

**You want to keep track of:**

- a record of your achievement
- your promise to yourself
- your promise to your reader
- what next?

# Your Growth Ring

The primary role of a tree trunk is to protect and support the tree. A tree trunk represents harmony and balance in nature. It also guides us through the seasons, of hope, rebirth and renewal and calm and acceptance. Trees also remind us of our individuality and of our connection between the earth and the illusive and the earth and living beings. Trees give us strength, they symbolise independence and also the interconnectedness of what is the whole thing. Trees signify positive growth in a calm and creative environment.

Creativity is all about decision making. When we write, we're constantly required to make decisions and those decisions, we know, will take us forward. We're never quite sure whether we're going in the right direction so there's a weight behind these decisions that we feel in both mind and body. Our minds might be foggy, messy and inaccessible. Our body might feel tired, depleted, heavy. Our writing might feel all of these things. Instead of a journey we feel like we're trapped in a whirlpool with no way of swimming to safety. Not all decisions do this to us and not all of us will experience this level of indecision. Your **Growth Ring** encourages you to examine your process and maintain a healthy balanced harmony to your writing process, making the journey that bit easier and a lot more enjoyable.

**Your progress at a glance.**

This framework is a quick reminder of your commitment to yourself and your creative life purpose. It remains by your side for the entirety of your writing project and beyond. You can track your progress if that's something that appeals to you. Even if it doesn't, you have an at-a-glance record of how you feel you're progressing. At any point, you can decide you need to focus on a particular aspect of your writing process, if you feel it's lacking and creating barriers for you.

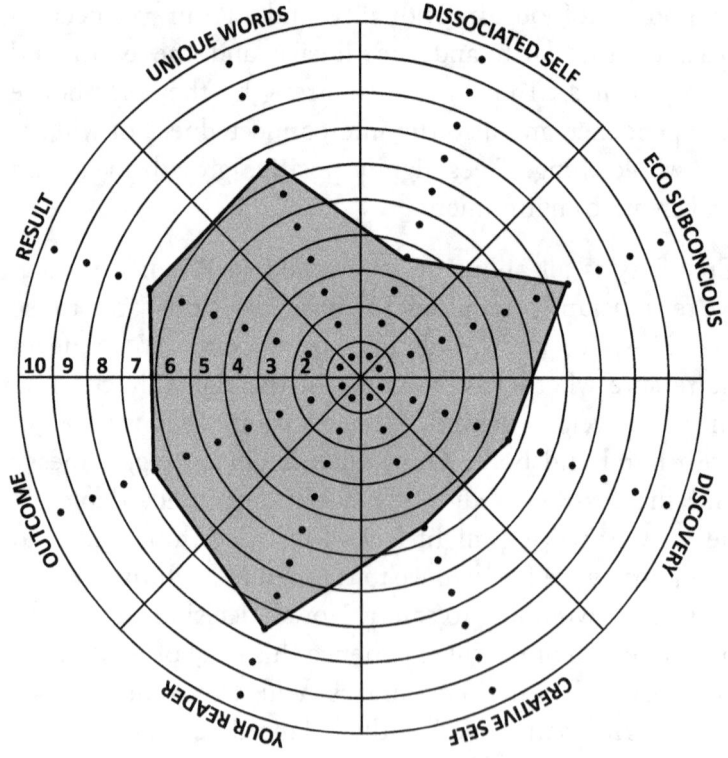

Use the Growth Ring to visually map your progress at a glance. You'll see that each domain of the ring refers to a specific heading in the previous chapter. And each domain has ten layers of progress (one being the lowest, ten being the highest) Using a pen or pencil, join the dots for each domain to the level at which you feel you are working. over time. Shade in the the resultant shape. You'll be able to clearly see any 'dents' that need hammering out and any areas where you're working well. Aim to fill the Growth Ring with a large, even octagon!

It works in two ways. You have a journal within which you can record your feelings on any point of the method, make decisions and strategies for going forward.

You can also incorporate your Growth Ring into your daily practice and take five minutes each day to fill in your ring. This will alert you to areas you may want to focus more on as you proceed.

Use the method in whatever way works best for you. The Growth Ring is simple and easy to use. The journal is designed to prompt you into thinking about your connection, your Illusive Self and your Elliptical Presence, as well as your writing progress, your messy drafts and your hopes for the future.

In the subsequent pages you will find a journalised version of the Growth Ring to track your progess over 3 months. Use the notes area in each week for any key observations or insights

## Week One

..................................................
..................................................
..................................................
..................................................
..................................................
..................................................
..................................................

## Week Two

..................................................
..................................................
..................................................
..................................................
..................................................
..................................................
..................................................

## Week Three

..................................................
..................................................
..................................................
..................................................
..................................................
..................................................
..................................................

## Week Four

........................................
........................................
........................................
........................................
........................................
........................................
........................................
........................................

## Week Five

........................................
........................................
........................................
........................................
........................................
........................................
........................................
........................................

## Week Six

........................................
........................................
........................................
........................................
........................................
........................................
........................................
........................................

## Week Seven

..................................................
..................................................
..................................................
..................................................
..................................................
..................................................
..................................................

## Week Eight

..................................................
..................................................
..................................................
..................................................
..................................................
..................................................
..................................................

## Week Nine

..................................................
..................................................
..................................................
..................................................
..................................................
..................................................
..................................................

**Week Ten**

........................................
........................................
........................................
........................................
........................................
........................................
........................................
........................................

**Week Eleven**

........................................
........................................
........................................
........................................
........................................
........................................
........................................
........................................

**Week Twelve**

........................................
........................................
........................................
........................................
........................................
........................................
........................................
........................................

# Anxiety and Transformation

*My child, then put aside your fear:*
    *Unbar the door and walk outside!*
    *The real tiger waits you there;*
*His golden eyes shall be your guide ...*

D. Hope

What do you think about when you think about anxiety? What if I invited you to reconsider your perception of anxiety and be open to the idea that anxiety can actually be a force for transformation? With this Write Wild Method, I'm asking you to keep such an open mind to the idea that your anxiety may help you embark on a transformative journey, one that offers a supportive presence along the way towards a deep and meaningful understanding of who you are and where you belong and an awareness of your own ability to exert a positive impact in your life with your strong connection to nature.

Part of all of this is that you have the freedom to choose. Anxiety can be entirely debilitating and prevent us from writing a single word. Connecting with nature helps you discover that freedom, recognise that you have choices and harness the empowerment that will get you the transformation you need to get to where you want to be. It will help you see where you are now, what you need to do to take the next step and give you the courage to take that step, in spite of the anxiety.

Remember all of this is about trusting the journey. Give yourself permission to feel courageous, you don't have to believe it, just be it. Get out there and take the next step, and if you can't right away, get out and roll yourself in the grass, smell the salt of the sea, get wet in the rain. As a child you knew how to connect to nature and when you were feeling anxious you most likely felt better once you were outside playing. If you have a dog, watch how your dog connects to nature. My dog Hugo's favourite thing is to roll about in the mud. I never stop him, even though it's exhausting to get him clean again, he has about ten layers of coat, but the joy we both experience is far outweighed by the effort it takes to clean him.

You want to feel a sense of enlargement. As if you are a hundred times larger than your physical self. You want what is buried deep in your Illusive Self to have the freedom to rise into your conscious awareness. Creative anxiety smothers creativity but you have a choice. Creative anxiety is often at the root of procrastination, but you have a choice. Creative anxiety is the manifestation of fear, but you have a choice. When you choose to connect with nature, you have that connection to help liberate you out of your anxiety and into your creativity. You are responsible for the choices you make, regardless of everything. Transformation is about changing as a person rather than simply changing behaviours. You want to make that whole transformation.

Believe that you can solve all your problems and that you can take the next step. If you're stuck ask yourself the following questions:

Where am I now?

Where do I want to be?

What is the next best step I can take to move me along the journey?

How do I know I can do it? Because I've done it before and I can do it again.

What choice can I make that will best serve me and my purpose in life?

*A note on anxiety*: Of course, nature and/or the Write Wild Method are not going to solve all your problems for you and as I talk about anxiety here I'm mostly referring to writing anxiety/creative anxiety. General and specific anxiety can be debilitating and may require medical/professional attention. It's important to get that attention. The Write Wild Method is not a substitute for professional help. From a writing perspective, the method itself may not be enough if your anxiety is deep rooted and interfering with your writing process to an extent that you can't commit to writing. If you've sought the help of medically trained doctors and/or therapists and you want to move forward with your writing you may like to think about Write Wild coaching as a step that will support you in transforming anxiety into creativity, if and when the time is right for you.

## Problem Solving

When you get hit with a problem and you feel stuck, this section may help you become unstuck or it may inspire you to find a way to become unstuck or it may simply give you a break from your 'stuckness' as often that's all it takes.

### Nature before writing

- I can't start
- Is it worth it?
- Which project?
- I've no time
- I've no motivation

- I'm starting, but what is the mystery of the beginning?
- I can't seem to commit

What we're really talking about when we talk about writing is that we want to be vital. To mean something to ourselves and to others. We want to make our mark. Is that true for you? Do you have the urge to make the most of your short time on this earth? How often do you acknowledge this to yourself? How much do you trust yourself to actually see your lofty aims to fruition?

There's some kind of conflict between societal expectations and individual desire that encourages us to be humble about our deepest creative longings, I think. Something that is at the root of difficulties that arise even before we start writing.

Polly has been writing for as long as she can remember but she keeps her writing secret, it's a hobby, she's never thought anyone would be interested in her words. Approaching retirement, she naturally began to have ideas about using her free time to make more of her writing. After retiring she enjoyed spending more time with her grandchildren and it turned out that she was spending most of her time babysitting and was too exhausted to do anything else. As much as she loved her grandchildren, she felt she was losing control of her life and began to lose the confidence and the desire to do anything. When she finally had enough of her life feeling less worthwhile than she wanted it to be she decided to do something about it. But as the days rolled on and she still hadn't come up with a solution that felt meaningful to her she became even more despondent.

The urge to be creative, if being creative is one of your life purposes, will never leave you. It is a part of your make-up, intertwined with your personality and your physical being. It becomes a real problem when the urge is strong but the action towards being creative is non-existent. Taking action is the first step on the journey to exercising your creative muscle and making a start. Talking about what you might do, or could do, or want to do is simply procrastinating. You may start with a plan but if even that's too daunting or you're not wholly committed to the plan you've made you're going to find it frustrating and difficult to move forward.

This is what happened to Polly. She made the decision to do something about her predicament, but she didn't know what that something was. That's fine. But what was Polly searching for?

Polly hadn't learnt to trust the journey. Instead of trusting the journey she spent her time musing about the writing. She did not take action. Less musing, more action. And action leads to experience. Polly was telling herself she wanted to do something. But instead of telling herself, she should have been experiencing. Taking action and experiencing is moving forward and trusting the journey is what will keep Polly moving.

Fed up with musing, Polly got up from her chair and took herself out for a walk to the nearby forest. She soaked up all that nature happily showered her with. She sat on a rock and watched a twig being thrust along by the river. It had rained a lot recently, so the river was overflowing and speedily winding its way to its destination. Polly imagined herself as the powerless twig, being carried along by the powerful river and it came to her to ask herself why be the twig, why not become the river?

Almost instantly the river and the twig became characters in Polly's imagination and this wildly excited her to the extent that she devised an entire story in her head. She quickly took out her phone and using the voice recorder, recorded the entire outline of the plot. She was so excited by this that for the rest of that day she wrote notes about characters, setting and conflict and a book appeared to her along with the enthusiasm of knowing she had a story to tell.

A year later Polly sold her book to a publisher and took time to reflect on the journey she's just taken. She thinks about all the times when she almost gave up. But she knew she wasn't taking this journey alone. She remembers that first experience watching the twig and the river and when she feels low she knows to trust that her natural self will show up for her whenever she gives it time to breathe, when her mind is quiet, whether she's in nature physically or refreshing her imagination, she has grown to trust that her natural self will show up with new ideas and new perspectives that will get her moving forward again. She trusts the journey.

There's no mystery to our fictional Polly's story. The mystery is why don't we know this stuff already? Why aren't there a thousand books on the subject of how crucial nature is to creativity for writers and all other creatives?

## Nature and first ideas

- Too many ideas
- Not any ideas
- Conflicting ideas

Ideas are born in our Illusive Selves, in the same place as courage and all the other things we need to be a writer. And like all those other things, ideas need to be released. They may come bursting forth or reveal themselves to you in the order of a trickle, the order being decided by the unknown, but again, we must trust the journey.

- Ideas and the imagination
- Combinatory play
- Intention

These three components come into play when we're thinking about ideas. But do writers think about ideas too much? There's that old adage that when a writer tells someone they're a writer, the first question they're asked is, 'Where do your ideas come from?' I can't remember this question ever not being asked at a literary festival event. And I've been asked the question myself.

Do you ask yourself the question? Where do my ideas come from? I suspect writers don't but instead worry about where and how they're going to get ideas and that ideas they think may or have run dry.

There's no 'searching' of ideas. And ideas cannot run dry. You can and should look for inspiration in all that you observe. I might be halfway through a draft of a novel and feeling a bit stale and I'll reach for a poem or a fairy tale or an interesting non-fiction book. Or I may watch a movie or documentary and tell myself I'm searching for ideas but really what I'm doing is looking for inspiration.

The difference is that inspiration is something that motivates you to take action. I get inspired by a line in a poem and use the line to kick off the short story I've decided to write.

The definition of inspiration is:

'The process of being mentally stimulated to do or feel something, especially to do something creative.'

How does that compare to how you, personally, would define the word, idea? If inspiration is a process, what is an idea?

It turns out that the word, idea, is a lot harder to define. The dictionary doesn't give much value other than an idea being a thought or a suggestion. The word originates as far back as Plato who used the term to refer to logical classification. But do we really know what *idea* means and if we don't, do we care?

Isn't it common to say, when you come across a problem, to say something like, 'I have an idea' or 'I have no idea'. And equally as common we refer to others in the same way. It was so-and-so's idea.

There's a belongingness to the concept of idea. Whereas inspiration is something external, ideas come from within. And if ideas exist at all, we should care about them, nurture them because they help us categorise our words. Perhaps Plato was on to something after all.

You have an idea for a novel. Perhaps it was inspired by something you watched on the telly. The first thing you do with that idea is attempt to put it into some kind of structure (category). Perfect. You may even end up with ten ideas. Perfect. If you have no idea, you know how to make one spring to mind: you take action to get yourself inspired.

Let's say you have three ideas for a novel and don't know which one is best. You may want to play about with investment theory and work out which idea looks to be the one that will get you a return on your efforts. A good rule of thumb is to choose the one that no one else in the world would choose to write.

Back to your three ideas. With or without investment theory, you have decisions to make. You could write all three but if I was your mentor I would make you work to try as best you can to see how this would fit with your schedule, you energy and commitment and your goals and purpose.

It all comes down to the decisions you make. The stumbling block for decision making is anxiety and by now you know that anxiety is the devil to the creative mind. You can imagine anxiety as foam that solidifies your Illusive Self and prevents ideas from reaching your awareness.

I'd like to invite you to develop a practice of increasing your ability to tolerate anxiety. Writing is an anxiety-inducing endeavour for most writers.

Take this hypothesis from Rollo May (May, 1977, p370)

'By moving through anxiety-creating experiences – [like rejection, fear of the unknown] – one seeks and partially achieves realisation of himself – [moving toward achieving your writing life purpose] – He enlarges the scope of his activity and, at the same time, measure of selfhood. – [self-confidence. Self-worth] – It is also a prerequisite to working through the anxiety – [feel the fear and do it anyway].'

It's important to make the distinction here between normal anxiety and neurotic anxiety and I'm going to paraphrase Rollo May's (May, 1977, p355) very clear differentiation so that you can assess your own anxieties better informed. Neurotic anxiety is a result of 'unfortunate learning'. It's a term I quite like and refers to learnt experiences most usually as a child forced to deal with 'a threatening situation and naturally incapable of coping directly or constructively'.

Compare this to constructive anxiety, the anxieties of our everyday, where we are able, with good strategies in place, to succeed in problem-solving anxious experiences as they arise, thereby avoiding the potential for further unfortunate learning.

I hope this makes it clear to you that not all anxiety is bad. To be sure, I'm not talking here about neurotic anxiety, simply the anxiety that all creatives are required to overcome in order to succeed.

How might you problem-solve anxiety as it arises and negate the potential for what you may call writer's block, or any of the other bumps in the road you may encounter along your writing journey?

Rather than trying to escape anxiety (which you can't do without causing yourself more problems further along the line so you may as well discover a way to embrace anxiety) how might you confront it and move through it?

The temptation of course is to escape, our survival instinct sends out vibes urging us to turn away, ignore or depart from what's causing the anxiety. Before I go on to give you one method that might work for you in terms of moving through anxieties that arise for you during your writing journey, I want to quote once again from Rollo May because his emphasis on the use of 'value' as a driver in moving through anxiety can't be underestimated for writers who want to succeed.

> 'A person is subjectively prepared to confront unavoidable anxiety constructively when he is convinced (consciously or unconsciously) that the values to be gained in moving ahead are greater than those to be gained by escape.' (May, 1977, p370)

Give yourself time to pause here and think about this. Write down the value – to you – of your writing journey.

For example, let's say you submit your novel to an agent. It's your debut novel and you're super excited (definitely celebrate this) and of course you should be. But a couple of weeks later the agent rejects your novel without any explanation whatsoever. This has the potential to be hugely anxiety inducing. It's quite natural to feel anxiety over this experience. Perhaps your first reaction is to cry. Or you may feel like sending the agent an angry email. Or, on this same day of your rejection, a friend calls you up and tells you she's just gotten a three-book deal and you take all your frustrations out on her and shout at her instead of celebrating with her. Or you celebrate but inside you're seething with jealously. What a jumbled mess of anxiety. And what? I'm going to ask you to get your boots on and wade through the sludgy path? Seriously?

Well, yes.

Here's a method you can use when anxiety spills over:

Take a walk. It can be a long walk or a short walk. Take the day and find a wild place if you can but you can do this exercise wherever you are outdoors. On your walk, practise a bit of wild mindfulness, seasonal breathing. Pick something up and take it with you, a twig, a stone, a leaf. Hold it comfortably in your hand. When you feel like it, find a safe place where you can sit in peace and quiet, away from other people.

Practise the following:

Fix your gaze on the path, pavement, river, road or track ahead of you. Take a long deep breath in and hold it for a beat or two.

Release.

Repeat x2.

After your third release say out loud: I can cross whether you are rock, sea or sand.

Repeat the breathwork.

Then say out loud: Rock, I have the right boots, strong hands and fierce determination.

Repeat the breathwork.

Then say: Sea, I can swim, my arms are strong and your waters are my courage.

Repeat the breathwork.

Then say: Sand, I can traverse you whether you're shingle or sinking, you are the earth beneath my feet and my friend.

The item you collected on your walk can be returned to the earth as a symbol of your gratitude for its support.

OK, this may sound a bit woo-woo but that's the point. You are re-committing to your writing life purpose and reminding yourself of your limitless courage. Doing this in a way that perhaps feels strange and uncomfortable reignites a belief in yourself that you matter, and that your creativity matters.

On the walk back, remind yourself of your meaning

statement and make the decision that success in your creative journey is what you're aiming for, anything that isn't success will not stop you from ploughing on. Return to your writing space straight away and journal your experience and reaffirm in your journal the value of what matters to you.

The rock, sea, sand, in other words, the natural world is there to support you on your journey.

Try to embrace rejection. Rejections are a great way of helping you move forward because they encourage you to refocus and problem solve and you continue to move forward. Embrace rejection.

Embrace anxious moments, every anxious moment is a step further towards the other side of the river.

*Somewhere someone is travelling furiously toward you,*
*At incredible speed, travelling day and night,*
*Through blizzards and desert heat, across torrents, through narrow passes,*
*But will he know where to find you,*
*Recognise you when he sees you,*
*Give you the thing he has for you?*
                       First stanza of 'At North Farm', John Ashbery

## Nature and first rewrites

When you have your first full draft in front of you and you're ready to begin the editing process, it can feel a bit daunting, even if you've done it many times before. Each story is different and demands different things from you. However, there are four key areas that are crucial for all books (including memoir and non-fiction) and those are:

- testing ideas
- narrative structure
- reader empathy and experience
- storytelling

It may feel that at this point you just want to get on with the work and don't want to invest time in nature or exploring wild places and that's fine. If you've practised the 10 Write Wild Principles while writing your first draft and have reached a point where you can feel your experience of being in nature while you're sitting at your desk, perfect.

There is good reason though to wonder about what nature can offer you at this editing stage of your writing journey. Let's look at each of these crucial processes in turn and find out.

*Testing Ideas*

It may seem pretty obvious that getting outdoors and exploring is a good way of testing ideas, or it may not. After all, you're testing the ideas you came up with in your first draft, this is editing, not exploring. Or is it?

One of the great things about the Write Wild concept is that it gets you away from your desk, creating some objective space from your words. And it helps you get out of your own way. Objectivity, as much as is possible, is the key to testing your early ideas for the first draft and/or future drafts.

Of course you will want to test all of your 'best' ideas as you make your way through your edits. But at this early stage, the first ideas that matter will be the ones that get you thinking how this book you've written will present to your reader. You want to be able to map the gap between where you think your book sits in terms of distance to your reader and where you want it to sit when it's physically or digitally in the hands of your reader.

None of this is simple and straight forward, you won't be surprised to learn.

Take yourself out for a walk and ask yourself why this part of the process isn't and shouldn't be straight forward. Your answer to this question should act as a driver, it should feel solid, like the ground underneath your feet.

Now, while you're out, find a quiet spot to sit and wonder, observe, experience the space directly in front of you. Imagine holding your finished, beautifully edited and polished book in your hand. You've just finished reading it. Answer the following:

- How did it make you feel?
- Was it a satisfying read? If not, why not?
- Were one or two characters memorable? In what way?
- What was the atmosphere of the book?
- What compelled you to read to the end?

These questions will help you solidify the kind of book you want your readers to read. Ideas will come to you about how you get from where you are presently with this first draft to where you want to be by the time a reader buys your book. This exercise is something you can do through all your edits and reimaginings. The reason for getting outdoors at this particular point is that you want that objectivity and finding a quiet spot in nature, where you can connect with your natural self, you are being who you are, and not the person that has to do all these edits. You may find that the natural you is a useful cheerleader, acting as your reader. Having conversations with yourself in the wood, or on a beach or any quiet spot is where you'll be able to see new perspectives that will help you edit and refine your book into something you mean to create and something your readers will thank you for creating.

*Narrative Structure*

I am inviting you to look at how you structure your writing in a different way. It's helpful, once you have a first draft, but even before you begin writing that first draft to understand narrative structure as the framework that will help your readers understand your story. But I want to give you a fresh perspective on what it actually does for you in terms of your creative process and how you can imagine it for your reader.

For this I want to briefly delve into the world of evolutionary theory, keeping it simple and specific and meaningful. Andreas Wagner is an evolutionary biologist who has devoted his life to discovering something that's rarely, if ever, discussed in the world of writing: that there are similarities between the creativity of the natural world and human creativity (Wagner, 2020, p4). I'm going to keep this relatively simple and just draw on what's relevant for you to reimagine your narrative structure and test your ideas.

When you've created some distance between you and your first complete and thorough draft you'll want to (among other things) note down any problems you feel are hampering your readers' understanding of your story.

Get out your notebook and imagine your manuscript as a landscape and draw a horizontal line on the page. On this line I want you to map each problem you've discovered in your manuscript as if it were a mountain peak: small peaks for small easily fixable problems and larger peaks for the larger ones. You're aiming to leap from peak to peak solving each problem as you go.

This idea comes from the scientific concept called adaptive landscape. In ecology, scientists are interested in the imperfections in natural selection to surmount a landscape of several to many peaks. Put simply, 'natural selection never accepts the worse for the better' (Wagner, 2020, p6), meaning that an ant that's evolved to breathe thin air climbs to the top of the peak but even if there's a higher peak in sight the ant has hit a problem in its evolutionary journey because it can't go back, it must keep striving forward, and therefore can't crawl down the other side of the mountain into the valley between the mountain it's on and the higher one across the valley. This is a problem for evolution but it's a great analogy for writers.

With your own adaptive landscape in front of you, you can see at a glance where the valleys are. This means that rather than focusing in on one problem, you're able to see how to link your story as a whole. You're seeing the journey of your plot and your characters (and your setting). It's the journey that counts, not the problem. As a writer, you have all the skills you need to get you from one peak, through the valley and onto the next peak. With each problem that you solve, you're reimagining the journey and treating your reader to greater depth and a more experiential read. And what's so brilliant about this framework is that as you're traversing the valleys, you're gaining more control over the direction of your story.

*Reader empathy and experience*

As well as adaptive landscapes we have adaptive energy. What do you think of when you think of reader empathy?

Write a few ideas down, then confront those ideas and see if you can reframe them. How did you do?

When you think of reader empathy, if you haven't already, I want you to think of energy. Why? Well, because your reader wants more than to simply understand and relate to your story. Your reader wants energy.

You want to be able to energise your reader. Energy creates what Rollo May (May, 1977, p101) describes as the 'zest and commitment of the person for the task at hand'. Just as our bodies are made for movement, our brains demand energy to stay healthy and function well. You're not writing your story to keep your reader healthy, but you do want to give them pleasure and for that, they require from you something that creates within them zest and commitment to your book. In other words, a memorable experience.

Beautifully written prose can bring us that energy of a memorable experience but as often as it does, it doesn't. It takes more than beautifully written prose therefore.

How do you inject zest and commitment to your words? You don't, you bring it to your story. You cause the energy. How do you do that? You feel it and bring it to your work as your own natural brand of energy.

This is the kind of energy you experience when you swim in the sea, climb to the top of a mountain, traverse the forest or smell a rose. Nature gives you thousands of ways to capture the energy you need for your reader. Capture it, reimagine it and when you return to your work, recapture, reimagine and bring it to every aspect of your story. Have it as you climb the mountain peaks of your adapted landscape and use it to propel you through the valleys. On every step of your journey you want to experience that energy and channel it into your work.

*Storytelling*

What actually is storytelling? We know about the storytelling of ancient times and the oral storytelling tradition but what is modern storytelling? How often do we sit around the campfire these days compared to watching a movie in the cinema or on a big screen TV? Has storytelling really changed or has it adapted to our modern world? Storytelling is by definition an activity. Preferably an interactive activity that involves both the storyteller and the listener/observer/reader. Nothing has changed in that respect, I'm sure. The nature of writing isn't about putting words together on a page, it is about the telling of experience. You are sharing your nature with your reader, the nature of you, how you interact and interpret the world around you. The 'how' you do this is the actual words but it's the doing that's important. The 'doing', the telling of your story, is an act that you must perform for yourself before your audience gets to see it and that means you must experience it.

Think about every day, you tell one story or another; what happened in the supermarket queue, how you missed the bus, why you were late for that meeting and so on. These are all stories that you've experienced. Think of the emotion, the passion, the anger or fear or humour you use to communicate these stories. Taking the same approach with your writing makes sense, doesn't it?

Pay attention to the stories you tell on a daily basis. Without labouring it too much, wonder at the emotions you employ, the passion or otherwise you display.

Nature's energy is freely available to you and with it you

can reimagine your story as you explore and wonder at being in the moment outdoors.

For example, if your story has your character trapped in a cellar or trapped by a relationship or trapped in a lift, dig your hands into the earth and pay attention to the sense of aliveness you feel in your hands. You can capture that alive energy and develop your character with it. Then you may have a character who acts (externally or internally) rather than one who is passive and feeling trapped. Feeling trapped and acting brings energy to the story and helps you find a way forward through the valley. Your character moves from passive to active via your own sense of aliveness.

This works the same way for non-fiction. If your book is to solve a problem, you begin by describing the problem and take your audience from passive to active.

Digging your hands in the earth is an experience you can reimagine over and over again for different elements of your narrative or your story. The act of digging your hands in the earth is also a symbol of your commitment to your writing, your natural self and to your connection with the natural world. You are opening a channel that will bring you so much more than ideas for plots and ways to develop character. It will help you discover the storyteller within you, the confident and self-assured believer in what you are achieving and what you aim to achieve in the future.

## Nature and rewriting

- Rewriting for more
- Rewriting for less
- Rewriting for your reader

I've been writing a section of this book and found myself so involved and absorbed in the process that when I took a break I was sure I must've written forty thousand words in that sitting. I'd actually written just over three thousand. I was truly scunnered and put my boots on and took myself out up the hill. Driving to the hill I had this notion of word count in my head and that led to thoughts of how much versus how little the reader needs to know, then, underwriting, overwriting and by the time I'd driven to the bottom of the hill I was too exhausted to make the walk up it. So I sat at the bottom on a patch of damp moss, lay back and asked the sky for an escape from this relentlessness.

The sky shrugged its shoulders and told me I was getting in my own way again.

Eventually, after I'd given myself some breathing space, felt the wet ground against my back and shoulders and legs, listened to my body's weird sounds, I saw, stretched across the light blue sky, the adapted landscape I'd made for this book. There it was, right in front of me. I thought about what I had to do to climb the first peak, what steps to take and where and how to position my feet. I realised that climbing those peaks involved no word counts, no fancy sentence structure, all it involved was deciding where each foot went and why and how.

When you're rewriting and reimagining, this is effectively what you're doing. It's so easy to get caught up in all the other stuff, like word count, because that's your brain procrastinating on your behalf. Your brain is procrastinating because it wants you to take the easiest route to the finishing line so that you conserve energy. By taking yourself outdoors, you're replenishing energy. So apart from it making sense to spend a lot of your writing time outdoors doing this method, it also makes sense to actually see more clearly what the problem is and resolve how to fix it.

Let's say, for example, that you read a chapter of your book and you sense intuitively that there's a problem but you're not quite sure what the problem is. You've charted your story on your adapted landscape and are sure it's not a problem related to the overall framework of the story but instead one that's affecting just this chapter. You are outdoors and you're thinking about this problem. Gather a twig or a leaf or a stone, one for each critical point in your story – each foothold. Now, examine each foothold and ask yourself if there's enough here to keep your foot from slipping. Or is there too much and your foot can't get purchase enough.

Being active with your creative problem solving has so many benefits, the most important of which are energy replenishment for your brain (to appease it because it's being forced to actually work on your behalf rather than procrastinate) and revelations for your creative problems.

## Nature and plot

- Plot circles
- Subplot circles
- Tying up loose ends

On your adapted landscape, plot is the earth that your characters traverse, up the hills and down the valleys, it's what keeps your characters, especially your protagonist/s moving forward. You can plot each of your major footholds on your landscape and map the sequence of interrelated events of your plot. In this way you have an at-a-glance visual of the pace and intensity of your story. Intensity describes the stakes for your characters, the higher the peak, the higher the stakes. The highest peak represents your climax and resolution.

This is all well and good but there are points where you might find yourself going round in circles with your plotting. I've discovered that plotting isn't as simple as it sounds. I've also discovered that some people are brilliant at plotting and others struggle a bit. But whether you're a genius at plotting or not, your plot is likely to send you off around in circles and that's how it should be.

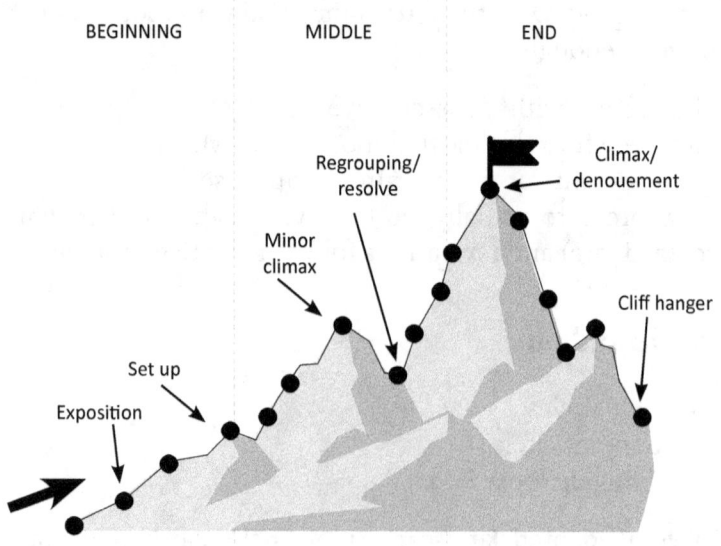

THE PLOT MAP; MILESETONES, PEAKS AND TROUGHS

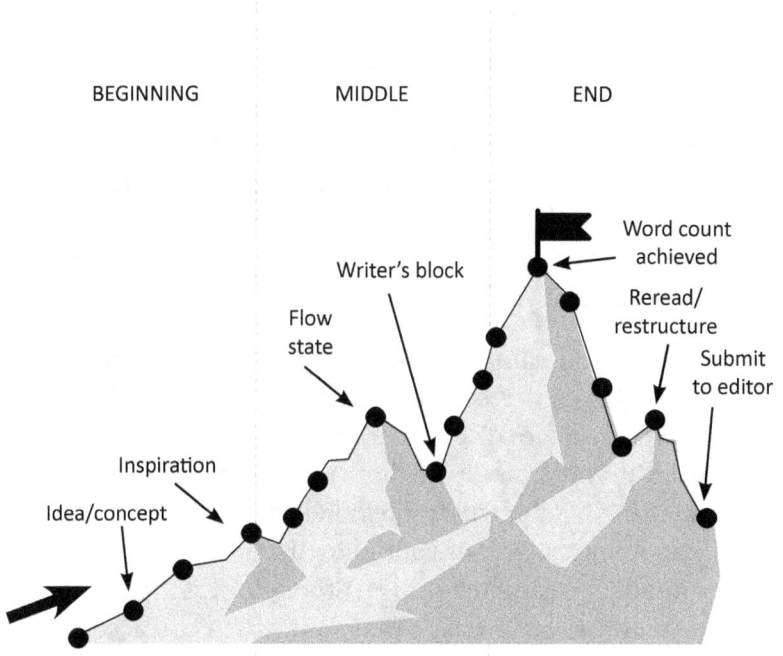

THE CREATIVE PROCESS (WRITING) FOR COMPARISON

I am one of those less fortunate non-genius plotters. It wasn't until a good writer friend and critique partner of mine, Michael Lynes, who happens to be one of the genius plotter kind, told me that plotting is like solving a mystery. Most of us love mysteries (don't we?) so this was a really helpful analogy for me but as I thought about it a bit more I finally understood that plots are circular. Let me explain. When I let myself believe that plotting was as exciting as solving a murder mystery, I began to embrace plotting a bit more and investigate it within my own writing. Plotting is a sequence of interrelated events, yes. But each of those events also has to return back to itself. It's not just the interrelation that counts, it's the clarity of the plot point itself and to find clarity each plot point must have a beginning, middle and end, and the best plots return to the beginning so that makes them circular.

Think of your entire plot. Does the end of your book return to the beginning in some shape or form? If not, shouldn't it? If it shouldn't, why not? The beginning is where you direct your reader to the main question of your story and the end is where your reader discovers the answer. See, circular. If you take this circular approach to each plot point you can't go wrong.

So when you think you're going around in circles with your plot, you are so don't fight it. Figure out the circle and you'll have discovered something you may have missed if you'd taken a lighter more superficial approach to plotting. And it will feel less like you're going around in circles if you figure out your plot circles before you get too far in your writing-rewriting. Although often these circles aren't all that apparent at first so it's better to accept that the creative process can send you around in circles and take a deep breath and hold your nerve.

The same goes for subplots but I suspect you can be less strict with yourself here. Some subplots are ripe for leaving you hanging by a thread and this can give the reader great enjoyment if you do it right. What I mean is that you make sure to tie up all the major plot circles but if you're careful and deliberate about it, you may want to leave a subplot with an unanswered question.

Of course, you want to make sure you don't get this wrong and end up frustrating your reader.

The best way to make sure this doesn't happen is to write your novel as a one-page fairy story. Practise reading your fairy story outside, aloud to nature then gather a few friends and read it out loud to them and see their reactions, also ask for feedback.

Apart from helping you write your synopsis (preferably before you write the first draft), it will also help you acknowledge where reader information is required and identify if you can ignite reader curiosity and delight by leaving them with an unanswered question regarding a subplot.

This brings us to the *experience of* tying up those loose ends. Even if you do decide to leave a subplot hanging, you'll want to tie up enough of it to make sure your reader doesn't throw your book at you.

Tying up loose ends, like most of the creative act of writing, is an experiential process. You first experience the plot for yourself. You do this from the moment you begin planning/writing to the moment you write The End on your final draft, it's not a one-off experience, it's a growth experience.

You want to feel each plot circle as if you've lived it. This is how you write with authority and authenticity and this is how you compel your reader.

Get yourself a map of your area or any area you can easily access that has some appeal to you. Draw yourself a circular route and actually go out and experience the walk for what it is, a circular walk. Employ all your wild mindfulness techniques as you walk, sit, explore and discover. Do this several times over the journey of your creative project. Each time will be different and each time will bring some new value toward your creativity. Once the route starts to become welcoming and familiar to you, you can always take along one or other of your characters, especially the intuitive one and/or the difficult ones. Have a conversation with them as if they're walking right alongside you. This is a great way to iron out any difficulties you have with plot and to ensure that you're writing from within the story and not grabbing for ideas outside of it. Just as everything you need to write the story is within you, everything the story needs is within it. Remember the difference between ideas and inspiration. You can be (externally) inspired but your ideas come from your lived experience with your story.

## Nature and endings

- Nature and intention
- Nature and genre
- Nature and fulfilment

It's been my experience that the only way to get to the finished polished version of your book, or indeed any creative project, is with intention. It is without a doubt necessary to work through all the uncomfortable feelings that come with creating and that are often coupled with resistance, procrastination and fear. Unless you're happy to take a surface level approach to your work, you will want to be marching forward strategically and not be searching for a way up and over or turning on your heels in the opposite direction or throwing a blanket over your head and hoping for the best. You will want to choose to be in control and take each tiny step brimming with intention.

Your creative purpose is your intention to matter and it's this that drives whatever course of action you desire to take in service of your journey, your happiness and fulfilment. You have a desire to finish the novel you're currently working on but, as you may have already discovered, desire isn't enough. You have to commit and you have to intend.

What if right now you took the time to write the synopsis of your story, if you haven't already? When you write a synopsis for your book before you begin writing the book, this signals a kind of action plan of your intention to write the book. But wherever you're currently at with your writing journey, stopping to write a synopsis of your story is confirming your intention to write the story. Whether you write the book or not is dependent on your level of commitment to the project and your purpose. Put simply, the only way to finish your book is to take action and continue taking action until the project is complete. There are resources and exercises in this book that will help you do that. But let's explore intention a little further by moving into the realm of genre.

When we intend to do something, we will rarely succeed unless we have a plan. Whether you consider yourself a 'planner' or 'pantser' isn't really relevant here. I find that these are superficial labels that don't really help your best interests. For instance, you may simply say to yourself that you're going to sit down for the next two hours and start your novel and see what comes up. You may not have an outline and are starting with just an idea but you are starting, you are planning to write for two hours – you have planned. Alternatively, you decide to take the next two hours to write a detailed outline for a new novel before starting the novel. Great, this is still planning. Each action is a step toward writing and finishing the novel. Planning is good in both cases. But it's intention that matters, intention that will get you to the next step, the next two hours, the next chapter and so on. When you decide on the genre for your book, that is a clear intention and if your decision has come from your creative purpose all the better. It's not genre that matters, or how you write necessarily. It is strengthening your connection between your intention and your creative purpose that will help you move along each step of your creative journey. If you have a strong urge to write in a particular genre, if you're drawn to a genre then that may be your creative purpose trying to push you in the right direction for you at this moment in time. On the other hand, you may choose a genre based on marketing trends or because that's the genre choice for all your writer friends or your writing hero; you have to decide whether this genre will sustain you, will you have as strong an intention, as powerful a commitment to this genre over one you're inexplicably drawn to? This is a difficult question and whatever way you choose to go is a way of exploring and discovering. There's nothing wrong with your choices in genre or your reasons for those choices, as long as you're clear on those reasons and it feels right to you in the moment. Curiosity is transformational.

Exploring genre in this way is a good measure towards defining your creative purpose if you're not already fully convinced you know what your creative purpose is. Any form of exploration is exciting and necessary and if one or more creative projects don't quite work out in the way you planned that's a meaningful learning experience in service of your creative purpose and the goals you make for your future.

Genre, if you're not already sure, is simply a means of marketing your book in the publishing or digital world. It helps publishers, agents and readers find your book. The concept of genre helps you also, to a certain extent. There are conventions for every genre (even the literary genre has conventions) and this helps you keep your book tight and helps you provide your readers with the basics. For example, if you write crime genre, your reader wants to follow the journey to solving the crime. Likewise, a reader will be upset with you if you don't have the boy and girl get together at the end of your romance novel. There is no denying that genre is important in today's publishing landscape, but how that landscape looks to each of us individually isn't and shouldn't be conventional. If you want a fulfilling writing life, your choice of genre has to come from within. Genre is an intention that comes from our creative purpose. This doesn't mean that while it's your life work to write fiction for young adults, you can't also write literary fiction for adults if that's something that appeals to you at some point along the way. The one thing we know is true about life is that everything changes. Everything, except that is your creative purpose to write. This will exist within you until the end of your life. But how else do we learn what we truly need without testing the water? Just be careful that's not all you're doing all of the time.

*'Dogen Zenji chastises a young monk for drawing too much water from the stream, then tossing what isn't to be used onto the bank. Because stream water, like everything else, has inoch, or "life integrity," it should be treated respectively. Unused water should be returned to the stream with gratitude and with as little waste as possible.'* (White, 2016, p238)

I know this section is about nature and endings and here we are talking about synopses and beginnings and choosing genre which generally is a thought we should be having before beginning a story, even if that thought is to not choose a genre. But in nature, there are no endings until we die as an individual or a species. In your writing journey, there are no endings until your life ends. There is now, and now is what we're committed to. Now you begin a story, you write it, you finish it, you write another. It's like the seasons, we have spring, summer, autumn, winter and there is a flow, an order, a certainty but never an ending, or a beginning for that matter. There is now and there is no better time to write.

While it is crucial to write to the end of our stories, for all of us who have writing as one of our creative purposes, there also is no end until the end. Just as in nature, there is constant growth and transformation until it ends. Life and death. Evolution and survival. Strength, resilience, courage and support. Nature is committed to it all. Nature has a plan for it all. Within nature's plan, there is no exit strategy. If suddenly you woke up one morning and it was yesterday, where would you be? Nature we know, even if, for some deathly reason we don't exist into tomorrow, that there will be a tomorrow for certain, whether we wake up to it or not. We can be certain about nature but it's impossible to be certain about our existence. So we have now, with no beginnings and no end and we must plan with intention and commitment. Because now is all we have. Genre, when it really comes down to it, is you the writer deciding to matter. You will deliver your words to the world, that is what you do and that is why you matter. Wherever in the world your words find a place is not why you matter. You matter because your words matter. And wherever your words land, they will continue to matter long beyond your own physical existence. So when you're thinking about genre, think about what matters to you and your creative purpose and imagine what your place looks like, how it feels to be there, what's happening to your senses and your sense of aliveness. Would you wake up happy and fulfilled being in that place? This is how nature teaches us about genre. It also teaches us that when we work towards our creative purpose we are leaving a meaningful legacy behind when we make our final exit on this planet. I repeat, there is now and there is no better time to write.

*'To the extent that we can learn to tolerate failure ... we will approach our full potential to create a world of our choosing.'* (Wagner, 2020, p222)

## Nature as Person: The Power of Our Stories

I'm sure you want your stories to have memorable impact on your reader and even on the world at large. What does that impact look like? What's the shape of it? How are you feeling it? How are you writing it? These are all difficult questions that are likely to send us off searching in places where we're unlikely to find any answers. Hopefully you've grasped the concept by now that the first place to search is within yourself and let that search stretch beyond your human form boundary and out into the natural world. This is where the answers are. We create the answers via our breath as it sucks in all that nature is.

What does that actually mean? The easiest route to this meaning is to ask the people who already know the answer.

The Okanagan people of Canada already understand that the human body is the earth itself.

*'Our body is pieces of land, the soul, water, air and all other life forms contributed parts to be our flesh. We are our land/place.*

*Not to know and to celebrate this is to be without land. It is to be dis-placed.'* (Roszak et al., 1995, p323)

How would you treat nature if it were a living, breathing member of your family?

The natural world shows us that with great belief comes great power.

I invite you to begin thinking about how you feel about the natural world and in what ways you are, if at all, connected to nature.

- I often feel a sense of oneness with the natural world around me.
- When I think of my life, I imagine myself to be part of a larger cyclical process of living.
- I have a deep understanding of how my actions affect the natural world.
- I often feel part of the web of life.
- My personal welfare is independent of the welfare of the natural world.

(Mayer et al., 2004)

We know from reading myths and fairy tales, and from connecting to our Fairy-Tale Selves, that there are many types of power we can draw from our creative ideas to present to our readers. We needn't think of power as a weapon, it's not a sword, a whip or a poison. The power we bring to our stories comes partly from belief and partly from good old practice. We understand that we are a part of a reciprocal relationship with the natural world, one of nurturing and sustainability. We also understand that practice is necessary if we want to reach for great writing and/or a writing career. And for good measure we need only turn to the Tale of The Story-Wise Icelander for corroboration.

*'... your luck will now be with you. Be welcome here with me, and I will grant you whatever you want.'*

(Thorsson & Scudder, 2001)

## Releasing the Orangutan: What Can Nature Tell You?

I wonder if, when I was little, I realised that I was making a profound connection with the orangutan that was blowing kisses to me and that this connection would remain with me throughout my life. Can you think of a similar past or present experience?

For example, I said earlier that I believe the orangutan was urging me to look inside of myself so that together we may share the wild places. This belief ignites something deep within me that encourages me to keep seeking and exploring and learning and growing. I've so far discovered that to search within ourselves is an act of searching outside of ourselves. It's almost as if our gaze begins within and extends beyond the boundary of our bodies, to our environment and what that can tell us about ourselves and about how we may choose to perceive and interact with the world around us.

When I rest my body on the forest floor and fix my gaze on the sky I soon begin to feel a part of the world around me and that quickly becomes a sense that I am an integral part of the forest ecosystem. I am asking nature to include me, and it does. And it reveals to me things that I am otherwise unaware of. I begin to feel the magnitude of my own breath and the significance of my being. I feel my strength and resilience supporting me and often I sense the courage that flows through this ecosystem that I am a part of.

I strongly believe that if we could scientifically measure these experiences, our connection with nature would be seen as more than just a spiritual encounter. It would be recognised as an integral part of our mental and physical being, an essential aspect of what it means to be human in both body and mind. We would acknowledge that as humans, our well-being relies heavily on this connection with nature. However, our dependence on science for understanding reality means there's still much we don't comprehend.

To rekindle our connection, we must actively choose to do so and allow nature to reveal its powers to us, even if we cannot fully grasp them. For me, this comes easily as I've never felt the need to understand everything. Some things, like how a TV works or the intricacies of the internet, may or may not interest me. Yet, when something does capture my curiosity, I find immense fulfilment in exploring it further and remaining open to new experiences.

Now, what if you're the type of person who isn't all that open to experience? Do you have a strong urge to understand every experience? There's nothing wrong with that. For a writer it can be a positive trait. All fiction requires research and we have to write authentically so that our stories feel real for our readers. The great thing about being a writer is that we can choose what we write about. What makes connection to nature something real for me is that it can be real for everyone, in fact it is real for everyone, and it simply requires you to choose.

Sit for a moment and try to conjure up your childhood self. Then imagine it's you in the zoo, standing in front of the orangutan blowing you kisses. What are you imagining, what are you thinking, how are you feeling? What is the orangutan telling you?

Are you beginning to trust the orangutan?

We don't get far in life without trust, as you might imagine. We're currently living in a world of international and civil war, of famine and pandemics, of hackers and scammers, deteriorating ecosystems and unsustainable practices, celebrity obsession and corporate greed. A world that is becoming increasingly difficult to trust that as a people, humans are trustworthy. Literature, as it has done for centuries, can and should be a mechanism for change, for revelation and for healing. It really doesn't matter what genre you write in, whether that's highbrow or lowbrow fiction or non-fiction, commercial or literary, there are readers for every book. What does matter is that you write so that your reader can trust you. Without that trust, your story will have little to no impact on a reader.

Yes, you have to write well. You have to learn the ropes, learn how to write, or at least, how to not write badly. You have to put in the practice. You most likely have to write badly before you can write well. You have to get those neurons in your brain firing off in the right direction and making the right connections and this takes lots of practice. A trainee neurosurgeon knows that he's not going to get good at his job without practice, where does he start? Does he practise on living brains? I actually don't know. But I can be certain that he doesn't practise on living brains on his first day at medical school. Most likely, you're not going to be a great writer with your very first story (I say most likely because there are always those outliers ...), or even the first draft of your tenth novel. But wherever you are on your writing journey, you can't go far wrong if you understand that your readers have to be able to trust you. If you keep this idea at the forefront of your mind while you're developing and writing your stories you will, without much doubt, write better stories.

The most non-taxing way of garnering trust in your reader is by developing and reigniting your nature connection. This connection can support you in creating a sense of trust between you and your reader. This happens because you are establishing a reciprocal and mutually supporting relationship between you and the natural world, one based on trust and understanding (Buzzell et al., 2009, p148). And quite naturally, without any effort on your part, you will bring this trusting relationship to your storytelling and consequently to your reader.

**Trust in Nature**

As a writer, trust in nature is not just a concept; it's a fundamental relationship that infuses depth and authenticity into my work. Nature is my collaborator and my sanctuary. I trust in its ability to inspire, to heal, and to teach. When I immerse myself in nature, whether it's a dense forest, a local park, or a rocky shore, I listen for its wisdom. I trust that nature has stories to tell, secrets to unveil, and lessons to impart. Its ever-changing beauty, its rhythms, and its mysteries all fuel my creativity and shape my perspective as a writer.

But trust in nature goes beyond mere inspiration. It's about recognising my place within the natural world and honouring the interconnectedness of all living beings. When I think about nature, I strive to capture its essence with honesty and respect. I trust in nature's ability to surprise me, to challenge my preconceptions, and to remind me of the vastness of the universe. I trust that by being a part of its intricacies and complexities, I can foster a deeper appreciation for the natural world through my work.

Trust in nature invites a sense of humility. It's humbling to stand in the presence of vast oceans, ancient trees or a wild meadow to realise the insignificance of our individual existence in comparison to the grandeur of the natural world. As a writer, this humility grounds me and reminds me to approach my craft with reverence and awe. Moreover, trust in nature means acknowledging resilience and adaptability. Despite human interference and environmental challenges, nature persists, offering endless opportunities for discovery and growth.

We exist in a world of climate change, habitat destruction, and biodiversity loss. Trusting in nature carries with it a duty to champion its conservation and safeguarding. I trust in the power of storytelling to raise awareness, inspire action, and ignite a sense of stewardship for the planet. As a writer, I embrace this reciprocal relationship and trust in nature's resilience to inspire hope and resilience in my own storytelling.

Trust in nature is a guiding principle that shapes my writing process and perspective. It reminds me to listen, observe, and learn from the world around me. It encourages me to approach my craft with humility, curiosity, and gratitude. In essence, it is both a guiding principle and a profound source of inspiration. It reminds us of our place within the natural world, calls us to action in its defence, and nourishes our creativity and natural self. Through trust in nature, we as writers have the opportunity to illustrate the beauty, complexity, and interconnectedness of the world around us, inviting readers to join us on a journey of discovery and wonder.

# Nature's Impact on Creativity: Voices from the Wild

Welcome to a chapter that uncovers the intricate relationship between nature and creativity through the lived experiences of others. Here, we embark on a journey to explore how the natural world serves as a source of inspiration, shaping our creative ambitions in profound ways.

Within these stories, you'll encounter a variety of voices, each offering a unique perspective on the profound connection between nature and creativity. From a psychotherapist capturing the ethereal beauty of the desert to a bestselling psychological suspense novelist harmonising with the rhythms of the sea, these narratives paint a vivid portrait of the transformative power of nature on creativity.

As we immerse ourselves in these stories, we can embrace the depth of this bond and the conviction with which it influences our lives. We can ponder the moments when a walk in the woods ignited a new commitment or a sunset sparked a burst of inspiration. Through these shared experiences, we'll uncover the depth of nature's influence on our creative journeys and, if we choose to, reaffirm our commitment to honouring and preserving this invaluable connection.

So join me as we delve into the heart of nature's influence on creativity, guided by the conviction that with a deep and meaningful connection to nature, we discover not only artistic inspiration but also profound truths about ourselves and the world around us.

## ELIZABETH MORRIS

A compassion-focused psychotherapist, neuropsychologist with over forty years of experience, Elizabeth is founder innovator at the Centre for Applied Compassion. A mindful self-compassion skills teacher and a bestselling author, Elizabeth will tell you that if you don't believe in yourself nobody else will. www.instagram.com/compassionchannel

The story involves a time when I was fortunate enough to travel to Namibia and be invited by a friend to drive out into the desert and camp overnight.

It was many, many years ago when there were almost no restrictions on doing this kind of adventure. It was wild nature, wild landscapes and wild, wild women. There were two of us, two young women in our early thirties. We lived in a very busy, sophisticated city and we both longed to escape to simple, to space, to silence and the purity of clean air. We wanted to enter and experience the space, the silence and the mysteriousness of the desert.

And so a quick flight to Windhoek and a night there to shop, pack the car and early the next day we were off.

Every mile we drove took us into a landscape of stunning light, greater and greater vistas of space and beauty. Blue skies. Eventually sand dunes appeared and the real bare, very bare desert. This was where one tuft of grass every two feet or so was what the local farmers called a 'good year' for grazing for the animals.

We drove on and on and ended up at nightfall well beyond the reach of humanity, deep into a deserted empty landscape. We stopped, pulling off the sand road and decided to do our camping out for the night right there. One outcropping of rock would give some shelter from any wind that came up and the soft sand would give us a comfortable enough sleep if we decided not to cram ourselves into the car.

A quick lighting of a fire with wood paper and matches we had brought with us and then opening up the basics of steak, sausages and salad, also brought with us, and we had the makings of a good African braai. So, we grilled our meat on an old grid of metal we had also brought and ate that delicious food with our fingers. No meal in any restaurant in our sophisticated city ever bettered that one! Our light came from the brilliant stars above, the glow of the fire and a couple of lanterns we had brought too. We felt the hustle of the city seeping out of our tired bodies into the earth. And relaxed.

Scraping a hole in the ground and throwing a blanket down we curled up like puppies and fell sound asleep.

Rudely awakened a few hours later, in what felt like the dead of night, by a great growling and clattering very close by. Blearily I looked around but could see nothing at first until my dark-adjusting eyes caught sight of movement – an odd shape just out of range of the still glowing embers, I peered harder and began to make out the hunched shape of hyenas prowling round and round snapping and snarling over the scraps they were pulling off the ancient grill we had laid across the fire. The smell of decay and putridness filled my nose as they moved around. I had never been so frightened in my life.

I had no idea if they would attack us. We had no means of defending ourselves. We probably looked vulnerable – and we were very vulnerable! I closed my eyes again and hunkered as far down in our hastily made little donga as I could and froze into terrified stillness. This was my only defence. My friend slept on, quite oblivious.

The next day I woke to a beautiful dawn, pawprints all round our hollowed-out donga and such a glorious feeling of having lived through intense fear and then still to be alive! It poured through every cell of my body. I was acutely aware of the beauty all around me. The wildness, the complete unspoilt rawness of nature all spoke to my whole body and I was filled with a weird, wild energy that could only express itself through movement and speed.

I stood up, shook off the sand from my crumpled clothes and began to run, run, run. And run …

Wild and free in the great vastness where the only footprints were the ones made by the fiercesome four-legged visitors and by many tiny critters who had wandered by minding their own business – and my own.

And I knew. Somehow. Intuitively. Deeply. That this was my destiny. That in the desert there are no pre-made paths. No other roadways. There was only the path I made in the virgin sand as I moved through it. I knew then that I would never follow someone else's path. That what I needed to do was always make my own pathway. In a vast, unknown spaciousness and into deep mystery. And that only that would work for me.

It is what I have done ever since.

# CRAIG RUSSELL

Award-winning, bestselling and critically acclaimed author, Craig is author of *The Devil Aspect*, a riveting 1920's thriller about the making of the most terrifying silent film ever made and a deadly search for the single copy rumoured still to exist. Craig also writes a Hamburg-set thriller series featuring detective Jan Fabel which have been translated into 25 languages and are dark, atmospheric and spine tingling. www.craigrussell.com

A writer's nature.

Each writer's nature is different.

Each has his or her own unique perspective, own experience to share, and voice to express. And each creates their work in their own context. Inspiration comes in a variety of environments: some authors will find the buzz and bustle of a city, the presence of large numbers of people, as the source of their stories and as the environment that best suits them to work. Others, like myself, will find being surrounded by nature, by open spaces and wildlife, inspirational.

But the role of nature in maintaining balance and perspective – and good mental health – for writers goes far beyond it being a source of inspiration.

For me at least, nature is about a great deal more than sparking ideas. When I wrote the Fabel series, set in contemporary Hamburg, I spent a great deal of time in the city getting to know its geography, its culture, its people, its *feel*. It allowed the city to exist in my head as I sat down to write the novels. That writing, however, took place at home, in rural Perthshire, surrounded by the sights and sounds of nature.

As writers we create entire worlds in our heads, invent topographies and architectures, populate them with invented characters, then share our creations with readers. It is arguably the most introspective occupation there is. It is our job to live inside our own heads. I am a great believer that nature allows us to take frequent, essential breaks from that introspection: to engage with something wider, something bigger. The real world doesn't get more real than when you are surrounded by the sights, smells and sounds of the natural world.

I'm sure neuroscience has a dozen proven reasons why stepping away from your desk and into nature has such a positive effect; all I know is that it does. I can't tell you how many times an idea has come to me, or a problem with a plot point has been resolved while walking through a wood, by the loch, or up a hill or watching deer or birds from a distance. One thing I can say is that these revelations have come to me when I *wasn't* thinking them through, when my mind was disengaged from my writing and engaged with the natural world around me. And, invariably, when I return to my desk and reimmerse myself in the universe of the novel on which I'm working, I feel invigorated and energised.

We are, of course, enormously blessed in Scotland – I consider myself incredibly lucky to live in a dramatically beautiful part of Highland Perthshire – but engaging with nature doesn't mean you have to live remotely or go the full Thoreau. George Bernard Shaw was an immensely prolific writer on a staggering range of subjects – and all of his writing was done in his garden, where he had a writing shed set on a turntable so he could push it to get the best of the sun and the garden throughout the day. Shaw died after falling from a tree he was pruning in the same garden. At the age of ninety-four.

In today's world, it's all too easy to cocoon and insulate ourselves from nature, to distance ourselves from the changing seasons, the shifting moods of the climate. It's particularly easy for writers. But I cannot stress enough the physical, psychological and professional benefits of getting out there and embracing nature. All it takes is for you to take a break from your desk and go out and find it.

It is, after all, quite literally all around you .

## JULIE ROBERTSON

A nutritional therapist and menopause wellness practitioner, Julie is founder of Harmony Health and Menopause and a highly acclaimed speaker, educator, coach and soon-to-be published author. www.instagram.com/harmonyhealthandmenopause

WINTER

She emerges from the red-brown carpet of autumn, embracing us in her warm, protective arms, encouraging us to move onward, rest, reflect and recharge.

Encouraging the trees to shed their green cover, revealing the magnificence of their sturdy trunks and branches, she guides the animals to retreat into their packs, where they can recuperate and reflect, returning in spring rejuvenated and ready to flourish.

This year I'm embracing winter's hug, welcoming her into my world with open arms. In her presence, I feel a stirring of creativity, sparked by moments of reflection and deep contemplation. Taking her hand, we embark on tranquil woodland walks, where the rustle of leaves beneath our feet and the whisper of the wind through the trees create a cacophony of nature's melodies. Each step brings a new revelation, as winter encourages me to slow down and appreciate the subtle beauty of the changing landscape.

In this quiet sanctuary of the woods, I am free to delve into the depths of my soul, to fully immerse myself in the present moment without the distractions of modern life. Winter's gentle nudge reminds me to bundle up against the chill, allowing me to stay warm and cosy as I venture deeper into the wilderness of my own mind.

Standing amidst the hushed tranquillity of winter's embrace, I feel a profound sense of clarity and purpose. The crisp crunch of frost beneath my feet and the icy bite of the air serves as a reminder of the fleeting nature of time, urging me to seize the moment and embrace my creativity with passion.

Amidst the serene backdrop of the forest, I encounter a robin redbreast, perched upon a branch with an air of quiet contemplation. In its poised stillness, I see echoes of my father, whose calm presence and thoughtful gaze have always inspired me. Moved by this poignant moment of connection, I feel compelled to write a letter to him, expressing gratitude for his enduring influence on my life.

So, let us respect winter and thank her for allowing us to be part of this magnificent circle of life, and when the time is right, take her hand and bid her farewell as she retreats down through the fields, busy preparing to bloom into life and grow.

Let her depart with a smile on her face and a loving wave, back into the loving arms of Mother Earth, passing the baton and giving a weary but loving smile to spring, waiting patiently to burst into life. It's her time now to reflect, recharge, rejuvenate, knowing her part of the circle is complete.

I can sense spring's tentative steps in the emergence of every tiny snowdrop and shoot, filling me with excitement. Standing amidst this transition, my heart swells with a sense of wonder and anticipation, eagerly awaiting the vibrant new beginnings which spring promises to unfold. I stand waiting, arms open wide.

## SOPHIE HANNAH

Sophie Hannah is an award-winning and *Sunday Times* and *New York Times* bestselling writer of crime fiction, published in forty-nine languages and fifty-one territories. Her books have sold millions of copies worldwide. In 2014, with the blessing of Agatha Christie's family and estate, Sophie published a new Poirot novel, *The Monogram Murders*, which was a bestseller in more than fifteen countries. She has since published four more Poirot novels.

Sophie's murder mystery musical, *The Mystery of Mr E*, co-written with her friend and composer Annette Armitage, has been released as a movie. She has also published two short story collections, five collections of poetry and two self-help books. Her poetry is studied at GCSE, A Level and degree level across the UK. Sophie has recently helped to create a master's degree in Crime and Thriller Writing at the University of Cambridge, for which she is the main teacher and course director. She is also the founder of the DREAM AUTHOR coaching programme for writers.

Sophie Hannah: www.sophiehannah.com/books
Dream Author: www.dreamauthorcoaching.com

## Songs in the Sea
### Please imagine me saying this loudly:

At the age of not-quite-53
It's high time I admitted, and proudly,
That I like to write songs in the sea.

Every tune goes through quite a few passes:
One hour's swimming yields two drafts, or three
And though last year the waves stole my glasses,
Still, I love to write songs in the sea.

I would not write a serial killer
Murder mystery while doing front crawl,
Nor a taut psychological thriller,
But I'm happy to answer the call

Of the ocean for choruses, ditties,
Soaring notes at the end of each line.
I will gladly write novels in cities,
But on Porthkidney Sands, I'd decline

(Which, by now, must be hardly surprising
Given what I've revealed about me.)
At Porthminster, I'd start harmonising,
Since I love to write songs in the sea,

And in winter, when sands are frostbitten,
At Porthmeor and Porthgwidden: new rule —
It appears songs can also be written
In the Carbis Bay Spa's heated pool .

## NORMAN BISSELL

Writer, educator and director of the Scottish Centre for Geopoetics, Norman grew up and lived much of his life in Glasgow and now lives on the Isle of Luing in Argyll where he writes poems, fiction and essays, and co-edits the online journal Stravaig. Geopoetics is deeply critical of Western thinking and practice over the last 2,500 years and its separation of human beings from the rest of the natural world, and proposes instead that the universe is a potentially integral whole, and that the various domains into which knowledge has been separated can be unified by a poetics which places the planet Earth at the centre of experience.

Geopoetics: www.normanbissell.com/geopoetics
Norman Bissell: www.normanbissell.com

### A Place to Think, a Place to Be

One Easter I bought a CalMac Island Rover ticket and fitted in visits to as many islands from Islay to Lewis as I could in a week. The following summer I drove right up the west coast to Cape Wrath and back down via Dornoch and the Black Isle in search of a special place to live. However, it was to the Isle of Luing in Argyll that I was drawn after I came across it by chance one bright May morning in 1995. I visited Toberonochy on Luing's east coast and was charmed by its sheltered harbour, its white-washed cottages and hanging baskets. At Blackmill Bay, Scarba loomed large like some west coast Bali Hai. And who should I meet there but David MacLennan, the artistic director of the Wildcat Theatre Company, whom I knew well, and his wife Juliet Cadzow. I had got to know David through the many Wildcat musical shows he wrote, often with Dave Anderson, which always had a strong socialist message. At my urging, the Lanarkshire Association of the Educational Institute of Scotland sponsored each Wildcat show by booking them for the Cardinal Newman Theatre in Bellshill. We built up a regular audience of teachers and others for their shows and usually I would meet David afterwards. That day he told me about the beauty of the wildflowers in the Dubh Licher on Luing that changed with the seasons. I took meeting him there as a good omen.

But as I came round the corner towards Cullipool, I was bowled over by the sight that befell me. Out west was a string of small islands in the midst of a sparkling blue sea, the long coast of Mull stretching out towards the Atlantic, and Fladda lighthouse twinkling white in the vast ocean. I fell in love with that view at once and pulled up the car to knock on the door of a house with a For Sale sign outside. That wasn't to be, but, after several years of searching, I eventually found a cottage in the conservation village of Cullipool on Luing's northwest coast which suited me down to the ground. The village had been built to house the workers in the nearby slate quarries and it had been a busy place until the last quarry closed in 1965.

It was here that I fell in love with a woman who was also drawn to that place, and it was she who helped pull me through the greatest challenge of my life. My first winter on Luing was not what I had foreseen, for it was spent recovering from an operation to remove prostate cancer which, though successful, led me to deep-going thinking about death and life.

On the island I learnt from divers and marine scientists about the precious underwater reefs and teeming marine life which have made the Firth of Lorn a Special Area of Conservation. I spoke to fishermen and their families about their fears for their livelihoods if conservation prevented them from fishing and tried to reconcile these conflicting interests in ways which gave long-term hope to island communities.

From the slate quarries in Cullipool you can see trails of basalt which run over the seabed to their origin on a volcano on Mull. It also flowed from there to the Isle of

Staffa (truly one of the wonders of the world) and all the way to the Devil's Causeway in Ireland. I began to learn about the significance of the geology of the area and of the work of Scottish geologists. I met George Orwell's postman in Oban one day and visited Barnhill where he lived on Jura and wrote *Nineteen Eighty-Four*, and I began to look into how William McTaggart, Joan Eardley and Kenneth White were each in their own way deeply influenced by the sea and coast and, in different ways, have tried to capture its essence in their work. At Na h'In Ban, the Isles of the Sea, I explored the remote islands where Brendan came from Ireland seeking contemplation and renewal before his journeys across the Atlantic, and I found inspiration in the nature poetry of Celtic monks which encouraged me to establish a resource and research base for the Scottish Centre for Geopoetics in Cullipool.

### Slate, Sea and Sky

> an island on the rim of the world
> in that space between slate, sea and sky
> where air and ocean currents
> are plays of wild energy
> and the light changes everything.

Of course, geopoetics can be practised anywhere – whether it be in an urban or rural setting, on an island or on the mainland – since it's a heightened way of perceiving and expressing creatively the world we live in. But it does involve becoming much more aware of the natural world of which we are part and that's certainly made easier if you're living by the sea and can witness Atlantic weather systems approaching, and basking sharks and dolphins feeding along the coast. That said, my years living on Luing haven't exactly worked out as I had expected. I wrote a feature film script and a novel about

George Orwell's last years rather than the poems inspired by this beautiful place that I'd intended. And I took an active part in the Isle of Luing Community Trust and its efforts to obtain £1.3 million funding to build an Atlantic Islands Centre here as a focus for the regeneration of the Luing community. You can take the man out of Glasgow...

However, in a way the island has inspired all of this activity since it has given me the urge to be more creative and to reconnect with the childhood I spent in the city and by the sea. I have found the island where I want to spend the rest of my days and it has helped me to find myself and to lead a productive, creative life. The Community Trust interpretation panels which are scattered around the island bear the legend 'The Isle of Luing: a place to think, a place to be'. And that's exactly how it feels, now that my life's journey has brought me to these shores.

This is an extract from Norman Bissell's book *Living on an Island Expressing the Earth* to be published soon by Alba Editions: www.normanbissell.com. He is the director of the Scottish Centre for Geopoetics: www.geopoetics.org.uk.

## TERENCE BLACKWELL

Terence had long thought about writing a short story about a cat that he had looked after for a year. Once he had started to write, lots of memories came flooding back. He had great fun writing

about Smudge, showing all the traits that she showed and putting words to her actions.

### CHAPTER FIVE
### Nature Lessons

Pepper moved off, going deeper into the woods and I followed feeling very excited now about what else we might meet tonight. As we wandered further along the paths that Pepper knew about, she would know how the paths had been made, and by which animals. All of which was absolutely fascinating to me as I had never heard of any of these creatures before.

Some of them sounded a bit frightening to me but I felt that Pepper would keep me safe as she was full of confidence about being here. As we went on further into the woods, Pepper would stop every now and then to point out something of interest to me. Some funny looking plants that looked as if they were growing on an old fallen tree.

"Those are a fungus that actually live off the rotting wood of that old tree, but even if they look tempting because they look nice you should not eat them as some are poisonous to animals and humans. Any way, we would not normally eat anything like that, would we," Pepper said with a very knowledgeable look on her face.

A bit further on Pepper pointed out something that looked like very small tunnels in the long grass. "Those little tunnels are very likely made by small field mice or other small animals. Very interesting but not worth chasing, sometimes an owl will swoop down and catch it just as you are getting ready to pounce, which is why it is not worth the bother, you see."

"What is an owl?" I asked.

"Well, it is a biggish bird that hunts for small animals such as mice and voles for food for itself and to feed its family. As it is almost silent when it is flying, you cannot hear it coming until it drops down on what you thought was your meal. That can be very frightening as you are not expecting it," said Pepper.

"Goodness me, I hope that I do not see one tonight!" I replied.

As we go along, Pepper keeps pointing out objects to me such as a large bush or an odd-shaped tree. "Try to remember these things as they will help you to find your way home if we get separated," Pepper said.

"Thank you, but I will be sticking to you like the leaves on Henry's back," I replied.

"Good, I did not doubt that for a moment, but just in case I thought that it was a good idea to show you how to find your way back".

The evening light was fading faster now and the deeper we went into the woods, the darker it became. I was not worried at all about this as by now I was very happy to be with Pepper and trusted her instincts. All my own instincts and senses were working like mad as if I had never used them before. Now there were some even more interesting sounds and some very strong smells in the air. All very fascinating.

## IAN BANYARD

Ian Banyard a well-being author, nature connection guide, guide trainer and the founder of Nature Connection World. https://community.natureconnection.world/

When Ian set out to write his own book in 2016, he frequently experienced writer's block and often found himself so easily distracted. It always amazed him that when he felt 'one with nature' – connected to the experience of nature in the present moment – understanding and creativity would flow. Here is a small extract that he included in his book. It beautifully captures this natural mindfulness moment:

*As I am writing these words in my notebook, I am sitting on a bench in the centre of a town. Tall buildings, busy shoppers and noisy traffic surround me. As I look around and shift my attention, I notice the abundance of Nature which shares this moment and space too. I can hear the birdsong. There's a warm breeze on my face. There are trees coming into bloom and spring flowers immerging. A small white pigeon feather floats slowly down in front of me, drifting gently on the breeze. The feather lands on the pavement drawing my eye to a new green shoot. The shoot has forced its way out of the darkness through a crack in the pavement. It instinctively grows towards the sunlight, forever reaching for the clear blue sky above me. While sensing the natural world around me, I stop writing; all thoughts of anything other than that present moment stop. I experience an overwhelming feeling of calm, clarity and connection. I am having a Natural Mindfulness experience and it feels wonderful. When I return to my writing, everything flows.*

## MARY LUNAN

Global Life Coach & Magic Carpet Ride guide at Dare to Blossom www.daretoblossom.co.uk

My connection with nature is deep, profound and hard to put into words. And it is not necessary to do that – even though often the words do come when I surrender to the joy I feel being in nature. That joy cannot be contained, it is too big, too limitless for that: yet it can be channelled. By this I am not thinking of 'channelling' in the specific sense of receiving and passing on messages in the way a medium might. For me, it is about simply being – being out on the clifftops, on the beach, in the woods, beside a river, in my garden. Simply being in, and a part of, nature. Feeling the joy of being a thread in the weave of life that encompasses all. Then, then that joy is effortlessly channelled through my writing.

## LIZ WEBB

Liz Webb is a hugely popular thriller writer. Her second novel, *The Saved*, was published on 25 January 2024. Her first novel, *The Daughter*, was published in 2022. She worked as a stand-up comic and radio drama producer before becoming a novelist. www.lizwebb.co.uk

### Wild Writing with Sarah Clayton
By Liz Webb,
author of *The Daughter* (2022) and *The Saved* (2024)

I'm a scared, doubting, self-sabotaging cynic of a writer. I dismissively wave away advice; I heavily criticise myself and my writing; and I don't easily believe that a writing coach can be of any real help to me. But I believe in Sarah Clayton and her 'writing with nature' approach. Without her I could never have written my second novel *The Saved* or be starting my third book. She knows what she's talking about from her own writing experience and her coaching training, and she advises with boundless kindness, wit and flexibility and with a unique focus of connecting with nature that even gets through to a tense wary curmudgeon like me.

Crafting any piece of writing, but especially a novel, you need lots of things: some innate talent, some learnt techniques, time, perseverance, support and luck. But most of all, you need the right frame of mind: the confidence, focus and joy required to write and to keep on writing. And having and maintaining that frame of mind is no mean feat. Cos writing is haaaaard. You're alone in your turret/bed/coffee shop, doubting you deserve to write, doubting what you've written, awed by and jealous of the writers you see succeeding around you, crushed by criticism and setbacks, and so easily forgetting what you actually really enjoy about writing. Sarah has been a lifeline through my writing negativity, cascading fears and self-imposed roadblocks.

I met her two years ago when I was starting my second book, *The Saved*, the premise of which meant that it needed to be set in a very cold, watery, isolated place. My lead character had to experience hypothermic cardiac arrest, a heart attack in freezing conditions, from which he was brought back to life six hours later, apparently fully recovered, but to his partner, sinisterly unrecognizable. Sarah was a total stranger to me, who happened to be attending the same writing course I was doing. She mentioned that she was herself running a writing course later in the year, on the slate island of Easdale off the west coast of Scotland. Umm, cold, isolated, watery? Perfect for my book. So I cynically signed up, purely so that I could research the island as the setting for my novel. I fully expected to tune out during the dull predictable writing course bits, but I intended to just blank off and fake looking engaged.

The slate island was indeed perfect for my book, but unexpectedly, the course and Sarah herself, started to get through to me, despite my cynicism. She chivvied us participants out the door, to get out and about on the beautiful windswept island. And we were not just looking at the scenery, we were trekking through spiky gorse, come rain or shine, clambering up steep hills and across mossy rocks, and taking off our shoes and socks and wiggling our toes in the sparkling sea water off the deserted hard-to-reach coastlines we discovered. We did lots of writing exercises out in the wild, inspired by what we saw, found and experienced. I gradually stopped worrying about myself, my writing and the publishing world and connected with the wonderful island experiences. I wrote without analysing. It was a transformative experience. And I'm soooo not a person who ever uses the word 'transformative'!

I finished the course in love with the island, confident and inspired, and all the writing exercises I'd done during the course, without ever overthinking and struggling, ended up in my final novel.

I live in London and Sarah lives in Perth but I've continued to work with her over Zoom, doing writing exercises and talking about my writing problems. She helps me to let go of my seizing self-sabotaging, focus on doing the writing and to get out in nature when I especially need to get over myself and find an even keel to enjoy my writing.

# Embracing the Write Wild Coaching Programme

The Write Wild Method explores the profound and transformative potential of the connection between writers and nature. It demonstrates the extraordinary ability of a deep relationship with the natural world to bring healing and personal transformation, providing comfort and purpose while creating an environment where creativity and productivity can flourish.

At the heart of the Write Wild approach is a simple yet profound truth: our creativity is deeply intertwined with the natural world. From the gentle rustle of leaves in the wind to the fiery brilliance of a sunset sky, nature speaks to us in a language that transcends words – a language of beauty, wonder and infinite possibility. It is from this interconnectedness that we draw our strength, our vision and our deepest insights as writers.

But it requires more than just passive observation; it requires active engagement – a willingness to immerse ourselves fully in the sights, sounds and sensations of the world around us. This is where the Write Wild Coaching Programme comes into play. Through personalised coaching sessions, tailored exercises and immersive experiences in nature, we guide you on a journey of self-discovery, working with you to unlock the full potential of your creativity and find your unique voice.

One of the key principles of the Write Wild approach is

the idea of alignment – aligning our creative process with the natural rhythms of the world. Just as the seasons ebb and flow, so too does our creative energy wax and wane. By attuning ourselves to these rhythms, together we can learn to work with, rather than against, the natural ebb and flow of your own creativity, leading to greater productivity, deeper insights, and a more authentic connection to your work.

The Write Wild Coaching Programme is more than just a series of techniques and exercises; it's a philosophy – a way of life. It's about embracing the wildness within us, tapping into the energy that lies dormant, and bringing it to the page with fearless commitment. It's about recognising that our greatest strengths as writers – our intuition, our empathy, our capacity for wonder – these are all gifts of nature, and by embracing them, we unlock the full potential of our creative selves.

The Write Wild Coaching Method isn't just about improving writing skills; it's about transforming lives. Here's how:

1. **Unlocking Creativity**: Through personalised coaching sessions and tailored exercises, the Write Wild Programme helps you tap into your creativity. By fostering a deep connection with nature and encouraging you to explore your own inner wilderness, we empower you to unleash your imagination and create stories that resonate on a profound level.

2. **Overcoming Creative Challenges**: Writer's block or getting stuck is a common hurdle for many writers, but with the Write Wild Method, it becomes a thing of the past. By aligning with the natural rhythms of

creativity and learning to trust your instincts, you gain the tools you need to overcome obstacles and keep your creative purpose alive.

3. **Finding Authentic Voice**: One of the most powerful aspects of the Write Wild Programme is its emphasis on authenticity. By encouraging you to embrace your vulnerabilities, quirks and unique perspectives, we help you find your authentic voice – the voice that sets your writing apart and draws readers in.

4. **Cultivating Discipline and Consistency**: Writing can be a solitary and sometimes daunting task, but with the support of the Write Wild Programme, you gain the motivation and accountability you need to stay disciplined and consistent in your practice. Through workshops, retreats and online groups, you come together to share your experiences, offer encouragement and hold each other accountable, creating a supportive environment where creativity can flourish.

5. **Deepening Connection with Nature**: The Write Wild Method isn't just about writing; it's about forging a deeper connection with the natural world. By immersing yourself in nature and connecting with the sights, sounds and sensations around you, you gain a renewed sense of wonder and awe that infuses your writing with vitality and depth.

6. **Creating Lasting Change**: Ultimately, the Write Wild Coaching Programme is about creating lasting change in writers' lives. By guiding you on a journey of self-discovery, artistic exploration and profound connection to the world around you, we empower you to tap into your full potential, both on and off

the page. With the Write Wild Method as your guide, you emerge transformed – more confident, more creative and more deeply connected to yourself and the world around you.

Together, we'll explore the wild landscapes of your imagination, forge deep connections with the natural world and unleash the full power of your creativity upon the page.

Whether you're a seasoned writer or just starting out on your creative journey, the Write Wild Coaching Programme is here to support you, inspire you and empower you to embrace your fullest creative potential and write your wildest ambitions into reality.

For more details and to schedule a discovery call visit: https://www.writewildbooks.com

## The Golden Bird
*A fairy tale by the Brothers Grimm*

In times gone by there was a king who had at the back of his castle a beautiful pleasure garden, in which stood a tree that bore golden apples. As the apples ripened, they were counted, but one morning one was missing. Then the king was angry, and he ordered that watch should be kept about the tree every night.

Now the king had three sons, and he sent the eldest to spend the whole night in the garden; so he watched till midnight, and then he could keep off sleep no longer, and in the morning another apple was missing. The second son had to watch the following night; but he fared no better, for when twelve o'clock had struck he went to sleep, and in the morning another apple was missing. Now came the turn of the third son to watch, and he was ready to do so; but the king had less trust in him, and believed he would acquit himself still worse than his brothers, but in the end he consented to let him try. So the young man lay down under the tree to watch, and resolved that sleep should not be master.

When it struck twelve something came rushing through the air, and he saw in the moonlight a bird flying towards him, whose feathers glittered like gold. The bird perched upon the tree, and had already pecked off an apple, when the young man let fly an arrow at it. The bird flew away, but the arrow had struck its plumage, and one of its golden feathers fell to the ground. The young man picked it up, and taking it next morning to the king, told him what had happened in the night. The king called his council together, and all declared that such a feather was worth more than the whole kingdom. "Since the feather is so valuable," said the king, "one is not enough for me; I must and will have the whole bird."

So the eldest son set off, and relying on his own cleverness he thought he should soon find the golden bird. When he had gone some distance, he saw a fox sitting at the edge of a wood, and he pointed his gun at him. The fox cried out, "Do not shoot me, and I will give you good counsel. You are on your way to find the golden bird, and this evening you will come to a village, in which two taverns stand facing each other. One will be brightly lighted up, and there will be plenty of merriment going on inside; do not mind about that, but go into the other one, although it will look to you very uninviting."

"How can a silly beast give one any rational advice?" thought the king's son and let fly at the fox, but missed him, and he stretched out his tail and ran quick into the wood. Then the young man went on his way, and towards evening he came to the village, and there stood the two taverns; in one singing and dancing was going on, the other looked quite dull and wretched.

"I should be a fool," said he, "to go into that dismal place, while there is anything so good close by." So he went into the merry inn, and there lived in clover, quite forgetting the bird and his father and all good counsel.

As time went on, and the eldest son never came home, the second son set out to seek the golden bird. He met with the fox, just as the eldest did, and received good advice from him without attending to it. And when he came to the two taverns, his brother was standing and calling to him at the window of one of them, out of which came sounds of merriment; so he could not resist, but went in and revelled to his heart's content.

And then, as time went on, the youngest son wished to go

forth and try his luck, but his father would not consent.

"It would be useless," said he. "He is much less likely to find the bird than his brothers, and if any misfortune were to happen to him he would not know how to help himself; his wits are none of the best." But at last, as there was no peace to be had, he let him go.

By the side of the wood sat the fox, who begged him to spare his life, and gave him good counsel. The young man was kind, and said, "Be easy, little fox, I will do you no harm."

"You shall not repent of it," answered the fox, "and that you may get there all the sooner, get up and sit on my tail." And no sooner had he done so than the fox began to run, and off they went over stock and stone, so that the wind whistled in their hair. When they reached the village the young man got down, and, following the fox's advice, went into the mean-looking tavern, without hesitating, and there he passed a quiet night.

The next morning, when he went out into the field, the fox, who was sitting there already, said, "I will tell you further what you have to do. Go straight on until you come to a castle, before which a great band of soldiers lie, but do not trouble yourself about them, for they will be all asleep and snoring. Pass through them and forward into the castle, and go through all the rooms, until you come to one where there is a golden bird hanging in a wooden cage. Near at hand will stand empty a golden cage of state, but you must beware of taking the bird out of his ugly cage and putting him into the fine one; if you do so you will come to harm." After he had finished saying this the fox stretched out his tail again, and the king's son sat down upon it; then away they went over stock and stone, so that the wind whistled through their hair.

And when the king's son reached the castle he found everything as the fox had said. He at last entered the room where the golden bird was hanging in a wooden cage, while a golden one was standing by; the three golden apples too were in the room. Then, thinking it foolish to let the beautiful bird stay in that mean and ugly cage, he opened the door of it, took hold of it, and put it in the golden one. In the same moment the bird uttered a piercing cry. The soldiers awaked, rushed in, seized the king's son and put him in prison.

The next morning he was brought before a judge, and, as he confessed everything, condemned to death. But the king said he would spare his life on one condition, that he should bring him the golden horse whose paces were swifter than the wind, and that then he should also receive the golden bird as a reward.

So the king's son set off to find the golden horse, but he sighed, and was very sad, for how should it be accomplished? And then he saw his old friend the fox sitting by the roadside.

"Now, you see," said the fox, "all this has happened, because you would not listen to me. But be of good courage, I will bring you through, and will tell you how you are to get the golden horse. You must go straight on until you come to a castle, where the horse stands in his stable; before the stable door the grooms will be lying, but they will all be asleep and snoring; and you can go and quietly lead out the horse. But one thing you must mind – take care to put upon him the plain saddle of wood and leather, and not the golden one, which will hang close by; otherwise it will go badly for you."

Then the fox stretched out his tail, and the king's son seated himself upon it, and away they went over stock and stone until the wind whistled through their hair. And everything happened just as the fox had said. He came to the stall where the golden horse was and as he was about to put on him the plain saddle, he thought to himself, "Such a beautiful animal would be disgraced were I not to put on him the good saddle, which becomes him so well." However, no sooner did the horse feel the golden saddle touch him than he began to neigh. And the grooms all awoke, seized the king's son and threw him into prison. The next morning he was delivered up to justice and condemned to death, but the king promised him his life, and also to bestow upon him the golden horse, if he could convey thither the beautiful princess of the golden castle.

With a heavy heart the king's son set out, but by great good luck he soon met with the faithful fox. "I ought now to leave you to your own ill luck," said the fox, "but I am sorry for you, and will once more help you in your need. Your way lies straight up to the golden castle. You will arrive there in the evening, and at night, when all is quiet, the beautiful princess goes to the bath. And as she is entering the bathing house, go up to her and give her a kiss, then she will follow you, and you can lead her away; but do not suffer her first to go and take leave of her parents, or it will go ill with you." Then the fox stretched out his tail; the king's son seated himself upon it, and away they went over stock and stone, so that the wind whistled through their hair.

And when he came to the golden castle, all was as the fox had said. He waited until midnight, when all lay in deep sleep, and then as the beautiful princess went to the bathing house he went up to her and gave her a kiss, and she willingly promised to go with him, but she begged him earnestly, and with tears, that he would let her first go and take leave of her parents. At first he denied her prayer, but as she wept so much the more, and fell at his feet, he gave in at last.

And no sooner had the princess reached her father's bedside than he, and all who were in the castle, woke up, and the young man was seized and thrown into prison. The next morning the king said to him, "Thy life is forfeit, but thou shalt find grace if thou canst level that mountain that lies before my windows, and over which I am not able to see and if this is done within eight days thou shalt have my daughter for a reward." So the king's son set to work, and dug and shovelled away without ceasing, but when, on the seventh day, he saw how little he had accomplished, and that all his work was as nothing, he fell into great sadness and gave up all hope.

But on the evening of the seventh day the fox appeared, and said, "You do not deserve that I should help you, but go now and lie down to sleep, and I will do the work for you." The next morning when he awoke, and looked out of the window, the mountain had disappeared. The young man hastened full of joy to the king, and told him that his behest was fulfilled, and, whether the king liked it or not, he had to keep to his word, and let his daughter go. So they both went away together, and it was not long before the faithful fox came up to them.

"Well, you have got the best first," said he; "but you must know the golden, horse belongs to the princess of the golden castle." "But how shall I get it?" asked the young man. "I am going to tell you," answered the fox. "First, go to the king who sent you to the golden castle, and take to him the beautiful princess. There will then be very great rejoicing; he will willingly give you the golden horse, and they will lead him out to you. Then mount him without delay, and stretch out your hand to each of them to take leave, and last of all to the princess, and when you have her by the hand swing her up on the horse behind you, and off you go! Nobody will be able to overtake you, for that horse goes swifter than the wind."

And so it was all happily done, and the king's son carried off the beautiful princess on the golden horse. The fox did not stay behind, and he said to the young man, "Now, I will help you to get the golden bird. When you draw near the castle where the bird is, let the lady alight, and I will take her under my care; then you must ride the golden horse into the castle-yard, and there will be great rejoicing to see it, and they will bring out to you the golden bird. As soon as you have the cage in your hand, you must start off back to us, and then you shall carry the lady away." The plan was successfully carried out, and when the young man returned with the treasure, the fox said, "Now, what will you give me for my reward?" "What would you like?" asked the young man. "When we are passing through the wood, I desire that you should slay me, and cut my head and feet off."

"That were a strange sign of gratitude," said the king's son, "and I could not possibly do such a thing." Then said the fox, "If you will not do it, I must leave you; but before I go let me give you some good advice. Beware of two things: buy no gallows-meat, and sit at no brook-side." With that, the fox ran off into the wood.

The young man thought to himself, "That is a wonderful animal, with most singular ideas. How should any one buy gallows-meat? And I am sure I have no particular fancy for sitting by a brook-side." So he rode on with the beautiful princess, and their way led them through the village where his two brothers had stayed. There they heard great outcry and noise, and when he asked what it was all about, they told him that two people were going to be hanged. And when he drew near he saw that it was his two brothers, who had done all sorts of evil tricks, and had wasted all their goods. He asked if there were no means of setting them free.

"Oh yes! if you will buy them off," answered the people; "but why should you spend your money in redeeming such worthless men?" But he persisted in doing so; and when they were let go they all went on their journey together.

After a while they came to the wood where the fox had met them first, and there it seemed so cool and sheltered from the sun's burning rays that the two brothers said, "Let us rest here for a little by the brook, and eat and drink to refresh ourselves." The young man consented, quite forgetting the fox's warning, and he seated himself by the brook-side, suspecting no evil. But the two brothers thrust him backwards into the brook, seized the princess, the horse, and the bird, and went home to their father.

"Is not this the golden bird that we bring?" said they; "and we have also the golden horse, and the princess of the golden castle." Then there was great rejoicing in the royal castle, but the horse did not feed, the bird did not chirp, and the princess sat still and wept.

The youngest brother, however, had not perished. The brook was, by good fortune, dry, and he fell on soft moss without receiving any hurt, but he could not get up again. But in his need the faithful fox was not lacking; he came up running and reproached him for having forgotten his advice.

"But I cannot forsake you all the same," said he. "I will help you back again into daylight." So he told the young man to grasp his tail, and hold on to it fast, and so he drew him up again. "Still you are not quite out of all danger," said the fox. "Your brothers, not being certain of your death, have surrounded the wood with sentinels, who are to put you to death if you let yourself be seen." A poor beggarman was sitting by the path, and the young man changed clothes with him, and went clad in that way into the king's courtyard. Nobody knew him, but the bird began to chirp, and the horse began to feed, and the beautiful princess ceased weeping.

"What does this mean?" said the king, astonished. The princess answered, "I cannot tell, except that I was sad, and now I am joyful; it is to me as if my rightful bridegroom had returned." Then she told him all that happened, although the two brothers had threatened to put her to death if she let out anything.

The king then ordered every person who was in the castle to be brought before him, and with the rest came the young man like a beggar in his wretched garments; but the princess knew him, and greeted him well, falling on his neck and kissing him. The wicked brothers were seized and put to death, and the youngest brother was married to the princess, and succeeded to the inheritance of his father.

But what became of the poor fox? Long afterwards the king's son was going through the wood, and the fox met him and said, "Now, you have everything that you can wish for, but my misfortunes never come to an end, and it lies in your power to free me from them." And once more he prayed the king's son earnestly to slay him, and cut off his head and feet. So, at last, he consented, and no sooner was it done than the fox was changed into a man, and was no other than the brother of the beautiful princess; and thus he was set free from a spell that had bound him for a long, long time. And now, indeed, there lacked nothing to their happiness as long as they lived.

# Acknowledgements

This has been a mesmerising but mammoth journey and I'd like to thank **Eric Maisel**, psychotherapist, teacher, coach and author for introducing me to the idea that writing is a life purpose and giving me the confidence to reach for my creative and coaching ambitions.

**Ian Banyard**, well-being author, nature connection guide, guide trainer and founder of Nature Connection World, for showing me a route to finding my own unique nature connection. I look forward to our nature journey together.

**Norman Bissell**, Centre for Geopoetics, for his gracious welcome and deep convictions that nature is a part of who we are as a species and bringing geopoetics into the limelight.

**Sophie Hannah,** bestselling author and founder of *Dream Author* for her long-term support and encouragement and her belief in me and my writing journey. And for bringing to me and many other writers the Dream Author coaching programme that is now and always will be an important part of my own writing journey.

**James Willis and the team at Spiffing** for their patience and insight and for their critical guidance and support in bringing this project together.

**Dr Elizabeth Morris,** compassion-focused psychotherapist, for her undying support and cheerleading and her accountability magic and for her beautiful presence that encompasses all that nature is.

My **Critique Group Partners** – my greatest allies, each with their own critical eye and unyielding support for each other. With a tiny part of them in everything I write, I know I am in safe hands.

**The Write Wild Method contributors** for the value you've brought me and brought to The Write Wild Method, and for your belief in my project.

**Mike**, my husband, whose support in my writing and coaching ambitions never wavers and who has developed the most wonderful means of calming me and ensuring I stay on my path.

**Iceland**, the most breathtaking landscape with the most interesting nature-fuelled humans I've ever met. The ground under their feet and their natural souls will always be an inspiration to me.

**Argyll and Bute** for reasons unknown to me, a place that feels like home.

**Easedale and Jan and Daz** for their passion and direction and their amazing outlook on life and also their appreciation and fulfilment of the beauty of their local wilderness.

**Skye** forever a part of me, where my natural journey began and for the seaweed and the sky that gave me the greatest gift of all, a reason to be.

**Kinnoull Hill** for its beauty, its trees and its changing seasons.

**Pennan** for huddling me and keeping me safe while I worked out what this Write Wild Journey was all about.

**Kirsty Gunn**, novelist and professor of the MLitt at Dundee University, for making me understand that writing is something more.

**Past and future clients** who have and will share this journey with me, together we will thrive.

And for **Rollo May**, author and existential psychologist, for giving me the courage to create.

# Glossary

**Authentic self**: Being conscious and active in your own possibilities and facing up to the temporal nature of human existence. In other words, none of us can escape death. But by confronting the inevitability of death, we are choosing to matter in this world we exist in.

**Barrier thought**: A thought that's getting in the way of you making creative progress.

**Best Interest thought**: A barrier though reframed to allow you to cherish your creativity. By experiencing your writing life as something that is intuitively linked with the natural world, and by including experiential practices into your writing process and trusting that your discoveries will make a difference, you are simultaneously strengthening your courage. That means, you are breaking the cycle, forming new neural pathways that allow you to see not what is but what might be.

**Bottom-up process:** You can't not respond. In other words, you are constantly observing, with all your senses and sensibilities and making decisions based on what you observe in the present (not what you experienced in the past). This allows you to strengthen your relationship between the inner you and the outer you. You are writing from the ground up, from the earth under your feet. This will give you an inner confidence that will flow through you and reach right into the heart of your reader.

**Closing Distance**: Measuring and reducing the distance between you, your story and your reader. Closing Distance refers to bringing the reader in, closer to the text and the meaning of your words. It's not about closing the distance between writer and reader or text and reader, the technique is more about bringing the reader closer to your natural self, you as the writer.

**Combinatory Play**: Opening yourself up to receiving inspiration from unexpected places; the act of opening up one mental channel (for example, language) by dabbling in another (for example, music).

**Connection**: Means you are choosing to matter.

**Continuity**: Means consistency, resilience and self-belief, all things a writer wants to aim for. With trust and continuity, we reach transformation, a state of Ergriffenheit.

**Courage Continuum**: Reminds you to trust your creative journey and to get your natural self asking questions that will help you achieve your writing goals. Courage – and we're talking about the courage to be creative here – helps you stand up, get out of your own way, and show up in spite of all the potholes along the way. Courage is what helps you finish one project and go on to the next regardless of how unnegotiable the road ahead feels.

**Dasein**: Being in the world. The act of being. We cannot be without the world. Being and the world are interlinked and both are necessary for one another to exist.

**Develop**: Develop courage and resilience to push through. What life looks like when you embrace the process and are able to tackle any bumps in the road easily and swiftly.

**Ebb and Flow**: Encourages focus and helps you become absorbed in your project. The writing process and the writing become less onerous if you develop your natural self and commit to being persistent with your writing process. If you put the effort in to show up to your writing with commitment and persistence, and you continue to develop your natural self this combination of activity will greatly strengthen your Ebb and Flow, that is, your ability to instantly become absorbed in your writing without any fuss, stress or confusion.

**Ergriffenheit and Humility**: Encourages you to develop your natural curiosity and reconnect to your inner wonder. To reach a moment of creative freedom. Describes the experience that occurs when two different selves come into conflict and the resolution of that conflict leads to an increase in our capacity to create. The conflict reaches the deepest part of ourselves and from this clash, we experience Ergriffenheit. Jung developed this idea and the definition of the word Ergriffenheit to describe moments of heightened emotion, marvel and wonder.

**Field-dependence**: A field-dependent person will have difficulty finding a geometric shape that is embedded or 'hidden' in a background with similar, non-identical lines and shapes. The conflicting patterns cause distraction. They appear to be hampered by a lack of structure in their environment.

**Field-independence**: A person who is field-independent can more easily identify the geometric shape, regardless of the background setting. Field-independent people are able to impose their own sense of order and structure on their environment. Importantly, field-independent people are able to distinguish and maintain their sense of self from the environment. Because you may require no fixed structure to understand yourself within it, you are open to greater experience, new, meaningful ideas and, above all, a greater connection to your world, your sense of self, your words, and your reader.

**Get Motivated**: a framework that will guide you along your writing journey and keep you on track with your sanity intact.

**Growth Ring**: A method to keep track of your progress and measure it at a glance.

**Human-nature connection**: Our deep and meaningful relationship with the natural world gives us the courage and strength to keep on creating despite self-doubt and the hundred other reasons that threaten to prevent us from showing up. It helps us embrace uncertainty and anxiety. It reminds us that we have a natural ability to become absorbed in our writing, and it allows our minds to remain open to spontaneous creativity.

**Imagination network**: Your brain working creatively on your behalf while you're out in the wild, or walking mindfully, sleeping or engaging in quiet time. Brain regions are recruited during the creative process and, depending on what you're attempting to create, several brain regions combine to form networks that help you achieve your creative task.

**Impossible Worlds**: A reminder that you begin a book by writing it for yourself, but your final draft must always be for your reader. The notion that during the reading process, readers construct imaginary worlds from the story that mean something particular to them. They do this by filling in the gaps in a story with a fictional world that resembles their own lived experience of reality.

**Inauthentic self**: If you choose not to take responsibility for your own existence and instead allow others to make all your choices for you, you're living a less authentic life than you may want. We do this when we're children. But at some point in our lives, we may want to embrace our own potential and realise our own possibilities.

**Incubation**: We allow the information to percolate while your Illusive Self (for now, let's coin it your unconscious or subconscious mind) takes over and engages in combinatory play.

**Illumination**: That moment of euphoria, or at least a moment of insight awakens in your conscious awareness. Your creativity has been given the freedom to rise to your awareness.

**Innate Releasing Mechanisms**: This is the idea that both humans and animals have fixed neural patterns in their brain that can be activated (released) by environmental stimuli. Essentially, humans possess inherent, goal-oriented neural pathways that rely on environmental cues to fulfil their potential.

**Interdependent relationship**: You engage in a deeper and more meaningful relationship with the natural world which, in turn, helps you engage in a deeper and more meaningful creative journey. A kind of push and pull string of activity that tests you and your ability to liberate yourself, to detach yourself from total control over the creative process, to not so much manage but be curious about the way in which your writing and your natural self are interdependent.

**Investment Theory of Creativity**: The idea that creative people have a willingness and ability to 'buy low and sell high' in the realm of ideas. Buying low means pursuing ideas that have growth potential but are unknown or out of favour. This involves assessing ideas in new ways and overcoming the myriad excuses we invent to avoid writing. However, if we persevere with our uncertain ideas despite the resistance, there's no guarantee of their merit. Yet, by persisting and overcoming the inevitable obstacles, we have the opportunity to achieve significant success, or in other words, to sell high.

**Mental stimulation:** A hybrid writing process – combining writing with time out to explore nature – may actually provide the most optimal environment for unleashing creativity.

**Motivation:** Nobody but you can understand what natural creativity means for you and how it will fuel your writing. You have to discover your own path to natural creativity, via your Illusive Self and your courage and investment in your writing life purpose. Your goal is to get to a point where you believe that you are the only influencer in your creative progress. To know that the concept of motivation can itself be a barrier to productivity – feeling motivated is not necessary to write and make creative progress. You may not feel very motivated but you can choose to write or not write regardless.

**Nature Connection:** Your connection with nature, your natural self, your meaning and writing life purpose.

**Natural Self:** A wildly creative state of being that is intertwined with the natural world and is where ideas exist. When we practise connecting to our natural self, we are opening ourselves up to the wild places where ideas exist. To where ideas may lead us closer to our potential.

**Organic Architecture:** Organic is natural/natural is organic. The landscape is the foundation of your organic storytelling – a reciprocal relationship with nature and creativity.

**Perspective taking:** Imagining other perspectives and scenarios, comprehending stories and reflecting on mental and emotional states, both your own and others. All of the Write Wild principles and techniques contribute to your ability to discover new perspectives, greater understanding and a more meaningful relationship with your natural self, your self as a writer and your optimal writing process.

**Personal meaning-making:** As you connect with nature, your Illusive Self is busy making sense of your creative ideas and it does this easily via the imagination network as it activates your unique and innate connection to the landscape.

**Prepare:** We often forget that writing is a whole body experience. The best road to success is to be prepared, physically, psychologically and emotionally.

**Preparation:** We begin and continue to gather information.

**Principle Application (PA):** How you apply your experience. Experience is everything. Experiencing your idea, your meaning, your intent, because once you do that, you will write authentically and with a better chance of producing writing that is compelling for both you and your reader.

**Progress:** Only you can write your story. This means getting the writing done and rewarding yourself at the end of each day.

**Reimagining-Reawakening:** Guides you to explore how to make meaning and tell a story. The quality of your story is a factor of the depths to which you are willing to explore meaning. To create is to continuously explore. Reimagine the problem, reawaken the solution and you'll find you've gotten yourself unstuck and back on the road to the finishing line.

**Re-presenting Story:** Consider the idea that the world is not given to humans in pure form and is instead always mediated or re-presented.

**Riff Writing:** To do with editing/rewriting/reimagining. Taking a piece of writing and reworking it on the basis of the anticipated emotional response of a potential reader. Helps us to be more specific in our writing, to pay closer attention in our observations and to focus at a deeper level on what matters most, delivering an experience for our readers. when you're riff writing, the way in which the words/sounds make you feel will be the route to allowing your reader to feel.

**Simplify:** Simplify the process. It's easy to spend a lot of time developing a daily practice only to find out that you've made it too difficult to sustain. Make sure that doesn't happen!

**Spontaneous Creativity:** Originates from the depths of our unconscious. It's like tapping into a hidden realm where ideas dwell, fuelled by our innate connection to the natural world. This connection serves as a gateway to unlock creativity and bring it into conscious awareness.

**Style:** Style is subjective but when carefully considered is a good means of attracting the reader to your story. Style isn't simply genre, for example, whether your story is a tragedy, comedy, romance or fantasy, etc. Once you're clear on the genre of your story (if you're writing for the commercial market), paying attention to style becomes important. Style is both genre-specific and unique to you. It is the intertwining of both these things because no one can write in the same style as you. You bring your own uniqueness to your writing. It has been said that you have to write ten thousand words before you can identify your own style. I say, write from deep within yourself and you'll find that your style is already fully formed, ready for you to discover.

**The Walking Writer**: Take at least a fifteen-minute walk per day. Keeps your writing muscle healthy and willing to show up for you daily.

**The Write Wild Experience (WWE)**: The work of your storytelling ought to grow not from words but from the experiential reawakening of your imagination – your natural self.

**Top-down process**: Ideas come from the mechanisms inside your brain. In practice, you sit, ready to write, and either hope for inspiration (that, by design, must come from past experience) or detail outlines, plans, character sketches and so on.

**Transform**: But above all, write!

**Trust**: Trusting your creative journey. Relates to challenging your assumptions and being open to experience.

**Verification**: Where you communicate creatively using words to describe the meaning of your insights and illuminations.

**Your Courage Continuum**: Reminds you to trust your creative journey and to get your natural self asking questions that will help you achieve your writing goals. Courage – and we're talking about the courage to be creative here – helps you stand up, get out of your own way, and show up in spite of all the potholes along the way. Courage is what helps you finish one project and go on to the next regardless of how unnegotiable the road ahead feels. You already possess the courage it will take for you to achieve your writing goals, the tricky part is accessing that courage. You are required to invest in and trust the journey. This is the Courage Continuum.

**Your Elliptic Presence**: Invites you to embrace the chaos of the creative process. This is about process. About fully embracing a mindset that is conscious of the present moment and is open and curious about the unknown. Getting outside, experiencing new and natural places, observing, being curious about your surroundings, experiencing the now of the landscape – all of these things can and I feel should be part of the writing process. Simply think of it as your journey to a mindset growth, a wild mindfulness, where you're opening yourself up to receiving inspiration from unexpected places. This is combinatory play: The capacity to invite your innate genius to step forward and fill the gaps. This is your Elliptic Presence.

**Your Fairy-tale Self**: Invites you to develop the part of you that will deliver the elements of your story without you having to force the writing. A measured way of tracking your progress towards your writing life purpose. Your Fairy-tale Self brings nature and the writing process together to form a connection and at the centre of that connection is YOU. Your natural self. Your natural self comes from being in nature and setting your Illusive Self free to roam and find the creative answers you need to keep going with your writing life.

**Your Illusive Self**: Where your creativity exists. The part of you that you have no conscious awareness of. Rediscover your imagination, your natural self, your courage, resilience and creativity. When you embrace a mindset of unwavering determination, when you are naturally unrelenting. The name for your creativity. It lives within you and it needs oxygen to come out to play and it is limitless when it is fully connected to your natural self. Not only does it need oxygen but your Illusive Self also requires you to believe in your creative self.

**Your Writer's Ecosystem:** Writing is a whole body experience. With your writer's ecosystem, you don't have to strive to believe in yourself, it simply comes naturally. In each of us there exists three parts. The part that is you – the physical you (including the brain). The part that is your mind. The part that is Illusive You. This is your writer's ecosystem. When each of these parts is connected, self-belief becomes less of an issue as it is a natural part of that connection. When the connection is broken, doubts and fears are able to creep in leaving your self-belief vulnerable. So, rather than attempting to improve on self-belief, it's worth investigating where your connection may be broken and fixing that.

**Wonder:** Every act of writing is value laden and symbolic. It has social as well as individual meanings. It relies on a degree of trust, continuity and being open to transformation. It relies on interactivity.

# Bibliography

Allan, T., 2021. *Myths of the World. An Illustrated Collection of the World's Greatest Stories.* Duncan Baird Publishers Ltd, London.

Aalto, K,. 2020. *Writing Wild.* Timber Press, Inc., Oregon.

Banyard, I., 2018. *Natural Mindfulness. Your Personal Guide to the Healing Power of Nature* Connection. Vision Maker Press, Great Britain.

Bettelheim, B., 1991. *The Uses of Enchantment. The Meaning and Importance of Fairy Tales.* Penguin Books, London.

Berns, G., 2010. *Iconoclasts a neuroscientist reveals how to think differently.* Harvard Business Press, Boston.

Bissell, N., 2007. *Slate, Sea and Sky. A Journey from Glasgow to the Isle of Luing.* Luath Press Limited, Edinburgh.

Bond, M., 2020. *Wayfinding. The Art and Science of How We Find and Lose Our Way.* Picador, London.

Bringhurst, R., 2006. *The Tree of Meaning: Thirteen Talks.* Gaspereau Press. Nova Scotia.

Buzzell, L., Chalquist, C. 2009. *Ecotherapy. Healing with Nature in Mind.* Counterpoint, Berkeley, CA.

Cain, S., 2012. *Quiet. The Power of Introverts in a World That Can't Stop Talking.* Penguin Books, London.

Chainey, D. D., Winsham, W. 2021. *Treasury of Folklore: Woodlands and Forests: Wild Gods, World Trees and Werewolves.* Batsford. United Kingdom.

Currie, G., Ravenscroft, I. 2002. *Recreative Minds.* Oxford University Press, Oxford.

Dunn, C., 2021. Rewilding the Urban Soul. Searching for the Wild in the City. Scribe Publications, London.

Heidegger, M., 2019. *Being and Time* MacQuarrie, J. & Robinson, Ed. (Trans). Martino Fine Books, Eastford, CT.

Higgens, P., 2020. *Dare to Be Great. Unlock Your Power to Create a Better World.* Flint, Gloucestershire.

Kaufman, S. B., Gregoire, C., 2016. *Wired to Create. Unraveling the Mysteries of the Creative Mind.* Tarcher Perigee, New York.

Lunnen, M., 2008. *Dare to Blossom Coaching and Creativity.* Dare to Blossom Books, Cornwall, UK.

Maisel, E., 2024. *Choose Your Life Purposes.* Yellow Pear Press/Mango Publishing, FL

Maisel, E., 2005. *Coaching the Artist Within.* New World Library, Novato, CA.

Mamet, D., 2002. *Three Uses of the Knife. On the Nature and Purpose of Drama.* Bloomsbury, London/NY.

May, R., 1975. *The Courage to Create.* W.W. Norton & Company, New York.

May, R., 1991. *The Cry for Myth.* Norton, New York.

May, R., 1977. *The Meaning of Anxiety.* W.W. Norton & Company, New York.

Mayer, F. S. & McPherson Frantz, C., 2004. 'The

connectedness to nature scale: A measure of individuals' feeling in community with nature.' *Journal of Environmental Psychology*, 24, 503–515.

Oppezzo, M., Schwartz, D. L., 2014. *Journal of Experimental Psychology: Learning, Memory, and Cognition*. Vol. 40, No. 4, 1142–1152.

Roach, M., 2022. *Animal Vegetable Criminal*. Oneworld, London.

Roszak, T., 1992. *The Voice of the Earth. An Exploration of Ecopsychology*. Phanes Press, Inc. Grand Rapids, MI.

Roszak, T., Gomes, M. E., Kanner, A. D., (Eds), 1995. *Ecopsychology. Restoring the Earth Healing the Mind*. Counterpoint, Berkely, CA.

Ryan, M., 1992. *Possible Worlds, Artificial Intelligence, and Narrative Theory*. Indiana University Press. USA.

Segal, L., Jarrell, R., Sendak, M. (Eds & Trans), 1973. *The Juniper Tree and Other Tales from Grimm*. The Bodley Head Ltd, London.

Thorsson, O., Scudder, B., 2001. *The Sagas of Icelanders*. Penguin Books, New York.

Wagner, A., 2020. *Life Finds a Way. What Evolution Teaches Us About Creativity*. Oneworld, London.

Welling, T., 2014. *Writing Wild*. New World Library, Novato, CA.

White, J., 2016. *Talking on Water. Conversations About Nature & Creativity*. Trinity University Press, San Antonio.

Wulf, A., 2015. *The Invention of Nature. The Adventures of Alexander Von Humboldt. The Lost Hero of Science*. John Murray, London.

www.ingramcontent.com/pod-product-compliance
Lightning Source LLC
Chambersburg PA
CBHW052131070526
44585CB00017B/1783